BIBLE EXPLORER'S GUIDE

JOHN PHILLIPS

BIBLE EXPLORER'S GUIDE

JOHN PHILLIPS

LOIZEAUX BROTHERS
Neptune, New Jersey

FIRST EDITION, MARCH 1987

A publication of LOIZEAUX BROTHERS, Inc.
*A nonprofit organization devoted to the Lord's work
and to the spread of His truth*

Library of Congress Cataloguing-in-Publication Data

Phillips, John, 1927-
    Bible explorer's guide.

    Bibliography: p.
    1. Bible—Hermeneutics.   2. Bible—Handbooks,
manuals, etc.   I. Title.
BS476.P49   1987   220.6'01   86-18565
ISBN 0-87213-682-5

PRINTED IN THE UNITED STATES OF AMERICA

Contents

Foreword

This is the kind of book I wish someone had given me when I first started studying the Bible seriously. I went on for years accumulating bits and pieces of information—a sermon here, some Bible study there, a commentary somewhere else—until I had at my finger tips a considerable amount of information about the Bible. I was familiar with Bible stories and the great doctrines. I had some knowledge of basic Bible themes. I thought I knew the Bible and how to study it. I thought I was equipped to teach others.

In actual fact, however, I was ignorant of great tracts of Scripture and had only the sketchiest of notions about how the Bible should be interpreted. Much that I passed on to others was secondhand information culled from my background and handily tacked on to a text or passage of Scripture.

If only someone had taught me how to interpret the Bible properly. It came as a revelation to me to discover that a whole science of *hermeneutics* existed (the very word was formidable), that there were right ways and wrong ways to go about discovering what the Bible actually said in any given passage. I had some knowledge of the importance of context: of seeing the whole before studying the part, of the dangers of allegorizing too freely. But it was like light in a dark place to discover that some general principles, mastered and applied to the Bible, could keep one on a safe course. (And how important that is. After all, the false cults and the great errors of Christendom have their roots in a failure to rightly divide the word of truth.)

In writing this book I have had in mind people like myself. This book is not written for those who have had the advantage of a course on hermeneutics in a Bible school or seminary. It is written for people who are cut off from such advantages. They may have bravely taken on the responsibility of a pulpit, a Sunday school class, a Bible study group, but they find themselves in the condition I have just described. My intention has not been to produce a scholarly study of the science of hermeneutics, but rather to state the great principles of interpretation. I will illustrate how those principles work and how important they are.

The book is in two parts. In the first part I introduce the reader to the ground rules for handling God's Word (I have done my best to make them interesting). I have given much of this material in church seminars over the years, usually with a very warm response from those taking the course. The second half of the book brings together information that will help the reader use some of those principles of interpretation. The list of books at the end is quite subjective. These are books that have helped me. Perhaps they will help others too.

I do not expect that everyone will like this book. Those who are already wedded to an allegorical scheme of interpretation will probably disagree with much that is said. Those, however, who embrace the "golden rule of Bible interpretation"—that God says what He means and means what He says and that when He speaks to us He does so using the usual laws of language and communication—will, hopefully, find much to encourage and help them in their task of "rightly dividing the word of truth."

Part 1

Hermeneutics

Introduction

I once had a friend do some rewiring for me. First he installed lengths of tubing through which the wires would pass. Then from box to box, from terminal to terminal, he pulled long lengths of thick, insulated wire. Each length of wire contained three other wires, each well insulated and each a different color—red, black, and white.

My friend kept those wires separate and paid careful attention to the color code. He did not indiscriminately link together red and black, white and red, black and white. He proceeded on the simple rule that those wires could be brought together only according to the laws of electricity—red to red, white to white, black to black. Suppose he had ignored that simple rule and mixed up the three wires. When the power came on, total disaster would have resulted. It is a simple law of wiring a building for electricity that such wires be kept separate and that the place and function of each be understood.

That is also true of Bible interpretation. Like wiring a house, Bible interpretation has its rules.

Three main lines of truth run through the Scriptures: *salvation* truth, *church* truth, and *kingdom* truth. We must distinguish the one from the other, keeping them separate in our thinking, bringing them together only in their proper place and for appropriate purposes. To mix them up results in confusion.

Salvation truth runs all through the Bible from Genesis to Revelation. God has always had just one way to save sinners. His answer to human sin is Calvary. No matter in what age they lived, Old Testament believers anticipated the cross. They looked forward to it by faith. Believers before the Flood, believers in the age of Promise, and believers living under the Law offered their sacrifices and laid hold by faith on the salvation offered at Calvary. Believers in the church age today, believers in the coming tribulation age, and believers during the millennial age all look back by faith to the cross. Calvary covers us all.

Church truth is found only in the New Testament and particularly in the Pauline epistles. The Church was not revealed to the people of the Old Testament but was a mystery hidden from them, first mentioned by Christ and brought to full light by the Holy Spirit in the Pauline epistles. Although church truth was not *revealed* in the Old Testament, it was *concealed* there. Today, New Testament in hand, we can go back and see it hidden away in the most unlikely places in types and shadows. Old Testament believers, however, could not see what we can see. Since they knew nothing of the Church, that fact must be kept in mind when interpreting the Old Testament Scriptures.

Kingdom truth, like salvation truth, runs throughout the Bible. God has always intended to set up a kingdom on earth and He has not abandoned that goal. Many of the psalms and most of the prophetic writings are rich with kingdom truth. A number of the Lord's parables deal with kingdom truth, and to try to read into them salvation truth or church truth leads only to confusion. Some of the parables, of course, do present salvation truth (the parable of the prodigal son, for instance) and some of the parables do hint at church truth (the parable of the pearl, for example), but we need to be careful not to get our wires crossed.

At the outset we are confronted with two possible roads to follow. Evangelical men and women will be found on both of these roads, so we need to find out where they lead. At times both roads look much alike but, in actual fact, their courses diverge widely. Some say a third road exists (if we can call it a road), but it is full of potholes and it leads far from Biblical truth.

One main road begins with the principle of *allegorical* interpretation and takes the grace of God as its controlling principle. God, it is claimed, does all things to manifest His grace.

The theology that emerges from this system of interpretation is known as covenant theology. The Biblical scheme is said to embrace two great covenants made by God with man, one a covenant of works and the other a covenant of grace.

This system runs at last into one of the major issues that confronts the Bible expositor, the relationship of the Church to Israel. The covenant theologian identifies the Church as spiritual Israel. To do that, however, does away with any future for the nation of Israel and also makes no allowance for the millennial reign of Christ on the earth.

The other main road begins with the principle of *literal* interpretation, with the premise that any passage of Scripture must be interpreted literally, grammatically, and culturally. The controlling principle of this system is not the grace of God but the glory of God. God, it is claimed, does all things to manifest His glory—a far wider and more satisfying unifying principle, it seems to me, than the grace of God.

The theology that emerges from this system is dispensational theology. The Bible is seen to embrace a number of "dispensations," or periods of time, during which God made plain man's sinfulness and demonstrated man's failure, no matter how God has approached him.

This system of interpretation likewise runs into the issue of the relationship between Israel and the Church. The literal rule of interpretation postulates a sharp distinction between the two. The

Church is not spiritual Israel; rather, Israel and the Church are two separate entities in God's dealings with mankind. The Church and Israel are dealt with in entirely different ways and have wholly different futures. The future of the Church climaxes in "the rapture." The future of Israel climaxes in the great tribulation, the battle of Armageddon, and the millennial reign of Christ on the earth.

Among evangelicals, both the allegorical and the literal systems of interpretation affirm the doctrine of salvation for sinners through the Lord Jesus Christ. Both affirm the eternal state: glory for the believer and the eternal woe of the lost. These points of agreement, however, should not blind us to the radical differences of the two systems. This handbook follows the literal method of Bible interpretation.

What about an alleged third "road"? This is not really a Biblical road at all. It usually begins with some man-made dogma, philosophy, or experience and uses proof texts from the Bible to bolster a position already adopted.

The so-called "charismatics," for instance, start with an *experience*: a supposed baptism of the Spirit, an outburst of speaking in tongues, or an alleged miracle. The "experience" may be a personal one or someone else's. It seems to be Biblical, since the Bible certainly does refer to healing, miracles, prophecy, and speaking in tongues. All kinds of texts can be paraded to support the view that these things are part of normal Christian experience and are still valid. A favorite text with some, for instance, is "forbid not to speak with tongues" (1 Corinthians 14:39). A not-so-favorite text is "whether there be tongues, they shall cease" (1 Corinthians 13:8), especially since this statement in the original text indicates that tongues would "cease in and of themselves." They would come to an automatic end because they were only a temporary phenomenon.

Roman Catholics start with *dogma*: the immaculate conception of the Virgin Mary, purgatory, prayers for the dead, the "real presence" of the Lord Jesus in the consecrated wafer. Such dogmas are not supported by a thorough-going exegesis of Scripture but by proof texts, by appeals to tradition, by the writings of the Church fathers, and by the Apocrypha. One needs only to procure a copy of *The Baltimore Catechism* and to study Catholic dogma from its pages to see that no solid Biblical support exists for those dogmas. Dogmas are based on texts taken out of context. The vast Roman Catholic edifice is built on this foundation of sand.

Before people can drive a car they are first required to learn the rules of the road and satisfy the authorities that they have done so. This is for their own safety and for the safety of all those who use the highways. Nobody can be a law unto himself on public roads. We cannot arbitrarily drive on the wrong side of the road, operate our vehicle at high speed in school zones, or ignore traffic signals.

Likewise, before people interpret the Bible they need to master the rules of Biblical interpretation. Failure to do that makes a Bible teacher a danger to all he encounters. The first part of this book gives the salient rules. These rules are not arbitrary. Most of them are simple common sense—the same kind of rules we apply to the interpretation of all writing.

The Bible is unique, of course, in that the unregenerate cannot unravel its truths at all (1 Corinthians 2:14). Moreover, even the most devout believers need the Holy Spirit to reveal its mysteries and wonders (John 14:16-17; 16:12-15). At the same time, the Holy Spirit used the laws of language when writing the Bible and He uses the laws of language when making its truths plain. We need to know what those laws of language are so that we can rightly divide the word of truth (2 Timothy 2:15).

1
The Golden Rule

If the plain sense makes common sense, seek no other sense. *That* is the golden rule of Bible interpretation. God says what He means and means what He says. We are to read the Bible just as we read any other piece of writing, not trying to force some allegorical, mystical, or figurative meaning into its plain statements. That does not mean that spiritual lessons can not be derived from a passage of Scripture, even from a passage dealing largely with narrative. Nor does it mean that a passage has no deeper lessons than those lying on the surface. The Bible is the Word of God and is therefore inexhaustible. We must, however, apply to the Bible the same principles of common sense we would use in examining any other writing. We must look for the plain sense of what has been written. Once we have determined *that,* we can mine beneath the surface for hidden treasure.

1. In other words, *we interpret literally.* The ordinary or commonly acknowledged meaning of a word is the literal meaning of that word. When people write to us or speak to us, we take their words at face value, even when they are using poetic language. We do not look for all kinds of hidden meanings buried beneath the surface of what they have to say. We read papers, magazines, trade journals, novels, and textbooks literally. When we come across a figure of speech we recognize it for what it is, a poetic means of conveying a literal idea. We use idioms, symbols, and poetic expressions every day—not to convey secret meanings but to add color to our speech.

Thus, in the Bible, when we read the parable of the wheat and the tares, we recognize the aptness of the symbols because weeds do grow prolifically in a field of wheat. When the Bible refers to people as "dogs," we recognize the validity of the comparison. We know how gross the habits of dogs can be at times and how snappish or fawning, vicious or unclean, people can be in their lives. In the Bible people are compared with all kinds of animals: dogs, lions, wolves, swine, foxes, sheep. Characteristics of these animals illustrate human characteristics.

Before deciding that a passage of Scripture is figurative, we must first examine the literal meaning. Only when a literal interpretation proves to be either absurd or completely out of harmony with the context or the theme should we accept a figurative interpretation.

The book of Psalms, for instance, has many references to Zion. We have no right to read the Church into those references. Zion was a well-known stronghold in Jerusalem and was a name often used for the whole city. Prophetic references to Zion refer not to the Church but to the literal city of Jerusalem. It is true that the writer of Hebrews uses "Zion" in a figurative way, but does so, not to identify the Church with Israel but to contrast the two. When interpreting the Bible literally we make obvious allowances for figures of speech.

Some years ago an American businessman was asked to address a Chinese audience in Taiwan. He was provided with a translator whose familiarity with English idioms was less than adequate. The speaker rose to his feet and said, "I'm tickled to death to be here." A look of agony passed over the face of the interpreter. He shrugged helplessly. Then he announced to the waiting Chinese audience, "This poor man scratches himself to death in order to be here."

Interpreting a communication literally makes full allowance for poetic utterance and for idioms. The rule is to look for the primary, obvious, intended meaning to a passage and to interpret symbols, types, allegories, and figures of speech as we normally would. If someone says, "I completely lost my head," we know what he means. It does not mean he was decapitated; it means he acted without thinking. We must use the same common-sense approach when interpreting the Bible.

2. *We interpret culturally.* For an intelligent understanding of some parts of the Bible we need to know something about the geography and climate of the country and the customs and history of the times. The Bible was not written in the twentieth century, nor was it written in the West. It was written over a period of 1,500 years in places as far apart as Persia in the East and Rome in the West and it was written by people drawn from many walks of life. Moses and Daniel were statesmen. David, Solomon, and Hezekiah were kings. Amos was a cowboy, Joshua was a soldier, Ezra and Ezekiel were priests, Matthew was a tax collector. Peter and John were fishermen, Luke a doctor, Paul a scholar. The cultural background of Exodus is quite different from that of Hosea. Almost a century separated Jeremiah from Isaiah. During that century a whole new international situation arose. Four hundred turbulent years intervene between Malachi and Matthew. In studying Old Testament histories and prophecies, and the New Testament historical books, some understanding of the times is essential.

We also need to know something about Bible *geography*, which is rich and varied. We read of mountains, rivers, plains, cities, crops, climate, seasons, vegetation, and animals. A good Bible dictionary can be helpful since it specializes in giving information about these things.

Knowledge of Bible geography will help us, for instance, in understanding Psalm 29. It is really a description of a thunderstorm that left a lasting impression on David's soul. It broke out over the Mediterranean (verses 3-4), and David describes the spectacular display of the storm out at sea. Then it swept inland, shaking the mighty cedars of Lebanon and thundering through the ravines of Mount Hermon (Sirion) in the north (verse 6). From there the storm moved south over the wilderness of Kadesh (verse 8). Its tremendous reverberations caused calves to be prematurely born. Its wind and rain stripped the forests bare (verse 9). Thus David traces the progress of the storm from its first appearance over the Mediterranean to its final disappearance in the deserts of the south. He then makes observations and draws lessons from the storm.

Or take, for instance, Ezekiel, chapters 38 and 39. It is vital to remember that all geography in the Bible takes its center from Palestine. When we read of a coming invasion from "the uttermost parts of the north," we understand at once that this is north, not of Pittsburgh or Paris but of Palestine.

When we read of "the seven churches of Asia," we don't think of a handful of churches in India, China, or Japan. Bible geography directs our attention to the Roman province of Asia Minor, a part of what we now know as Turkey. Many of the incidents in the life of the Lord Jesus can be much better understood, given a knowledge of the geography of the Holy Land.

The Holy Land was really quite small, as the following table of distances (in modern Israel) shows. The distances are given in miles. See the chart on the following page.

Who would want to study the missionary journeys of Paul without some good Bible maps? (Be sure to see the list of helpful books listed in the Appendix.)

Bible history is just as colorful as Bible geography. The Bible was written against the background of the rise and fall of great empires. Egypt and Assyria, Babylon and Persia, Greece and Rome all march across its pages. Canaan and Syria, Moab and Edom, Ammon, Philistia, and Arabia all come and go. Jerusalem, Gaza, Damascus, and many other cities crowd its pages.

Draw a circle with a radius of 900 miles, with Jerusalem as its center, and you will encompass Athens, Istanbul, Antioch, Beirut, Damascus, Baghdad, Alexandria, Cairo, and Mecca. You will also encompass the area in which most of western civilization arose. From Jerusalem to Egypt is only about 300 miles; to Assyria or Babylon, about 700 miles; to Persia about 1,000 miles; to Greece about 800; and to Rome about 1,500 miles. Jerusalem lay on the line of march for the great imperial powers of antiquity. No wonder its history has been so turbulent. It had been besieged scores of times, and taken and sacked again and again.

	Beersheba	Caesarea	Capernaum	Damascus	Dan	Gaza	Haifa	Jerusalem	Megiddo	Tel Aviv
Beersheba	—	136	167	244	206	27	161	54	134	82
Caesarea	136	—	63	140	102	95	30	82	22	48
Capernaum	167	63	—	80	40	152	52	113	59	105
Damascus	244	140	80	—	63	229	123	190	136	182
Dan	206	102	40	63	—	191	86	152	98	144
Gaza	27	95	152	229	191	—	114	60	100	55
Haifa	161	30	52	123	86	114	—	101	20	67
Jerusalem	54	82	113	190	152	60	101	—	80	41
Megiddo	134	22	59	136	98	100	20	80	—	53
Tel Aviv	82	48	105	182	144	55	67	41	53	—

The Mount of Olives stands just a little higher than Jerusalem and serves to screen the city from the wilderness that falls away to the Dead Sea. Jerusalem itself stands 2,500 feet above sea level while the Dead Sea lies 1,290 feet below sea level. Thus, going down from Jerusalem to the Dead Sea, the traveler descends nearly 4,000 feet to a tropical climate. Snow can be lying on the streets of Jerusalem while twenty-five miles away at Jericho it can be hot. Jericho is not far from the Dead Sea. We can see the literal truth of the man in the Lord's story who "went down" from Jerusalem to Jericho. The Jordan Valley is part of a great rift system in the earth's crust and it remains hot all year around.

In Scripture we read of "Dan to Beersheba" as being the extremities of the land in historic Bible times. We think of it as a vast distance. It is less than a day's drive. It is just seventy-five miles from Jerusalem to Nazareth. Bethlehem is a scant five miles from Jerusalem. From Nazareth to Capernaum is barely twenty-five miles. When David stood with his sheep on the Judean hills around Jerusalem he could see the country of the Philistines only twenty miles to the west. All Palestinian Old Testament history took place in a country smaller than Wales or the Scottish highlands.

The great plain of Esdraelon, where the battle of Armageddon will take place, is a fertile valley filled with greenery and farms. Many an ancient army marched across that fateful field. The armies of Egypt, Assyria, and Babylon tramped across it. Somewhere there, Barak won his victory over Sisera and his nine-hundred chariots of iron. There good King Josiah met his death trying to halt an Egyptian invasion of his land. On the hills that gaze down on it King Saul crept furtively to meet a witch. Naboth's vineyard was not far from that great plain. The Carmel range, where Elijah smote the prophets of Baal, rises from the extremity of that far-flung area.

Nazareth itself, not far away, was a kind of great divide, not only between north and south, Judea and Galilee, but between the Old Testament and the New. Nazareth, geographically, is a frontier town, the bridge between two worlds. It was the place where the traveler said a final "farewell" to Judea and "hello" to Galilee when going north, and the opposite when going south. To the south was exclusive, aristocratic, formal Jerusalem. To the north was Galilee of the Gentiles, with Roman military roads from Syria and old trade routes from the distant east.

Turning eastward one went past Cana and on again into the hills, past a saddle-shaped hill in later times called the Horns of Hattin, where Saladin broke Crusader power in Palestine. Then travelers caught their first sight of the Sea of Galilee, a thousand feet below, with the winding Jordan River snaking into it at one end and twisting and turning out of it again at the other. The Sea of Galilee itself is some 700 feet below sea level. It is heart-shaped, thirteen miles long and about seven miles across at its widest part. It is rimmed around with mountains whose heads stand in a temperate zone and whose feet are in the subtropics where bananas, palms, and bamboos can grow. Far to the north Mount Hermon raises its snow-capped peak.

In Jesus' day the hills around the lake were clothed with trees. Aqueducts provided irrigation. The western shore was a chain of populous villages and towns with green gardens, busy markets, thriving wharfs, and humming light industries.

The chief town was Tiberius, a center of Roman life which Jesus never visited (as far as we know). There Greeks and Romans rubbed shoulders with native Galileans. The splendid Herodian palace was there, with its Greek sculptures that offended the sensibilities of orthodox Jews. There, too, was an amphitheater and theaters where one could watch performances of traveling entertainers or watch gladiators fight, as though it were Rome itself.

Capernaum, where Jesus made His home, was only ten miles from Roman Tiberius with its baths and famous spa. Across the lake the wild Gergesene hills crowded down to the shore.

This was where Jesus lived, where Roman soldiers marched, where Greek merchants flourished, where Phoenicians spread their exotic wares from distant lands across the sea, where caravans halted from the east, where soldiers and camp followers rubbed shoulders with gladiators and entertainers, where Jew and Gentile met in uneasy contact. Jesus chose to live not in the theological center of Jerusalem, not among the ascetic Essenes in the wilderness, not even in prim but dubious Nazareth, but in bustling Capernaum where people from many lands crossed and recrossed in their journeyings.

The sea of Galilee, usually placid and still as a mirror, is subject to sudden, violent storms that churn the lake into massive waves quite able to swamp small boats on its surface. The reason can be found in the surrounding hills. Westerly winds come swooping over the highlands, come howling down to the lake through scores of gorges and valleys, and then emerge like so many furies on the low lying water. As a result the sea of Galilee can be calm one moment and raging the next.

When the lake is calm it has another property, utilized by the Lord Jesus when addressing the great crowds that thronged its shores to hear Him speak. He would have the thousands of people sit on the slopes while He Himself either stood at the water's edge with His back to the lake, facing the crowds, or else sat near the shore in a boat. He would not need to raise His voice. He would speak in a conversational tone, and the lake behind Him, acting as a natural sounding board, picked up His voice, amplified it, and cast it up the slopes ahead. I once addressed a group of men in this way, near Capernaum where the Lord did so much of His teaching. The men sat a fair way off where they could not normally have heard someone speaking in an ordinary talking voice. But they heard every word I said as I read to them, in a dinner-table tone of voice, the story of the sower who went forth to sow. The lake was the Lord's microphone and amplifier, designed by and for Him when He created the world.

There can be no doubt that knowledge of Bible geography lends color and realism to our understanding of the Book.

A knowledge of the *history* and political intrigues of the times, of ancient kings and their campaigns, and of the political structure of nations in Bible days is also helpful in understanding some parts of the Bible. Daniel 11 is practically unintelligible apart from a knowledge of the political struggles in the Middle East after the collapse of the Grecian empire. The more we know about the history of Bible times the better equipped we shall be to detect some of the nuances in the text. For example, what light it sheds on the Absalom rebellion to know that Ahithophel was Bathsheba's grandfather. (Be sure to examine the synopsis of Bible history given at the end of this book.)

Knowledge of Bible *customs* is as important as knowledge of Bible history and geography. Anthropologists divide a people's culture into material culture and social culture. Such things as tools, houses, weapons, clothing, and utensils make up a people's material culture. Customs and practices, rites and ceremonies, religious customs, economic matters, and politics make up a people's social culture. Some things in the Bible that greatly puzzle the modern western reader would be perfectly understood by those to whom the Bible was originally addressed.

When the Lord gave His disciples instructions for locating a room in which to celebrate His last Passover, He told them to follow a man "bearing a pitcher of water" (Mark 14:13). Since only women generally did such work, the instructions were specific indeed. It would be uncommon to see a man performing that particular function in that day and age.

In Matthew 10:8-10 we read that the Lord sent out His disciples to "heal the sick, cleanse the lepers, raise the dead, cast out devils." He told them how they were to operate: "freely ye have received, freely give. Provide neither gold nor silver, nor brass in your purses: Nor scrip for your journey, neither two coats, neither shoes, nor yet staves" (see also Mark 6:8-9; Luke 9:3). The Greek word for "scrip" is *pēra*. From a study of the *papyri* (documents of all kinds from classical and Biblical Greek times: letters, contracts, accounts, receipts, school work, stories, bills of sale, etc.) we learn what a scrip was. It was a beggar's collecting bag (not a bag filled with provisions to sustain them on their mission). Wandering priests from heathen shrines would carry begging bags collecting money for the shrine. The Lord tells His disciples that they are not to earn money. Neither are they to *beg*. The One who commissioned them would take care of all their needs.

These and similar cultural highlights add greatly to our understanding of the Bible. Further examples are given in chapter 4.

3. *We interpret grammatically.* Because of that, some knowledge of the languages in which the Bible was written is desirable. Translations of the Bible can be helpful, but a translation, no matter how careful its translators have been, is still a translation. Something is always lost when a message is translated from one language into another. With the help of a good lexicon and several reputable volumes on Bible words, however, individuals who do not know Hebrew and Greek can overcome their handicap to some extent—at least as far as determining the etymology and meaning of words is concerned. Syntax (word arrangement), of course, is another matter.

God has communicated His mind to men in words, and the words He uses are all vitally important. He does not use them arbitrarily but with the most careful precision. Take, for instance, the word so often translated "hell" in our Bible. It comes from a Greek word, *hades,* which literally means "invisible." It thus denotes the place that is invisible, the abode of departed spirits. But other words are translated similarly in our Bible. *Sheol, gehenna,* and *tartarus,* for example, all refer to the invisible world. Students need to know exactly which word they are dealing with and in what sense the word is used in the passage being studied.

A knowledge of the original words of the Bible can enrich one's understanding of the Scriptures. Take for instance the word translated "transformed" in 2 Corinthians 11:13-14. The passage reads: "For such are false apostles, deceitful workers, transforming themselves into the apostles of Christ. And no marvel; for Satan himself is transformed into an angel of light." The word translated "transformed" is *metaschēmatizō,* and it means "to change the outward figure, to alter the shape, to alter one's bearing, look, or manner." It carries the idea of taking on an outward expression that does not truly reflect the inner nature. Kenneth Wuest, who has done much to popularize and explain the Greek New Testament for the average English reader, says that the English word "masquerade" exactly conveys the sense of the word. When Satan fell, he became an angel of darkness, but he masquerades as an angel of light. It is no wonder, Paul says, that false apostles masquerade as apostles of Christ.

Syntax requires a more thorough knowledge of the original languages than etymology. The arrangement of words in a sentence, at least in part, determines word usage. We arrange words in sentences to convey complete ideas. The diligent student must either become proficient in the original languages or else seek competent help in determining matters relating to the syntax of the sentences under study. (Obviously not everyone can be a grammarian or a philologist—and, after all, much of the Bible can be adequately interpreted without recourse to original languages—so no one should be discouraged at having to get such help.)

One example, however, will suffice to show how valuable the

grammatical interpretation of the Scripture can be. In Hebrews 1:1-2 we read that "God, who at sundry times and in diverse manners spake in time past unto the fathers by the prophets, hath in these last days spoken unto us by His Son." The verb "spake" is an aorist participle and should be rendered: "God having spoken." The verb "hath spoken" is an aorist indicative. The grammarian would understand from this that God began to speak in the Old Testament but He did not speak all His mind. In Christ, however, God has finally finished what He had to say.

Since the meaning of words is determined by the context in which they are found, attention must always be paid to the context. Take, for example, the much abused statement: "No prophecy of the scripture is of any private interpretation" (2 Peter 1:20). In the past, the Roman Catholic church has used that verse to bolster its position that Bible interpretation is the function of the church, not of individuals, and that the Bible can be interpreted only according to "the unanimous consent of the fathers."*

What does 2 Peter 1:20 say? How are we to understand the phrase "private interpretation"? The word "private" is *idios,* which occurs about 114 times in the Bible and is nearly always translated "its own." Not once is it translated "private" except here. The word *interpretation* is *epilusis* which means "to loose," "to solve," "to explain." The context gives the sense. The next verse says, "For the prophecy came not in old time by the will of man: but holy men of God spake as they were moved by the Holy Ghost" (verse 21). In other words, the writers of Scripture did not put their own construction on the God-breathed words they wrote. The reference in 2 Peter 1:20 is not so much to the way we interpret a passage of Scripture as to the way the writers handled it. It refers to the process of *inspiration* rather than to the problems of *interpretation.* The context makes that clear.

Most of us, in ordinary writing and conversation, do not try to hide what we want to communicate. We say, as plainly as we know how, just exactly what we wish to convey. God also does that. We should apply the same laws of language to the Bible that we apply to the words of Shakespeare or Einstein or the fellow next door.

Since the grammatical principle of interpretation is so important, the next two chapters in this handbook are devoted to explain it further and give additional examples.

---

*In actual fact there is no such thing as "unanimous consent," since many of the fathers have bitterly denounced what other fathers have written. Jerome, for instance, in the six volumes of letters from him still in existence, denounces Augustine to the extent that Jerome and Augustine agree on only one thing—to disagree about everything. In addition, the writings of the Catholic fathers fill at least 200 large volumes, and it would take years of continuous study to discover on what subjects, if any, they agreed. Something is obviously wrong with the official position of Rome on the matter of private interpretation.

2

Studying the Words of Scripture

The very words of the Bible, in the original languages and autographed documents, are "God-breathed." That is why, in seeking to find precisely what it is that God has said, we should go back to the original Hebrew and Greek languages and to the purest text available.

This handbook is designed to help men and women who are unable to do that. True, those who cannot read Hebrew and Greek will always suffer a measure of deprivation in expounding the Scriptures. But that in itself is not an insurmountable handicap. Diligent students of the English Bible today have numerous helps available to them. Besides various translations (of differing degrees of usefulness and reliability) and all kinds of critical commentaries, we can resort to lexicons and to specialized works that concentrate on the original Hebrew and Greek words of the Bible. (Be sure to see the listing of some of these at the end of this handbook.)

Three helps are essential:
1. Strong's *Concordance*
2. Thayer's *Greek-English Lexicon of the New Testament*
3. Gesenius's *Hebrew-Chaldee Lexicon to the Old Testament Scriptures*

With those three books, supplemented by W. E. Vine's *Expository Dictionary of New Testament Words* (be sure to get the edition published by Thomas Nelson, which has a corresponding dictionary of Old Testament words) and by W. E. Bullinger's *Critical Lexicon,* the diligent student can acquire a passable degree of proficiency in the vocabulary of the Bible.

The three primary works mentioned above open up a wealth of information about the original of any word used in the King James Bible. This is because in Strong's concordance every word in the English Bible is keyed to a lexicon at the back of the concordance and because the Thayer and Gesenius lexicons are keyed to the same number system. Half an hour with a King James Bible and these three tools should convince anyone of the value and helpfulness of such of study.

Take, for instance, the word *love* in the King James Bible. Suppose you were reading in John 21 the Lord's post-resurrection challenge to Peter: "So, when they had dined, Jesus saith to Simon Peter,

Simon, son of Jonas, *lovest* thou Me more than these? He saith unto Him, Yea, Lord; thou knowest that I *love* Thee . . . " (verse 15). From Strong's concordance you discover that these two words for *love* are not the same word in the Greek. You find the word *lovest* and run your eye down the column until you come to John 21:15. You find at the end of the line the number *25*. You make a note of it. You look up the word *love* and again run your eye down the column until you come to John 21:15. At the end of the line is the number *5368*. The difference in the numbers alerts you at once to the fact that you are dealing here with two different words for love—in the same Bible verse.

Now you turn to the Greek dictionary at the back of the concordance, to the second section that deals with Greek words. You look up the number *25* and discover that the word *lovest* comes from the Greek word *agapē*. You look up the number *5368* and discover that Peter's word for *love* was *phileō*. Moreover, Strong's lexicon gives a brief comment on each of these Greek words, indicating the significance of the particular word. As we shall see in a moment, this comment can sometimes be amplified by use of the other lexicons.

When the Lord used the word *agapē* He was asking Peter if he loved Him with a deep love, a spiritual love, a divine love (see John 14:21), the love that the Law demands (Luke 10:27), the kind of love that took Jesus to Calvary.

Peter, with a much better knowledge of himself now than he had displayed when he had boasted that, although all the other disciples might betray the Lord, he never would, dared not use the Lord's word for love. He used the word *phileō*. "Yea, Lord: Thou knowest I am fond of You, I have an affection for You."

The third time the Lord asked Peter that same question He used Peter's word for love: "He saith unto him the third time, Simon, son of Jonas, Lovest (*phileō*) thou Me?" (verse 17). Even then, Peter did not dare to use the higher word for love. In effect he said, "Lord, You know I can never, never love You as much as You love me, but I love You as much as my poor human heart is capable. You know that, Lord."

In many cases, further commentary on a given Greek word can be found in Thayer's lexicon. You just take the number of the word from Strong's concordance, look up that number in Thayer, and see what added light the lexicon sheds on the word. The same is true of the Hebrew words of the Old Testament. The Gesenius lexicon gives further commentary.

In addition, the numbering system in Strong's concordance enables you to see where else a given Greek or Hebrew word is used in the Bible. Take Peter's word, *phileō*. By noting all the other places where the number *5368* occurs at the end of the lines under "love" (and its cognates) you can compare Peter's use of the word with other uses of the word in the Greek New Testament. You can also see how frequently or how seldom a given word occurs in the original text of the Bible.

I am now going to give two extended word studies to show the value of giving this kind of attention to the words of Scripture.

For our first example, let us take the words for *sin* in the Hebrew Old Testament.

In the English language a number of words are synonyms for sin: iniquity, wickedness, evil, and so on. We tend to use these words carelessly.

The Hebrew of the Old Testament has about a dozen words for sin, which the Holy Spirit uses with great precision. Each word is chosen to express a specific shade of meaning. A working knowledge of these words and how they are used is helpful to a proper understanding of what God thinks and says about human wrongdoing. In this study we are going to look at these words and see how the Spirit of God employs them.

1. *Chātā*

The word *chātā* is the usual word in the Old Testament for sin. It means "to miss the mark." The word is used in a different but illuminating way in connection with certain warriors of the tribe of Benjamin. The Spirit of God says of these people that they could "sling stones at an hair breadth and not miss" (Judges 20:16). The word for "miss" is *chata*, the usual word for sin. Sin, then, is a matter of missing the mark.

God has set up a target. That target is His Word. He says to us, "That is My moral standard. You aim at that." The idea behind the word *chātā* is that of failing to hit the target. It does not necessarily imply willful sin, although of course it often does. We first meet this word in Genesis 4:7 in connection with Cain. He had brought what he considered to be a worthy offering to God, the work of his own hands, over which he had labored long and hard. God turned it down because it failed to take Cain's need for forgiveness into account. Cain was furious. God said, "If thou doest well, shalt thou not be accepted? And if thou doest not well, sin (*chātā*) lieth at the door." Cain's religion was sin. It missed the mark.

We have the same thing in connection with the kings of the northern kingdom of Israel. One refrain is repeated more than twenty times in the books of Kings. It says of them that they walked in the sins of Jeroboam "who made Israel to sin." The first occurrence is in 1 Kings 14:16. The word for Jeroboam's sin is *chātā*. He made Israel to miss the mark. He did it by setting up a false religious system. That is the trouble with mere religion. It causes people to miss the mark—and missing the mark is an Old Testament synonym for sin.

2. *Āshām*

The word *āshām* means "to trespass." It carries with it the idea of sinning through ignorance or by mistake. The word is frequently used in connection with the trespass offering (Leviticus 5:5-6 and elsewhere). The idea behind *asham* is that of breaking one of God's commandments through ignorance. Even though one was ignorant he was still guilty. Ignorance is legally no excuse. When one became aware of his trespass he had to make amends.

We are far too concerned with numbers. When David made up his mind to take a national census of his people, he did it in pride and self-will and without regard to what the law of God said about numbering God's people. Joab, usually a self-seeking opportunist, was right for once. He said, "The Lord make His people an hundred times so many more as they be, but my lord the king, are they not all my lord's servants? why then doth my lord require this thing? why will he cause trespass (*āshām*) in Israel?" (1 Chronicles 21:3). God did not want His people numbered just as a matter of publicity and pride. David went ahead and did it anyway—with terrible results. In confessing what he had done, David used the other word (*chātā*). He said, "I have sinned greatly" (verse 8). He had missed the mark. The amends he had to make were costly indeed, as the rest of the story shows.

We have fuzzy ideas about sin. We sin against God and His standards without even knowing we have done so. But God does not excuse us on that ground. Sins of ignorance are just as serious in His sight as any other kinds of sin. Thus we find in Isaiah 53:10 that God says of the Lord Jesus, "Thou shalt make His soul an offering for sin (*āshām*)." Some sins are committed in ignorance, but Jesus had to pay for those sins, too, at infinite cost.

3. *Āvēn*

The word *āvēn* carries with it the idea of iniquity. When David confessed to the Lord his guilt in numbering Israel, he not only used the word for missing the mark, he used the word *āvēn*. "I have sinned (*chātā*) greatly because I have done this thing: but now, I beseech Thee, do away with the iniquity (*āvēn*) of Thy servant" (1 Chronicles 21:8). He used the word that connotes perverseness.

In the Old Testament this word is often used in connection with idolatry. In 1 Kings 12:28-33 we have a classic example. Jeroboam, the first king of the northern kingdom, determined to keep his people away from Jerusalem and the Temple. He set up a rival religion. He built two shrines, the principal one at Bethel, a place of hallowed memories in Hebrew history. There he set up a golden calf to be worshiped by the people. It became a snare which led eventually to the complete ruin of the kingdom. The name Bethel means "the house of God." The prophet Hosea changed the name from Bethel to Beth-*āvēn*, "the house of iniquity" (Hosea 4:15).

In its general usage in the Old Testament, *āvēn* signifies not so much a breach of God's law as the general outflow of fallen human nature in bad behavior. We are not sinners because we sin. We sin because we are sinners. I do what I do because I am what I am. The word comes from a root meaning "to pant" or to exert one's self in vain. It often carries with it the idea of vanity. So much human thinking and activity are vain from God's point of view—worthless, coming to nought.

4. Āvon

The word *āvon* is often translated "iniquity" in the Old Testament. It means "to be bent," or to be crooked. It describes all the wrongness, the bentness, of fallen human nature. It stands for what we are by nature, for our natural perverseness. That condition is something never wholly eradicated from our nature in this life.

After David's terrible sin with Bathsheba and the subsequent murder of her husband, followed by weeks of stubborn hypocrisy and arrogant pretense that he had done no wrong, when finally the prophet Nathan came to him with God's message of wrath, David fell on his knees. From his heart poured the terrible confession of Psalm 32. "Blessed is he whose *transgression* is forgiven, whose *sin* is covered, blessed is the man unto whom the Lord imputeth not *iniquity*" (verses 1-2). David used three Hebrew words to describe his guilt. He called it transgression. The word is *pasha*, which means rebellion. We have not met this word yet. David's sin was an act of high-handed rebellion against God. He also called it *sin* (*chātā*). His sin was a terrible missing of the mark. He had fallen far, far short of the glory of God. He also called it *iniquity* (*āvon*), an act of perversion. It was an expression of the bentness of his nature, an exhibition of the ingrained wrongness of his being.

The word *āvon* is first used in Genesis 15:16, where God, having pledged the Promised Land to Abraham, told him that, although the title deeds were now his, actual possession of the property would be postponed for some time: "the iniquity of the Amorites is not yet full," He said. The word there is *āvon*. The bentness, the perversions of the Amorites, were not yet overflowing the cup of God's patience. Their idolatries and immoralities still had some way to go.

This word is used again to describe the horrible vileness of the people of Sodom with their perverted lifestyle which called for the vengeance of God. "And when the morning arose, then the angels hastened Lot, saying, Arise, take thy wife, and thy two daughters which are here, lest thou be consumed in the iniquity (*āvon*) of the city" (Genesis 19:15). The bentness or perversions of Sodom called for the vengeance of eternal fire. God was about to rain hell from heaven upon that city. He uses this word *avon* to describe its homosexual society.

The word is used by Shimei when confessing his sin to David. When David fled from Absalom, this wicked man gave free vent to the warped, bent, and twisted thoughts of his heart in vile oaths and curses against the Lord's anointed. When David came back, Shimei was desperately afraid for having thus given full rein to his wickedness. "Let not my lord impute iniquity (*avon*) unto me," he said (2 Samuel 19:19). People who oppose Christ reveal the same warp in their character.

The word is used in Leviticus 16:21 in connection with the Day of Atonement. On that day a goat was taken, and over its head was confessed all the guilt of the nation of Israel. "And Aaron shall lay both his hands upon the head of the live goat [both his hands for solemnity—and only here on this occasion], and confess over him all the iniquities (*āvon*) . . . and transgressions [the word *pasha* used by David in describing his rebellion] in all their sins (*chātā*), putting them on the head of the goat, and shall send him away by the hand of a fit man into the wilderness." Aaron used the three words that David used. The one that was first and foremost, however, was *āvon*—it was the incurable bentness of their human nature that first had to be confessed.

5. *Āmāl*

The word *āmāl* carries with it the idea of trouble, labor, and toil. It depicts the burden of sin: the trouble it causes and how grievous it is. This word is infrequent in the Old Testament and is translated in several ways.

Solomon, at the end of his misspent, wasted life, looking back over his follies and failures, wishing he could have his days to live over again, aware that he had lived for the wrong world, used this word. He used it in Ecclesiastes a dozen times in swift succession. He said, "Therefore I hated life; because the work that is wrought under the sun is grievous unto me: for all is vanity and vexation of spirit. Yea, I hated all my labor (*āmāl*) which I had taken under the sun" (Ecclesiastes 2:17-18). The word for *labor* can be made synonymous with sin. The great undertakings, the magnificent works he had wrought in Jerusalem, all at the expense of oppression and sweated labor, added up to *āmāl*, sin. No matter how magnificent and spectacular the end result might seem to others, in his secret soul Solomon, now that he was at the end of life, summed it all up as sin. What greater tragedy could one face than that? To realize that everything for which we have worked so hard adds up to sin because God has been left out.

Solomon uses the same word later. He says, "And this is a sore evil [here he uses a word we shall look at later, a word meaning "wicked" or "injurious," which carries the idea of obscenity and depravity], that in all points, as he came, so shall he go: and what profit hath he that hath labored (*āmāl*) for the wind?" (Ecclesiastes 5:16). Solomon sees life as obscene when people invest all their time, talents, and treasures seeking things that are empty and impossible to hold once they are attained. That is his assessment of his own life, so wretchedly wasted on the wrong world.

The word *āmāl* was thrown in the face of poor old Job by Eliphaz in his second address (Job 15:35). He put it in the third person, but he meant Job. He said, "They conceive mischief (*āmāl*) and bring forth vanity." He was comparing Job with the hypocrites. He was saying that Job was an oppressor, that he had caused trouble. He was saying that the terrible burdens now placed on Job by God were placed on him because he deserved them. His sin had found him out. While pretending to be good he had really been a hypocrite. Now mischief (*āmāl*) had come home to roost—so it served him right.

That was a terrible thing to say to a man whose integrity was the talk of heaven. Job's helpfulness to one and all, his generosity, kindness, and concern for the needy were beyond question. Few people have lived so free of all that the word *āmāl* implies as Job had.

6. *Āval*

The word *āval* means "unjust." It epitomizes the unfairness, deceitfulness, innate dishonesty, and unrighteousness of sin. Solomon used the word when he wrote, "An unjust (*āval*) man is an abomination to the Lord" (Proverbs 29:27). If we cheat someone or deceive someone or tell a lie, our behavior falls under the lash of this word.

Moses used the word in demanding the strict enforcement of justice in Israel: "Ye shall do no unrighteousness (*āval*) in judgment" (Leviticus 19:15,35). He illustrated this in demanding that no judge discriminate against the poor or be deferential to the mighty, and that no businessman use false weights and measures in conducting his affairs.

7. *Ābar*

The word *ābar* literally means "to go beyond." It carries with it the idea of transgression. David uses this word to describe sins of the tongue. "I am purposed that my mouth shall not transgress (*ābar*)" (Psalm 17:3). In no area of life are we more prone to go beyond prudent limits, to go beyond what is kind, true, and necessary, than in our speech. It is a fearful thought that Jesus solemnly said that "every idle word that men shall speak they shall give account thereof in the day of judgment."

The prophet Hosea, looking out on an apostate land and aware that the Assyrian army would soon be used as God's instrument of chastisement, said that Israel had "transgressed the covenant" (Hosea 6:7; 8:1). They had gone too far. They had crossed that hidden boundary line between God's mercy and His wrath.

8. *Rā'a*

The word *rā'a* means "wicked" or "injurious." It carries with it the idea of breaking up all that is good and desirable in life. It is often used to depict corruption, lewdness, and depravity. It occurs frequently in the psalms. In the Greek, an equivalent word is *ponēros* (from this word we get our word *pornography*). In the King James text it is sometimes translated "naughty," a wholly inadequate way to render the word.

We find *rā'a* used this way, for instance, by Eliab, David's elder brother. When David arrived at the front, sent there by his father, and heard the boasting of Goliath, he expressed astonishment that nobody in Israel dared to fight the giant. David's older brother maliciously said, "I know thy pride and the naughtiness [*rā'a*, the lewdness] of thine heart" (1 Samuel 17:28).

Eliab was jealous of his younger brother, who had been anointed by Samuel to be Israel's next king. His criticism of David was slanderous.

Solomon used the word in an interesting way in describing the way bargaining was carried on in an eastern market. "It is naught, it is naught [*rā'a*] saith the buyer, but when he is gone his way, then he boasteth" (Proverbs 20:14). We can easily picture the scene. We can see the buyer looking over the merchandise offered him for sale. "Bad, very bad," he says, shaking his head and deprecating the worth of the article in question. He used the strongest word he can think of to downgrade its worth (*rā'a*). But once the bargain his been struck he sings another song.

Then there is that famous statement of Jeremiah which so forcefully illustrates how the Elizabethan English of the King James Version has changed with the passing of the centuries. Describing Israel under the symbolism of figs the prophet had seen in a basket, he calls them "naughty" (*rā'a*) figs. The word *rā'a* in this case indicates that the figs were rotten, a fitting symbol for an apostate nation that was rotten to the core.

9. *Pasha*

The word *pasha* means "to revolt" or "rebellion." It speaks of sin as an act of rebellion against lawful authority. In several of his penitential psalms David uses this word. He uses it, for instance, in Psalm 51:1, "Blot out my transgressions (*pasha*)," he pleads. Then he promises that he will "teach transgressors (*pasha*) Thy ways" (verse 13). David's adultery and his assassination of Uriah broke God's laws high-handedly. Nowadays we tend to look on immorality as something excusable, something our society tolerates and permits. God labels it rebellion against His authority. He warns that it never goes unpunished.

In one powerful passage the prophet Isaiah records God's lament over Israel's continued neglect of Him. He says that Israel was weary of Him. And —He was weary of them. Then, against a sad catalog of Israel's sins of indifference, God says, "I, even I, am He that blotteth out thy transgressions (*pasha*, their rebellion) for Mine own sake, and I will not remember thy sins (*chāta*, missing the mark)" (Isaiah 43:25). What a revelation that is of God's motive in forgiveness. Our rebellion, our utter inability to reach the mark He has set, is put away

by God for His own sake. He does it to meet some deep need within
His own character as a God of compassion and love.

10. *Rāshā*

The word *rāshā* means "wickedness." It describes the restless, un-
ceasing working of our fallen human nature. In his first lament over
his losses, bereavements, and terrible physical affliction, Job regret-
ted that he had not died in childbirth. He would then be in a land, he
said, where "the wicked (*rāshā*) cease from troubling" (Job 3:17).

In one of his greatest prophecies (Isaiah 53) the prophet Isaiah
used *rāshā* in a striking way. Foretelling what people would do with
the body of the Lord Jesus, he said, "And He made His grave with
the wicked" (Isaiah 53:9). Or, as that can be rephrased, "One [or
they] made [appointed, assigned] His grave with the wicked." The
word is *rāshā*. Here it is in the plural. The idea is that they gave him a
grave with criminals. It was a final indignity that the authorities
planned for the Son of God, the Holy One of Israel. They were
going to dump His body in a common grave or else throw it into the
fires of Gehinnom. However, they reckoned without God and without Joseph of Arimathea, who saw to it that He was honorably
interred with the rich.

Another well-known use of this word is also by the prophet
Isaiah. "The wicked (*rāshā*) are like the troubled sea, when it cannot
rest, whose waters cast up mire and dirt. There is no peace, saith my
God, to the wicked (*rāshā*)" (Isaiah 57:20-21). So we see here that
the underlying thought behind this concept of sin is restlessness.
Whatever else the wicked man has, he does not have rest or peace.

11. *Māal*

The word *māal* carries with it the thought of treachery, of
unfaithfulness. It is the word used to describe a breach of trust, or
the breaking of a contract. It is used of the sin of committing an offense against "the holy things of the Lord" (Leviticus 5:15). The
word is used of unfaithfulness to the covenant. In warning Israel of
the penalties that would follow if they broke His covenant, God said,
"And they that are left of you shall pine away in their iniquity (*āvon*,
their bentness and innate crookedness) in your enemies'
lands . . . and if they shall confess . . . the iniquity (*āvon*) of their fathers, with their trespass (*māal*, treachery) which they trespassed
(*māal*) . . . then will I remember My covenant . . . " (Leviticus
26:39-42). In other words, sin is an act of high treason against the
throne of God. It brings about an annulment of God's promises.

The word is used in connection with marital unfaithfulness. "If
any man's wife go aside and commit a trespass (*māal*) against
him . . . " is the way the Law puts it (Numbers 5:12). Adultery is an
act of treachery.

Moses was kept out of the Promised Land for something he did.

At Meribah God told him to speak to the rock so that the living waters might flow for Israel. Once before he had been told to smite the rock. This time he was to speak to it. Moses, however, lost his temper with the children of Israel and, instead of speaking to the rock, he smote it. In recounting the incident to Israel and God's severe displeasure with him, he tells how God told him to prepare for death "Because ye trespassed (*māal*) against Me among the children of Israel at the waters of Meribah-Kadesh" (Deuteronomy 32:51).

What was so serious about this act of treachery? The rock had been smitten once. It was not to be smitten again. He need only speak to it now. The rock symbolized Christ. The Lord was only to be smitten once. Calvary was never to be repeated in the history of the universe. Only once would God smite His Son. All we need to do now to secure the blessing is to speak to Him. For Moses to smite the rock a second time was a serious offense, an act of high treason against the truth of God. It cost him his life and exclusion from the Promised Land at that time.

The same word is used in connection with the sin of Achan. God had declared that all the spoils of Jericho were to be His. It was the firstfruits of a life of victory. Achan, however, stole some of the spoils. Later when Israel fought against Ai they were defeated and when Joshua asked God for the reason, God uncovered Achan's sin. The Holy Spirit, in recording the incident, says, "But the children of Israel committed a trespass (*māal*) in the accursed thing" (Joshua 7:1). Achan's sin was an act of high treason against the law of God and against those principles of trust and obedience that made it possible for God's people to live in victory. He paid a high price for his treachery. Sin is a serious business.

12. *Shāgag*

The word *shāgag* is used to describe sin as an act of imprudence, of rashness—the result of being deceived. It is not used to describe willful sin. *Shāgag* is used to describe the kinds of sins people commit when they are carried away in the heat of passion or when they are drunk. Such sins are distinguished from sins of presumption, sins deliberately and flagrantly committed.

In Numbers 15:28 this word is used to describe a sin committed in ignorance. "And the priest shall make an atonement for the soul that sinneth (*shāgag*) ignorantly." Even though we might sin rashly, as the result of being deceived, or as a result of hot passion, it is still sin. We are still culpable. It still has to be atoned for.

The author of Psalm 119 uses this word on a number of occasions. He prays, "O let me not wander (*shāgag*) from Thy commandments" (Psalm 119:10). He says, "Thou has rebuked the proud that are cursed which do err (*shāgag*) from Thy commandments" (Psalm 119:21).

So there we have it: twelve words to describe all shades and varieties of sin. Sin as missing the mark and coming short of the glory of God. Sin as a trespass, as something done ignorantly. Sin as expressing the perverseness, bentness, and crookedness of fallen human nature. Sin in the light of all the trouble it causes others. Sin as an act of injustice and deceitfulness. Sin as going beyond the limits set by God. Sin as moral depravity, corruption, lewdness, a breaking up of all that is good—sin as pornography and perversion. Sin as high-handed revolt and rebellion against God. Sin as wickedness—the restless working of our fallen nature. Sin as an act of treachery against God or other human beings. Sin as a result of passion, as a result of imprudence, as a result of being deceived. Sin in all its cumulative horror. No wonder we need a Savior.

These are the Old Testament words for sin. The New Testament has an equally rich and versatile vocabulary for human wrongdoing:

—*harmatanō*, missing the mark.

—*paraptōma*, falling aside.

—*ponēria*, moral depravity.

—*kakos*, vicious desire.

—*anomos*, contempt for the law.

—*athesmos*, deliberate assault on all divine and human restraints in order to indulge one's evil desires.

—*asebeia*, impious, describing those who have no fear of God and no reverence for holy things.

—*apeitheia*, unwilling to be persuaded, or just plain obstinate.

—*parakoē*, disobedience, or the refusal to listen.

—*parerchomai*, to neglect, to go past.

—*parabainō*, to violate, or to overstep the mark.

—*adikia*, wrongdoing, unrighteousness.

—*paranomia*, to defy law or custom.

—*planaō*, causing someone to go astray (literally, to wander), used particularly to describe doctrinal error and deceit of a religious nature.

—*astocheō*, to deviate.

—*hēttēma*, to give less than full measure.

With a good concordance and lexicon the careful student can compile scores of examples of the use of these words. With a dozen Old Testament words and about two dozen New Testament words, the Holy Spirit has given us a vivid and dreadful picture of the damage done to the human soul by sin.

Now let us look at what the Holy Spirit says about the unseen world.

A careful examination of the words used in the original text, by the Holy Spirit, is essential if we are to make headway in understanding exactly what it is He has revealed to us about the *unseen world*. Several Hebrew and Greek words unfold for us the mysteries that lie beyond the tomb. In this study we are going to examine them with care.

The first word is:

1. *Sheōl*

The word *sheōl* is found 65 times in the Old Testament. It is translated in various ways in the King James Version: as "hell," 31 times; as "grave," 31 times; as "the pit," 3 times.

The basic idea behind the word *sheōl* is "the grave," *the* grave as distinguished from *a* grave or burying place. In Hebrew the words *geber* and *bōr* are used to depict the tomb, not *sheōl*. Diligent students will be greatly helped by taking a good concordance, one that gives the Hebrew words, and finding every passage where *sheōl* is mentioned and writing the word *sheōl* alongside whatever English word is used in all 65 places.

2. *Hadēs*

The corresponding Greek word for *sheōl* is *hadēs*. We learn this from Acts 2:27,31 where the Holy Spirit used the word *hadēs* to translate the word *sheōl* when quoting from Psalm 16:10. It is made up of the Greek stem *id* (which means "to see") with the prefix *a* in front of it. The two make up a composite word which literally means "the unseen." In other words, *hadēs* has reference to the unseen world. It occurs 11 times in the New Testament and is rendered "hell" on all but one occasion. The exception is in 1 Corinthians 15:55, where it is rendered "grave" with a marginal reading "hell."

Again, it would be a good idea, using a suitable concordance, to mark all the *hadēs* in your Bible. Where the context makes it clear that *hadēs* refers to the abode of human beings in the unseen world, it is best not to try to translate the word into "hell" but simply to transliterate it and let it stand as *hadēs*. Where the context would indicate that the word refers to the unseen world as a whole (not just the place of departed human beings) it would probably be best to translate it as "the unseen world." This occurs in two places:

1. Matthew 16:18, where the passage could be rendered "the gates [counsels] of the unseen world shall not prevail against it [the Church]." The gate, of course, was the place where business was transacted in a mideastern city and the place where the city fathers ruled. Jesus was assuring us that the rulers of the unseen world cannot prevail against His Church.

2. Revelation 1:18, where the Lord announced, "I . . . have the keys of death and the unseen world."

Where is *sheōl* or *hadēs*? In Old Testament times the abode of the dead is referred to as being in a downward direction. Thus, for instance, when the witch of Endor was asked by King Saul to summon Samuel back from the dead, he said, "Bring him *up* to me." When, much to the dismay of the witch (who was expecting her familiar spirit to do one of his impersonations) Samuel actually did appear, the outraged prophet demanded of Saul, "Why hast thou disquieted me, to bring me up?" (1 Samuel 28:8,11,15). Then, too, Paul says of the Lord Jesus that, at death, He *descended* into "the lower parts of the earth" (Ephesians 4:9). At death the soul of the Lord Jesus went downward. We can compare Psalm 16:10 with Acts 2:27 for confirmation of the fact that the Lord's soul went to *sheōl* (*hadēs*).

The story Jesus told of the rich man and Lazarus (Luke 16:19-31) tells us a great deal about *hadēs*. In the days when He lived on earth, *hadēs* was divided into two sections, the one divided from the other by an impassable gulf. The soul of the rich man went to one section; the soul of Lazarus went to the other section. Between them stood the Great Divide. The angel carried the soul of Lazarus to his resting place. We are not told how the rich man ended up in the place of torment. All that is mentioned is his burial, doubtless impressive enough on earth.

In his disembodied state, Lazarus was in what Jesus called "Abraham's bosom." That is a Hebrew idiom. It signifies a place of rest, fellowship, happiness, comfort, love, and security. The poor beggar was now consciously happy and content. Things he had craved and been denied on earth were now his.

The rich man, however, was in what Jesus called "a place of torment." He cried out in his agony, "I am tormented in this flame." Moreover, he was anxious that his brothers "come not into this place of torment," as he put it (Luke 16:24,28). Much more can be learned about this place by carefully studying the whole story in Luke 16. The rich man was dead but he was still alive. Death had severed him from his body but not from his consciousness. He was lost, tormented, beyond hope or help, aware that he was where he deserved to be and could look for no relief.

When the Lord Jesus hung on the cross, one of the two thieves repented of his sinful life and appealed to Jesus in a remarkable and bold statement of faith. Jesus said to him, "Today shalt thou be with Me in paradise" (Luke 23:43). There is a definite article in the text. Jesus said, "Thou shalt be with Me in *the* paradise."

The word *paradise* is especially interesting. In the Old Testament, Solomon said, "I made me gardens and orchards." The word translated "orchards" is the Hebrew word *pardēsīm*. Literally it means "paradises"—that is, parks or pleasure grounds. Such paradises were made by eastern monarchs for their relaxation and enjoyment. When Jesus said to the dying thief, "This day thou shalt be with Me in paradise," He was referring to the same place described as "Abraham's bosom" in Luke 16. In other words, He was going to the happy segment of the unseen world, one that would become an immediate paradise by the presence of the soul of the Savior.

In Ephesians 4:8 (compare Psalm 68:18), we learn that the paradise section of *hadēs* is now in a different location. The Holy Spirit says of the Lord Jesus that when "He ascended up on high, He led captivity captive." Or, as others render that: "When He ascended on high He led a multitude of captives." It is generally inferred from this statement that the Lord Jesus emptied the "paradise" segment of the Old Testament *sheōl* (*hadēs*) and took the souls of the believing dead with Him to heaven. Thereafter, when the New Testament has occasion to speak of believers in the unseen world, the location is *up* instead of down. Thus Paul speaks of being "caught up into paradise" (2 Corinthians 12:4) where he heard and saw things "not lawful to utter." It was something he could not talk about.

The expression "caught up" is also interesting. The Greek word is *harpazō*, literally meaning "to catch away" or "to snatch away." The King James text usually renders it "caught up." It is the same word used to describe the rapture: "For the Lord Himself shall descend from heaven with a shout, with the voice of the archangel, and with the trump of God: and the dead in Christ shall rise first: then we which are alive and remain shall be caught up (*harpazō*) together in clouds to meet the Lord in the air" (1 Thessalonians 4:16-17). Here the whole idea, in the sense of direction, is upward. The same word is used in Revelation 12:5 where we have a summary of the career of Christ, the "man child." We read that the woman (Israel) "brought forth a man child, who was to rule all nations with a rod of iron: and her child was caught up (*harpazō*) unto God, and to His throne."

So when Paul was "caught or snatched away" the King James text strongly implies that he was "caught up." The Lord ascended into heaven. He went up. He relocated paradise. Believers go now to be where He is and that is clearly indicated to be in an upward direction. In quite a different context Paul indicates the same thing when he says, "Say not in thine heart, Who shall ascend into heaven? (that is, to bring Christ down from above)" (Romans 10:6).

A study of the passages relating to the unseen world shows that those who have died can see, hear, speak, reason, and remember. They can recognize one another. In other words, they are fully alive and conscious of their state—for better or for worse. After his experience in paradise, Paul had what he called "a desire to depart, and be with Christ; which is far better" (Philippians 1:23). He also said that, for the believer, "to die is gain" (Philippians 1:21). In referring to his desire to depart and be with Christ, Paul used a number of interesting words. The word he used for desire (*epithumai*) literally means "the desire." In the King James text it is translated in three different ways: as "desire," 3 times; as "concupiscence," 3 times; as "lust," 31 times. The word was used by Jesus in describing His heart's desire to share the last Passover with the disciples. "With desire I have desired to eat this Passover with you before I suffer," He said (Luke 22:15).

In describing his yearning to see his beloved Thessalonican converts, Paul uses the same word. He wrote, "But we, brethren, being taken from you for a short time in presence, not in heart, endeavored the more abundantly to see your face with great desire" (1

Thessalonians 2:17). When he says that he desired to depart and be with Christ, he is literally saying that he lusted to go to heaven!

The verb he used for "depart" (*analuō*) is another interesting word. It means "to depart and return." The only other place this verb occurs in the New Testament is where the Lord urges His followers to be "like unto men that wait for their lord, when he will return [same word] from the wedding" (Luke 12:36). Paul uses the noun in writing his last note to Timothy. Expecting imminent execution, he wrote, "The time of my departure (*analusis*) is at hand" (2 Timothy 4:6). Scholars tell us that in classical Greek the word is used of a ship weighing anchor. Paul said, "I have a desire to depart." He wanted to weigh anchor. He was not anticipating a shipwreck. He was looking forward to weighing anchor and setting sail for another shore from which he expected one day to return freighted down with the wealth of another world. In this remarkable statement he says, not only that he had a desire (a lust) to depart (to weigh anchor) to be with Christ. He says that it is "far better." The expression is not strong enough in the King James text. It should read, "I have a desire to depart and be with Christ which is very far better." Death, for the Christian, cannot be described in comparatives. Death for the Christian can be described only in superlatives.

Such is the afterlife as incorporated in the words *sheōl* and *hadēs*. Now let us look at the word:

3. *Gehenna*

The story has another side: a dark, ominous, dreadful, awful side. The dark side of *hadēs* is only a prelude to the blacker shades of *gehenna*. The word *gehenna* is the Greek equivalent of the Hebrew word *topheth*. The actual Greek word is *geenna*. It occurs 12 times in the New Testament, and is always translated "hell." It refers to the final abode of the wicked dead. In the Apocalypse it is "the lake of fire" (Revelation 20:14,15). The Greek word is a transliteration of the Hebrew *Gai Hinnōm*, "the valley of Hinnom." The valley of the sons of Hinnom was a real place in Jerusalem. In the dark days of Jewish apostasy, children were sacrificed there. There they "passed through the fire" to the horrible god Molech. The image of Molech was hollow, and in his metal belly fierce fires burned. Little children, placed living on his red-hot lap, rolled down through a cavity into those fires. It was King Solomon who officially introduced this devilish worship into Jerusalem. "Then," we read, "did Solomon build an high place for Chemosh . . . and for Molech, the abomination of the children of Ammon" (1 Kings 11:7).

Centuries later, in the days of godly King Josiah, an end was put to this diabolical worship. We read that the king "defiled Topheth, which is in the valley of the children of Hinnom, that no man might make his son or his daughter to pass through the fire to Molech" (2 Kings 23:10). The valley referred to was the junction of the three valleys that unite south of Jerusalem. Topheth was a place in this valley.

By the time of Christ, the terrible idolatries of Israel were long over. No longer did little children die a dreadful death in Molech's lap, but the fires were kept burning in Hinnom. They were used for burning the refuse of the city. Thus the word *geenna* naturally passed into the language as a descriptive word for the place where burns "the fire that never shall be quenched, where their worm dieth not, and the fire is not quenched" (Mark 9:43,44,46,48).

In connection with the great white throne judgment of the wicked dead, the Holy Spirit writes: "And death and hades were cast into the lake of fire. This is the second death" (Revelation 20:14). At the time of this last judgment, the souls of the wicked dead, at present in the torment section of *sheōl* (*hadēs*), will be reunited with their bodies. They will stand at the great white throne for final judgment. Then they will spend eternity in what the Holy Spirit calls "the lake of fire." Thus *hadēs* will be emptied. It will no longer be needed as a place of imprisonment for the wicked. The lake of fire, what we think of when we think of hell, will be their final, dread abode. This is a real place, whether or not the language used to describe it is literal or symbolic. It is a terrible place, so much so that Jesus was willing to come and shed His precious blood in order that we might never need to go there.

4. *Heaven*

Heaven is an equally real place. In the Old Testament the word used is *shameh* or *shamayin*. The words come from a root meaning "lofty." It is the usual word for the sky, the stellar spaces, and hence for heaven. The same is true of the Greek word *ouranos*. The name for the sky, by extension, becomes the name of God's home.

When Solomon dedicated his Temple, he recognized that, magnificent as it was, it was a very small place indeed in which to expect God to dwell. "Thy dwelling place [is in] heaven," he said (2 Chronicles 6:21). Similarly Daniel, as he prepared to tell Nebuchadnezzar the meaning of his dream, said, "There is a God in heaven that revealeth secrets" (Daniel 2:28).

The idea is found repeatedly in the New Testament. When Jesus taught His disciples to pray, He taught them to begin by saying, "Our Father which art in heaven" (Matthew 6:9). When warning people against the abuse or exploitation of children, He said, "In heaven their angels do always behold the face of My Father which is in heaven" (Matthew 18:10). In the book of Revelation, just before he begins one of the most wonderful descriptions of the worship of heaven, John says, "Behold, a door was opened in heaven" (Revelation 4:1).

Heaven is a real place for real people. When Jesus announced to

His disciples that He was going home, He softened the blow by saying, "In My Father's house are many mansions [abiding places]: if it
were not so, I would have told you" (John 14:2).

It is from the full-length description of the celestial city that we
get our most vivid impression of what heaven will be like. It is true
that the language is highly figurative, and it is equally true that the
holy city, the New Jerusalem, is described in its relation to the millennial reign. Yet, just the same, it embodies all our ideas of heaven. It is
a perfect cube, 1,500 miles in all directions. Its materials are translu-
cent: light shines through. Even the gold is as clear as glass. It rests
upon twelve foundations ablaze with precious stones. Its twelve gates
are hewn from massive, single pearls. The crystal stream is there.
The tree of life grows abundantly there.

The throne of God is there. It needs no sun nor moon to light its
streets; the glory of God and the Lamb is all the light it needs. The
saints of all ages make their home there. There is no more curse, no
sin, no suffering, no tears, no night.

Jesus will be there, and we shall see His face. This is to be our eternal home. We shall dwell there in our resurrection bodies enjoying
this "inheritance incorruptible, and undefiled, and that fadeth not
away, reserved in heaven" (1 Peter 1:4) with "joy unspeakable and
full of glory" (1 Peter 1:8).

Finally, two other words connected with the unseen world deserve a brief comment.

5. *Tartarus*

Peter mentions *tartarus* as the prison house of the worst of the fall-
en angels (2 Peter 2:4). Many of the angels who accompanied Lucifer
in his rebellion against the throne of God are still free. They roam
what the Bible calls "the heavenlies." They are described by Paul as
"principalities and powers, the rulers of this world's darkness, wicked spirits in high places." They are mighty members of Satan's
hierarchy. Some of them rule the nations of the world under their
master who is called "the prince of this world."

But not all the fallen angels are free. Both Peter and Jude tell of
some who are now incarcerated by God. They are locked up in
Tartarus. It seems clear from what is said about these imprisoned
angelic beings that they were in some way responsible for the fright-
ful wickedness of the people who lived before the Flood. The
context in both cases links them with unnatural sex sins. Those beings are linked in Genesis 6 with the race of giants that inhabited the
world in Noah's day and helped to debauch the planet. For this second and even more debasing fall, God has imprisoned them. They
now lie in *Tartarus* awaiting the final day of judgment.

6. *Abussos*

The word *abussos* describes another of God's prisons. It is translated "the bottomless pit" in Revelation 9:1-21. In this mysterious

place certain terrible demons are at present incarcerated along with their leader, whose name is given in both Greek and Hebrew. In Hebrew it is *Abaddon*; in Greek it is *Apollyōn*. Both names mean "destruction." At a certain point in the future, after the rapture of the Church, these horrible creatures are to be let loose upon mankind. During the millennial reign of Christ, Satan himself is to be locked up in that abyss (Revelation 20:1-3,7-8).

These, then, are the words used in the Bible to describe the unseen world. It is a real world. Just because we cannot see it or sense it with our natural senses does not mean that this world does not exist. God says that it does.

From beginning to end, the Bible tells us that there is a heaven to be gained and a hell to be shunned. It tells us of a broad road that leads to destruction and of a narrow road that leads to life. It tells us that these roads cross at a place called Calvary. It is there that a person can get off the broad road that leads to destruction and onto the narrow road that leads to life.

These two word studies, one on the Biblical definition of sin and the other on the unseen world, show the importance of paying attention to the words used by the Holy Spirit in the Hebrew and Greek of the Bible. These studies were done simply by using the tools mentioned in this book and without any special knowledge of the original languages.

3

Figures of Speech in Scripture

Figures of speech express an idea more forcefully. The use of a figure of speech is always interesting, usually colorful, and generally arresting.

Picture yourself on a plane flying at a steady cruising speed above the clouds. As long as the plane flies on at a steady pace, you read, talk, or gaze out the window, but the moment the flight pattern changes, you are arrested. The plane suddenly banks, or hits an air pocket, or the pilot opens the throttle. Instantly you are alert and possibly alarmed. That is how it is with language. As long as words proceed smoothly our attention tends to drop, but introduce a deviation, a sudden departure from the norm, and at once attention is aroused.

The Spirit of God uses figures of speech with precision. E. W. Bullinger in his monumental *Figures of Speech in the Bible* has listed over 200 of them, several with a number of varieties within themselves. The Bible interpreter must determine when to take words literally or figuratively. Normally we take words literally, at their face value, unless doing so confronts us with a statement that is contrary to experience, to known fact, to revealed truth, or to the general tenor or teaching of Scripture.

It is not my purpose here to explore all the figures of speech used in the Bible, but to examine only some of the most common ones.

First, there is the *simile*, the most common of all the figures used in the Bible. We use a simile when we use a connecting word such as *like* or *as* to state an equivalence between two things. "He shall be *like* a tree planted by the rivers of water" (Psalm 1:3). "Ye were *as* sheep going astray" (1 Peter 2:25).

The second most common figure of speech is the *metaphor*. When we employ a metaphor we do not use a connecting word; we say that one thing *is* something else: "All flesh *is* grass" (Isaiah 40:6) is a metaphor. "All flesh is *as* grass" (1 Peter 1:24) is a simile. "The Lord is my shepherd" (Psalm 23:1); "Ye are the salt of the earth" (Matthew 5:13); "This is My body" (Matthew 26:26); "I am the bread of life" (John 6:35). All are metaphors.

The importance of recognizing metaphor is illustrated in a well-known historical incident. Martin Luther, confronted by one of his dissenting colleagues, entered into a heated debate over an issue of

Bible doctrine. The subject under discussion was the real presence of the Lord in "the host," the communion bread. Roman Catholics claim that the moment the priest consecrates the bread it ceases to be bread and becomes the body, blood, soul, and divinity of the Lord Jesus.

Martin Luther did not wholly free himself from that dogma and, like the Catholics, he supported his view with the verse, "This is My body." Luther's opponent, Zwingli, said, "He stubbornly insisted on taking this literally and at face value: 'If it says, "This is My body," then that is what it means, "This . . . is . . . My . . . body."' The bread becomes His body." After arguing with Luther in vain and pointing out that this was purely and simply a metaphor, Zwingli said at last, "Very well, Martin, and what do you propose to do with the text, 'I am the door'?"

The Bible contains a few examples of *allegory*. Like the simile and the metaphor the allegory draws its strength from comparison. A parable is an extended simile; it presents physical circumstances (for example, a sower going forth to sow) as spiritual truth—namely, the gospel being sent forth. Similarly, an allegory is an extended metaphor. It is more complex than a metaphor, however, because it continually represents one thing as another. John Bunyan's *Pilgrim's Progress* is the most famous allegory in the English language. An allegory may be a fictitious narrative with a deeper meaning than what appears on the surface, or, as in Galatians 4, it may be based on historical events. One of the purposes of allegory is to bring out teaching from past events. Psalm 80, Isaiah 5, and Matthew 12:43-45 are examples of such allegory.

Great caution needs to be exercised in reading allegory into a passage of Scripture, since the most fanciful interpretations can easily result. Just because the Bible uses this figure of speech is no justification for allegorizing whole segments of Scripture. More is said about this in chapter 5.

Another figure of speech found in Scripture is the *paradox*, a seeming contradiction. When we say, for instance, that we have to be cruel to be kind, we are employing paradox. Because God's wisdom often seems foolishness to human beings, there are numerous uses of paradox in the Bible: "Whosoever shall save his life shall lose it: and whosoever will lose his life for My sake shall find it" (Matthew 16:25). "She that liveth in pleasure is dead while she liveth" (1 Timothy 5:6). Both of those descriptions employ paradox.

There is also *irony* in the Bible. An ironical expression is one that expresses a thought in such a way that it naturally conveys the opposite meaning. Sarcasm, a form of irony, is often used, not to conceal the true meaning of a statement, but to add greater force to it. Elijah's comments to the false prophets of Baal are sarcastic, or ironical (1 Kings 18:27). Job used sarcasm on his critics; "No doubt but ye are the people, and wisdom shall die with you" (Job 12:2); Jesus used irony in Luke 13:33: "I must walk to day, and tomorrow, and the day following: for it cannot be that a prophet perish out of Jerusalem."

One of the most interesting and prolific figures of speech in the Bible is *personification*. It is employed when *things* are given the characteristics of persons. It is easily recognized: "Neither shall thine eye pity him" (Deuteronomy 13:8); "Let not thy left hand know" (Matthew 6:3); "The land mourneth" (Joel 1:10); "The stars in their courses fought against Sisera" (Judges 5:20); "Mercy and truth are met together; righteousness and peace have kissed each other" (Psalm 85:10); "When lust hath conceived, it bringeth forth sin" (James 1:15). The way we speak and write would be impoverished without such figurative language.

Then there is *anthropomorphism*. This figure of speech ascribes physical characteristics to God. Walter Martin, a writer on the cults, tells how he challenges Mormons to come to his meetings. At the end of his lecture on Mormonism he gives opportunity for them to question him. On one such occasion a young Morman asked Dr. Martin if he would acknowledge Joseph Smith and Brigham Young to be prophets of God if he, the Mormon, could demonstrate from the Bible that God has a body of flesh and bones (one of Mormonism's heretical doctrines). Dr. Martin agreed that he would certainly be impressed if such an idea could be proved from the Bible. Thereupon the Mormon began to reel off a number of verses such as Exodus 33:11,20, Job 34:21, James 5:4, and Isaiah 30:27—verses that speak of God's *face, eyes, ears,* and *lips.* "There," the Mormon cried, "God has a nose, God has eyes, God has feet—God is an exalted man. Now acknowledge that we are right. God has a body."

Walter Martin said to the young man, "And now will you please turn to another verse and read it just a quickly as you have read all the others? Read me Psalm 91:4." The Mormon turned to it and read, "He shall cover thee with His *feathers,* and under His *wings* shalt thou trust." "There," said Dr. Martin, "Now He's a big chicken! The same reasoning that makes Him a man makes Him a chicken." The young man sat down in confusion.

"Can't you see?" said Dr. Martin, capitalizing on the moment, "the verses you have been quoting are anthropomorphisms. God is not an exalted man. God is a Spirit. Jesus said so, and He also said, 'A spirit hath not flesh and bones.' God is not a man; He says so Himself. Look at Numbers 23:19. 'God is not a man that He should lie; neither the son of man, that He should repent.'" How careful we must be in recognizing figures of speech in the Bible and in understanding them correctly.

Similar to the anthropomorphism is the figure known as *anthropopathy,* which ascribes human feelings and passions to God. It is not that God necessarily has such feelings, but He has spoken of them to enable us to comprehend Him. Sorrow, grief, rejoicing, repentance, anger, hatred, vengeance, displeasure, zeal, and pity are all ascribed to Him under this figure of speech: "It repented the LORD that He had made man on the earth" (Genesis 6:6); "I the LORD thy God am a jealous God" (Exodus 20:5). When we read of the Lord forgetting or thinking or laughing or begetting or seeing or smelling or riding and all such activities, we are dealing with these two figures, anthropomorphism and anthropopathy.

The Bible also uses *hyperbole,* which means to say more than is literally meant in order to heighten the sense. This figure of speech is fairly common in Scripture: "All the dust of the land became lice throughout all the land of Egypt" (Exodus 8:17); "The cities are great and walled up to heaven" (Deuteronomy 1:28); "Every one could sling stones at a hair breadth, and not miss" (Judges 20:16). These are all examples of hyperbole.

One of the most common figures of speech in the Bible is *metonymy.* In this figure a related thing stands for the thing itself. Metonymy is founded not on resemblance but on some direct relationship. For instance, when we say that a person writes a good hand the word *hand* stands for the person's actual writing.

There are several kinds of metonymy. There is metonymy relating to cause, used when the cause is put for the effect: "Neither shall the sword go through your land." Here *sword* is substituted for war. "Purge me with hyssop, and I shall be clean" (Psalm 51:7). Hyssop was a small shrub used in ceremonial sprinklings. Hyssop is here substituted for the atoning blood connected with it. The same figure is used in Genesis 40:19, Galatians 3:13, and 1 Peter 2:24, where "tree" is substituted for gallows.

There is metonymy relating to effect, used when the effect is used for the cause. "Two nations are in thy womb" (Genesis 25:23). The word *nations* is substituted for the two infants whose descendants would become those nations. "Master, I have brought unto Thee my son, which hath a dumb spirit" (Mark 9:17, 25). The spirit itself was not dumb, but it produced dumbness in the person it possessed. "Lord, now lettest Thou Thy servant depart in peace, according to Thy word: for mine eyes have seen Thy salvation" (Luke 2:29-30). Old Simeon meant that he had see Christ, the One who was the Savior and who wrought salvation.

There is metonymy relating to subject, used when, for example, the name of a place is used for what is in the place, or when a vessel is used for what is in it: "This day is salvation come to this house" (Luke 19:9). The word *house* is used for what the house contained: Zaccheus and his family; "As often as ye eat this bread and drink this cup" (1 Corinthians 11:26). The cup stands for what it contains. (How many arguments as to whether or not grape juice or wine should be used in the communion service could be avoided by noting this figure of speech.)

It may sound complicated, but it really is not. We use these figures of speech in everyday conversation and never give a thought to their technical nature. In studying and interpreting the Bible, however, we need to know and recognize these figures, because failure to do so can sometimes lead to error.

Another figure of speech is *synecdoche,* used where a part of a thing is substituted for the whole thing: "Then shall ye bring down my gray hairs with sorrow to the grave" (Genesis 42:38). Here "gray hairs" stand for Jacob himself in his old age.

Ellipsis, while not technically a figure of speech, can be conveniently discussed here. It occurs when a gap is purposely left in a sentence through the omission of one or more words. The omitted words are grammatically necessary but can be left out without altering the sense. The device is used when a writer does not wish his readers to spend time on what is omitted but rather would have them dwell on the words emphasized by the use of the ellipsis. In Matthew 14:19 we read that Jesus "gave the loaves to His disciples, and the disciples to the multitude." Obviously the sentence does not mean that Jesus gave the disciples to the multitudes. The phrase "gave the loaves" is omitted from the sentence by ellipsis. If we supply the missing words we read that Jesus "gave the loaves to His disciples and disciples [gave the loaves] to the multitudes." The ellipsis shows that the important thing is not that the disciples gave the loaves—they were only the instruments. The Lord was the Giver.

The *polysyndeton* is another figure of speech. It is used to slow us down and draw particular attention to each item in a sequence. This figure of speech reveals itself by the constant repetition of the word *and.* The first chapter in the Bible contains that word at least 100 times. The feature can be detected in such famous passages as Genesis 22 and Luke 15. Although it pervades the whole Bible, most modern translations eliminate it and in so doing rob the reader of an instructive figure of speech.

The opposite figure of speech is the *asyndeton,* where a succession of clauses is found, each important but coming one after the other to hurry the reader to the climax at the end. For instance, we read the words of Jesus: "When thou makest a dinner or a supper, call not thy friends, nor thy brethren, neither thy kinsmen, nor thy rich neighbors . . . but when thou makest a feast, call the poor, the maimed, the lame, the blind: and thou shalt be blessed; for they cannot recompense thee: for thou shalt be recompensed at the resurrection of the just" (Luke 14:12-14). The list ("the poor, the maimed, the lame, the blind") is hurried over to focus attention on the blessing promised at the end of the sentence.

The Lord then told the story of the man who made a great supper and invited many. All made their excuses. The man, infuriated by the cavalier way his invitation was treated, sent his servants to fill his banqueting hall with more responsive guests. Note what Jesus said. We have the same listing but *this time* with the polysyndeton: "Go quickly . . . bring in hither the poor AND the maimed [the crippled]

AND the halt [the lame . . . the same Greek word as in verse 13]
AND the blind" (Luke 14:21).

The question arises, Why the polysyndeton here, in this list, but
not in the previous, identical list? Here the purpose is to draw attention to each, separate kind of person. The asyndeton hurried
us on to the climax at the end of the sentence, the list being important but less so than the climax. The polysyndeton draws attention
to the items in the list. The Holy Spirit in using this figure of
speech is saying to us: "Slow down. Think of this, now think of
this, now think of this."

Look at the list in the polysyndeton here. Examine the context.
You will see at once why the figure is used.

"Bring in hither the POOR [those unable to make the excuse of
verses 18-19: "I have bought . . . so I cannot come]; *and* the
MAIMED [those least likely to make the excuse of verse 20: "I have
married . . . so I cannot come]; *and* the LAME [those unable to make
the excuse of verse 19: "I have bought five yoke of oxen and I go to
prove them . . . so I cannot come"] *and* the BLIND [those unable to
make the excuse of verse 18: "I have bought a piece of ground, and I
must needs go and see it: I pray thee, have me excused"].

The word *and* is such a short word. In our everyday speech we do
not use it to link up many items or units of thought, to the extent that
the Bible does. A general rule in English grammar is that we normally use only one conjunction in a sentence. But examine your King
James Bible. Observe how lavishly the Holy Spirit uses this word
and. We hardly notice it in ordinary reading because of the beauty
and majesty of the language in which the surrounding text is
couched. But it is there—everywhere. Often a new chapter begins
with the word *and* (as, for instance, Genesis 22). Sometimes even a
new book of the Bible begins with this significant connective
(Leviticus, for instance). Translations that eliminate this figure of
speech do a disservice to the Bible-reading public by robbing them
of a Holy-Spirit-designed emphasis.

One more form of speech might also be mentioned here, the *euphemism*. We employ this figure whenever we wish to exchange a
harsh word for a more pleasant one. People use euphemism to cover
up sin. Hence to call a drunkard "an alcoholic" or to speak of a case of
adultery as "an affair" or to speak of a Sodomist as "gay" is to use euphemisms to cover sin. To call a garbage collector a "sanitary
engineer" is a kind of vanity; it uses this figure of speech to upgrade
the occupation.

In the Bible, euphemism is generally used to help when delicate
feelings or sentiments are involved. When David asked, "Is the
young man Absalom safe?" Cushi answered, "The enemies of my
lord the king, and all that rise against thee to do thee hurt, be as that
young man is" (2 Samuel 18:32). Cushi used two euphemisms to remind David gently of Absalom's treason and to intimate that he was

dead. "Spread therefore thy skirt over thine handmaid," said Ruth to Boaz (Ruth 3:9). It was a delicate way of suggesting that he marry her.

Here, then, are some of the more important figures of speech in the Bible. When someone says, "Oh, that's only figurative!" the implication is that its meaning is weak. Not so. A figure of speech may be a strong form of expression. The Holy Spirit never uses such devices without adding power and force to what is said.

4

The Importance of Culture

We cannot overlook the importance of the life and times, the culture and conditions, the background of code and custom, against which the Bible was written. Some knowledge of the way people lived is invaluable in interpreting all parts of the written Word. Never was this more so than in our modern, western world, so alien and different from the world of Abraham and the patriarchs and of Christ and His apostles.

This chapter will show the value of having some understanding of Bible times in grasping Bible truth.

THE TEMPLE

Jesus said, "Destroy this temple and in three days I will raise it up again." He was grossly misunderstood; the statement infuriated His enemies, and was used against Him at His mock trial.

Solomon built the original Temple in seven years. It was built around a rough slab of virgin rock, an outcropping from Mount Moriah that had been used as a threshing floor by Araunah the Jebusite. But centuries before that it had been used by Abraham as the site on which he was ready to offer up Isaac as a burnt offering to God.

In due course Solomon's Temple was destroyed and was eventually replaced with another one by the Jews repatriated from the Babylonian exile. The new Temple was a much humbler structure.

Then came Herod the Great, with his ambitious idea of ingratiating himself to the Jews by restoring the Temple to an even greater glory than it had before. The Jews were suspicious of the Edomite tyrant. To pacify their fear that he might somehow desecrate their place of worship, he promised not to move a single stone of the existing building until he was ready to begin work on the new one. Moreover, he had a thousand priests trained as carpenters and masons so that no unconsecrated hands might defile the Holy Place. Work began in the winter of 20 B.C. It took just a year and a half to rebuild the Holy of Holies, but work in the courts and cloisters went on until long after Herod's death. It was continued through the reign of Herod Antipas.

Every time the Lord Jesus visited the Temple He saw men at work on its reconstruction. When He made His famous statement about rebuilding the destroyed Temple (meaning His own body) in three days, the Jews, thinking He was referring to Herod's Temple, protested that already the work had consumed no less than forty-six years.

Just before He went to Calvary, the Lord made another prediction about the destruction of the Temple, this time referring to Herod's Temple. He told His disciples that it would be utterly destroyed. Nothing seemed more unlikely. Work continued on the Temple until thirty-four years after the crucifixion. Just eight years after it was finished, it was completely destroyed. The Roman soldiers besieging Jerusalem were given strict instructions by Titus to spare this architectural wonder. But the word of a Roman general, the son of a Caesar, no matter how powerful, could not countermand the Word of the Son of God. In the fierce fighting the Temple itself became a battle ground. Fire broke out and, in the consuming flames, the gold embellishments melted and ran down between the stones. To get at that treasure the victorious Romans pried the stones apart until, indeed, as Jesus had said, there was no stone left standing on another that was not thrown down.

THE PUBLICANS

Both Matthew and Zaccheus were publicans. In Jesus' day the name *publican* was an epithet of loathing and hatred among the Jews. The publican was a tax collector in the pay of the Romans and their client kings. No worse appellation could cling to a man than to be named a publican. The Romans farmed out the hated office of tax collector. The sum to be collected was set for a certain amount and the publican was responsible to turn that amount over to the authorities. Whatever else he could collect in the process was up to him. That was his reward. The publicans became very rich on the added revenues they squeezed out of the people over and above the stated sum. Thus the publicans were hated as traitors, tax collectors, and tyrants.

When the Lord called Matthew to be one of His disciples he was "sitting at the receipt of custom." The custom house occupied by Matthew seems to have been near the lake of Galilee, probably on the wharf. There Matthew collected taxes on all goods landed, including custom on all fish caught in the lake.

The whole area around the lake must have been infested with Matthew's colleagues, the other revenue officers. Since caravan routes converged there, tolls and duties were collected at this strategic spot. Matthew was likely employed by Herod Antipas to collect revenues from that district. There seem to have been at least two kinds of publicans, the general tax-gatherer and the custom house official.

Jesus was scorned by many Jews because He was "a friend of publicans and sinners." No self-respecting Jew would befriend a publican. Dr. Alfred Edersheim, an authority on the life and times of Jesus, pictures the call of Matthew. He says:

> We take it, long before the eventful day that forever decided his life, Matthew had, in heart, become a disciple of Jesus. Only he dared not, could not, have hoped for personal recognition—far less for call to discipleship. But when it came . . . it needed not a moment's thought or consideration. When He spake it, "Follow Me," the past seemed all swallowed up in the present heaven of bliss. he said not a word, for his soul was in the speechless surprise of unexpected love and grace; but he rose up, left the custom-house, and followed Him.

Much the same could probably be said for Zaccheus.

FUNERALS

One of the Lord's potential disciples was willing enough—on his own terms, that is. He replied: "Suffer me first to go and bury my father."

Among the Jews this was a duty that took precedence over all others. Moreover, funerals then (as now) were ruinously expensive and the bereaved were expected by the stern law of custom to raise the money to pay for them somehow. Families could be reduced to poverty by funerals.

Crowds of relatives, friends, and acquaintances would assemble. Refreshments had to be provided. Guests and mourners who came from a distance had to be housed and fed. These gatherings and feasts for the dead could extend over a period of forty days. The priests and religious functionaries employed for the funeral had to be well paid.

In Bible times, one who thus paid proper honor to the memory of a departed loved one was regarded as a person of integrity. Conversely, a man who neglected these duties, demanded by custom, would be regarded as an unnatural son and one not to be trusted. This would-be disciple then stated his case on what he considered to be the very highest, most sacred, and unchallengeable of grounds.

Jesus, however, did not accept the excuse of this man who wanted to delay becoming a disciple until his father had died. The call of custom, no matter how time-honored or socially sacred, must not be allowed to interfere with the call of Christ.

GRINDING AT THE MILL

The Lord Jesus spoke of His coming being swift and divisive, dividing even between "two women at the mill" (Matthew 24:41).

The mill was a hand mill made of two circular stones, one on top of the other. The grain was put into a hole in the center of the upper stone. This stone also had a handle by which it could be turned. The ground grain ran out from between the upper and lower millstones. The handmill was operated by two women sitting facing each other with the millstones between them. Both women grasped the handle, one woman holding it with both hands, the other keeping one hand free to throw in more grain as required. Both women retained their hold as the handle went round and round, either toward them or away from them. This was woman's work. A man would never do it. It was tedious and fatiguing and only slaves or the lowest servants were normally set to it. Grinding at the mill was a task often imposed on captives taken in war. The Philistines took great sport in setting mighty, fallen Samson to do this work.

The Lord's picture of two women grinding at the mill and one being taken at the rapture and the other left is a vivid one. The two women at the mill had their hands together on the handle as they faced each other across the stone, working steadily in unison and rhythm. Suddenly one is gone. The other sits there startled, alone.

ELIJAH RUNNING BEFORE AHAB

After the great battle with the false prophets of Baal on Mount Carmel, Elijah did an extraordinary thing. "He girded up his loins, and ran before Ahab to the entrance of Jezreel" (1 Kings 18:46). Why would Elijah do a thing like that?

On Mount Carmel, as God's avenging agent against the idolatries sponsored in Israel by King Ahab and his wicked consort Jezebel, the prophet overwhelmed Ahab with shame and defeat in the presence of his subjects. The natural result would be so to lower the king in the estimation of his subjects that rebellion and insurrection might have followed. This was no part of the divine plan. "The powers that be are ordained of God." What God wanted was to bring about repentance, not rebellion.

The prophet was therefore directed by God to restore to the king a measure of his self-respect and self-esteem and to warn the people that it was not up to them to overthrow constituted authority. That would come in God's own time and way. In the meantime the king must be given space to let the lesson of Carmel sink in.

The prophet chose a typically eastern way of restoring a measure of respect for the thoroughly humiliated monarch. He girded his loins and ran before the king's chariot. This was a method of doing honor to Ahab's office quite in keeping with the customs of that day and age. Great officials always employed runners to go before them, running ahead of the horses no matter how furiously they were ridden. In order to run with greater ease they not only "girded their loins" but also tucked up their flowing robes under the girdle lest they should stumble or get entangled in them.

The distance from the foot of Carmel across the plain of Jezreel was at least twelve miles. The august prophet ran across that expanse in the blinding rain, probably doing the distance in about two hours. No wonder it says that the hand of the Lord was upon the prophet. Otherwise he could never have done it.

THE WISDOM OF ANIMAL BEHAVIOR

W. M. Thomson tells of being in Tiberias one evening when droves of cattle and donkeys were brought down from the green hills where they were pastured during the daylight hours. There were large numbers of these animals. Thomson was curious to see if Isaiah 1:3-4 were true.

No sooner did the droves get inside the city gate than they began to disperse. Every ox, he said, knew perfectly well its owner, its house, and the way to it. Nor did a single animal get lost or bewildered by the maze of crooked, winding, and intersecting lanes and alleys. Every ass, too, went straight to his master's "crib." He followed one all the way to its owner's house and saw it take its appropriate stall and begin its evening meal.

Isaiah 1:3-4 was true, and the lesson forceful and sad. The animals were wiser than their owners, who neither knew nor considered the Lord but forsook Him and provoked Him with their rebellious ways.

Studying Bible culture and customs not only sheds light on difficult and sometimes obscure statements, it provides a sense that our Lord lived in a real time and place among people in many ways like ourselves.

5

Allegorical Interpretation

As was mentioned earlier in passing, one school of Biblical interpretation allegorizes much of the Old Testament, especially its prophecies relating to Israel. This peculiar approach to the Bible, that of covenant theology one suspects, stems originally from a desire to justify the unscriptural practice of infant baptism, a practice common to a major segment of the professing church.

When God entered into His covenant relationship with Abraham and his seed, the covenant sign was circumcision. Every male had to be circumcised when he was eight days old in order to be brought into that covenant relationship. Failure to have the ordinance of circumcision administered exposed the uncircumcised one to the peril of being "cut off " from God's people. A male Gentile who felt the attraction of Israel's religious faith and who wished to become a proselyte likewise had to be circumcised. Normally, however, the rite was administered to male infants on their eighth day of life.

The covenant theologian tends to equate Christian baptism with Jewish circumcision, but broadens it to include girl babies as well. Infant baptism is supposed to bring the baptized child into the good of God's covenant just as circumcision brought the Jewish male child into the Abrahamic fold. To bolster that kind of thinking, the Church is seen as "spiritual Israel."

It is claimed that the promises made to Israel under the Old Covenant are now being ratified in the Church under the New Covenant. To make a stronger case for this theory, many Old Testament prophecies are treated allegorically. Instead of the glorious prophecies concerning the millennial reign of Christ being taken literally, they are spiritualized. Thus the spiritual blessings of the Church are supposed to be a present-day realization of the promises made by the prophets to the nation of Israel. This method of Bible interpretation does away with any future for the nation of Israel and with the millennial reign of Christ. The rebirth of the state of Israel in our day confronts the covenant theologian with a rebuttal of that position. It proves that those who interpret the prophecies of the Old Testament literally are right. Israel is not the Church and the Church is not Israel.

So much, then, for that kind of allegorizing of the Old Testament.

It postulates two false propositions. One is the proposition that infant baptism brings babies into a covenant relationship with God (with the resultant tragedy that millions of lost people think they are going to heaven by virtue of their baptism, in infancy, into the Church—a Romish error from which much of Protestantism has never freed itself). The second is the proposition that, since the Church is Israel there is no future for the Jewish people as a people or for Israel as a nation (thus doing away with the reign of Christ on earth over a reconstituted and redeemed Hebrew nation, and robbing Christ of His exaltation in what was once the scene of His humiliation).

We recoil from such allegorizing but we must not abandon all allegorical interpretation of Scripture simply because the method has been abused. There *are* allegories in the Bible. Passages of Scripture *do* have deeper meanings, as Paul, for example, demonstrates in his handling of the Abraham-Sarah-Hagar triangle (Galatians 4:29-31). But those deeper meanings are secondary. They are not the primary interpretation of the Old Testament Scriptures on which they are based.

It is evident that Paul used the Genesis incident in an allegorical way to *illustrate* to justified believers, influenced by legalistic teachers, the folly of desiring to be under the Law. Paul's use of allegory, on that occasion, actually raises, for the *fifth* time in this epistle, the question: Is the Christian believer under the Mosaic law? (See Galatians 2:19-21; 3:1-3; 3:25-26; 4:4-6; 4:9-31.) The allegorical illustration was one more way of dealing with the issue.

Paul's use of allegory helps us understand its primary function. By taking the factual, historical narrative of Genesis 16:15 and 21:2 as an allegory, Paul was by no means undermining the grammatical-literal interpretation of the passage. He was finding a secondary, deeper meaning in the passage. Above all, his use of the passage as an allegory was purely illustrative.

This, then, is the value of an allegorical interpretation of a passage of Scripture. It can be used to illustrate a clear teaching of Scripture, a teaching that is well supported elsewhere in the Bible: plain doctrinal statements. Bearing that in mind, we can most certainly dig down beneath the surface of a passage of Scripture for deeper meanings—as long as we realize that what we are doing is illustrating truth that is clearly taught elsewhere in the Bible.

Here we have a legitimate handling of allegory, as can be demonstrated from numerous Old Testament passages. Genesis 1, for instance, deals with God's activity in creation. The plain, obvious, literal interpretation of the passage will bring out God's creatorial activity. Beneath the surface, however, is a built-in allegory. On the secondary level the passage can be taken to illustrate God's dealings in salvation with a human soul. It shows how the Holy Spirit moves on the darkness of the human heart, how He commands light to shine out of darkness, how He brings light, life, and loveliness to a realm where, before, there was darkness and chaos. Paul himself hints at this allegory in 2 Corinthians 4:6.

We can know when we have discovered such a hidden allegory because "things fit." The emerging illustration is not artificial and does not need to be forced. Rather, it is satisfyingly complete.

A good way to illustrate this is to show the hidden allegory in the book of Esther.

The literal interpretation of the book of Esther lies on the surface. The setting of the book is in Persia during the days of Xerxes. It shows how the king was influenced by Haman, his prime minister, to order the extermination of all the Jews in his realm. Through the activities of Mordecai, a Jew, and Esther, his beautiful young cousin, the schemes of the Jew-hating Haman were foiled. The book demonstrates God's providential activity on behalf of His people. There were no mighty miracles, as in the days of Moses and Pharaoh (indeed God is not mentioned in the book, though His name is hidden in acrostical form in the Hebrew text). God simply overruled natural events to effect a spectacular deliverance for the Jewish people. The story is told in graphic prose to show that "behind a frowning providence, He hides a smiling face."

But there is more to the book than that. Beneath the surface lies an awe-inspiring allegory of God's plan of salvation for lost and ruined human beings.

The story revolves around four people. First, there is Ahasuerus, by far the most important character in the book—he is named about 180 times. He represents the sinner. Then there is Mordecai, the Jew. In the book he is represented as the one who brings salvation. That is his role. He represents the Savior. There is Haman. He, clearly, is the enemy and represents Satan. Finally, there is Esther, the one who knows and loves Mordecai, the Savior.

With this key to the allegory in hand, the door to the secondary interpretation of the book opens easily.

In the opening chapter Ahasuerus is seen ruled by pride, pleasure, passion, and worldly policy. He is an individual who thinks only of himself and of what will enhance his ambitions, vanity, and enjoyment. Through circumstances beyond her control, Esther, who has been brought into Mordecai's family by adoption, finds herself married to the king. She tells her husband of salvation provided for him by Mordecai—only to have her tidings ignored.

Having turned from the message of salvation, the king comes completely under the influence of Haman and stoops to acts of wickedness. Haman has two chief hates: the person of Mordecai and the people of Mordecai, both of whom he attacks through his personal domination of the king.

At that point, Mordecai begins to deal with Esther about her understandable but inexcusable silence. She has long since ceased to speak to her husband about the salvation provided for him and the influence of the enemy in his life, sensing her lack of influence over him. Mordecai convicts Esther of her negligence. She promises to witness again to the king, as long as all God's people support her with prayer and fasting.

Now God steps in and personally deals with the king. One night, because of his insomnia, the king summons the court librarian to his bedroom and demands that he read to him. The librarian picks a book, opens it at random, and begins to read to the king about the salvation Mordecai had provided for him. Mordecai's great work had not been forgotten. It had been written into a book. Thus we have two unsaved men, sitting together in a bedroom in the middle of the night, the one reading to the other the story of salvation.

The king is convicted. He is ashamed that he has never acknowledged this savior of his. But who should turn up just then but the enemy Haman? He is too late, however, because the king has already made up his mind. He has made his decision for the savior and the very next morning he lets it be known that he intends to honor Mordecai and give him his rightful place.

Esther now has the delightful task of instructing her husband in what has really been happening. She exposes the enemy (wicked Haman) who is forthwith hanged on the gallows he had prepared for Mordecai. The king then gives his ring to Mordecai (the savior) who henceforth is allowed to control all his affairs.

The change of management in the king's life is soon felt far and near. Salvation is now extended to the Jews by Mordecai, and revival breaks out. It affects the Gentiles too: "The Jews had joy and gladness, a feast and a good day. And many of the people of the land became Jews for the fear of the Jews fell upon them."

The book of Esther ends with the institution of a feast of remembrance so that Mordecai's great work might never be forgotten.

Such is the allegory, a picture of God's dealings with the unregenerate. The Song of Solomon lends itself to similar treatment.*

That kind of allegorical interpretation of an Old Testament incident is quite different from allegorically cheating the Jewish nation out of the inheritance guaranteed to it by the covenant with Abraham.

---

*See the author's book, *Exploring the Song of Solomon* (Neptune, N.J.: Loizeaux Brothers).

6

The Application Rule

We sometimes sing a chorus that is popular because of the
sentiment it expresses and because it has a catchy tune. Regrettably, it teaches an untruth. It shows us not to take our theology from
our hymnbook:

> Every promise in the Book is mine.
>   Every chapter, every verse, and every line;
> All the blessings of His love divine,
>   Every promise in the Book is mine.

The chorus says twice that "every promise in the Book is mine." It
sounds good, but it isn't true. Every promise in the Book is not mine.
God made commitments to Abraham and to David, for instance,
that He never made to us. He has not promised to make of us a great
nation, nor has He promised that we shall found dynasties that will
never pass away. Obviously we must distinguish between the *meaning* of a passage and its possible *application* in other connections.

The interpretation of a passage must be sought in the occasion
that caused it to be written and in relation to the persons to whom it
was originally addressed. Only after that interpretation has been settled can we legitimately make application of the passage to ourselves.
Even then we should be careful that the application we made does
not conflict with other passages of Scripture. Applications of a passage can be rich and varied and, when made in harmony with
Scriptural teaching given elsewhere, such applications not only
prove true but reveal unsuspected depths in the passage.

Making applications in this way is quite different from
spiritualizing and allegorizing a passage by wresting it out of context
and importing into it all kinds of fanciful ideas. We would not dream
of treating other books in that way.

Imagine "spiritualizing" or allegorizing, for instance, a passage
from Shakespeare's *Julius Caesar*. Let us handle one the way some
people handle the Bible to see the folly of it. The great conspiracy
was successful and Julius Caesar was dead. His close friend, Mark
Antony, given permission to speak at Caesar's funeral, makes one of
the greatest speeches in English literature. He begins: "Friends, Romans, countrymen, lend me your ears; I come to bury Caesar, not to
praise him. The evil that men do lives after them; The good is oft interred with their bones; So let it be with Caesar."

To "spiritualize" that passage, as some expositors do with passages in the Bible, might produce something like the following interpretation.

> Antony was speaking of the death of the Roman republic and the birth of the glorious, new, imperial form of government.
>
> The expression "Friends, Romans, countrymen" is a reference to three forms of government: "Friends" refers to the paternal form of government which existed at the time of the founding of Rome. "Romans" refers to the patrician form of government that followed. Both Caesar and Antony were patricians. "Countrymen" refers to the plebian form of government, to democracy, the Roman ideal. Brutus is democracy in its purest form; Cassius is the political expediency which so often characterizes democracy; Caesar is the state and Antony the establishment.

It would be nonsense to handle the speech in such a way. Shakespeare was writing drama, based on historical incidents drawn mostly from Plutarch, and he had no thought of preaching a political sermon or of hiding secret meanings in his text. It would be silly to read things into his play. Anyone handling *Julius Caesar* like that would be ridiculed.

Evidently J. R. R. Tolkien feared that people might read all kinds of nonsense into his trilogy, *The Lord of the Rings.* He tried to safeguard against any such attempt in his *Foreword:* "Other arrangements could be devised according to the tastes or views of those who like allegory or topical reference. But I cordially dislike allegory in all it manifestations, and always have done so since I grew old and wary enough to detect its presence." He repudiates any suggestion that the trilogy is allegorical.

If we cannot take liberties with secular writings, still less can we take liberties with the sacred text. Unquestionably there are hidden depths in the Bible because God is its author. Many passages yield secondary and wonderfully consistent lines of truth, initially hidden and unsuspected. Because of that, the expositor is frequently faced with the temptation to go mining for these buried truths. And, as long as the results are consistent with the whole tenor of Bible truth, such delving can be profitable. But let us not mistake such burrowings for interpretation.

Many an excellent salvation message has been preached from the story of Rahab and her scarlet cord; from the story of Naaman and his cleansing from leprosy; from the story of the lost axe head; or from the story of David and Jonathan. Great gospel messages have been preached from Revelation 3:20 or from Lamentations 1:12 or Joshua 24:15. Such handling of the text is valid, but only as long as the lessons drawn do not violate the basic, underlying rules of interpretation.

A passage of Scripture has only *one* basic interpretation. Those who would handle the Word of truth honestly must seek to find *that* before making any other use of the passage. The application of a passage of Scripture must be governed by the same rules of interpretation that apply in all handling of the Scriptures.

When studying an Old Testament Bible character, for instance, the thing to look for is not some unsuspected "type" but the principles inherent in the story. Commands should be interpreted in the light of the cultural context. Promises may be applied to us only if they are addressed to us or are of a universal character. David's plea that God's Spirit not be taken away from him (Psalm 51:11) could obviously not be employed by a believer today, as is clear from John 14:16. To teach from Acts 1:4 that we should "tarry" for the Holy Spirit is to miss the point of 1 Corinthians 12:13. Sound principles of interpretation will keep us from drawing wrong conclusions from the sacred text. Just because a text is seemingly suitable to a present need does not give us the right to use it out of context as a convenient cloak for our own ideas without regard to its original intent.

Sometimes a passage does have several applications. The parable of the potter (Jeremiah 18) illustrates this. The parable has been used to depict God's remaking of the earth after the millennium, to describe our resurrection bodies, to show how God can overrule in our lives and bring something beautiful and useful out of even our failures, and so on. Those and similar uses of the text are applications. The interpretation of the potter scenario is given by God Himself and clearly has to do with the nation of Israel. We have no right to spiritualize the passage without first recognizing that basic fact of interpretation.

7
Bible Symbols

The use of symbolism is common in any form of communication. Many students of the Word believe that the Bible contains many symbols. Literal things such as the sun, moon, or stars are given a secondary meaning and are made to represent or symbolize something else. Symbols are forceful. Usually they communicate very quickly. Stars and stripes are a symbol of the United States of America; a maple leaf is a symbol of Canada; a bull dog is a symbol of Britain. In the heyday of its empire, Britain; was often symbolized by a lion.

Sometimes a symbol can stand for more than one thing. An eagle, for instance, might be a symbol of the United States, but it might also stand for Germany. So, obviously, the context in which a symbol is used is of prime importance in deciding exactly what the symbol represents.

The rule for interpreting Bible symbols is simple: God is His own interpreter. We do not have to go outside the pages of the Bible to get an explanation of its symbols. We must likewise avoid the extremes of either ignoring symbols or of reading too much into the text. Sometimes the symbol is explained in the immediate context. For instance, in Revelation 1, John, having seen the Lord walking between the lampstands holding seven stars in His hand, is told that the lampstands symbolized seven churches in Asia and the stars the angels of these churches. Sometimes the symbols are explained elsewhere in the Biblical book in which they occur. Certainly they are explained somewhere in the Bible.

In Revelation 8:8 we read, "And the second angel sounded, and as it were a great mountain burning with fire was cast into the sea." Here again the Bible explains its own symbols, only this time not in the immediate context but elsewhere in the Word. Thus in Jeremiah 51:25 we read, "Behold, I am against thee, O destroying mountain, saith the LORD." The context makes clear that the reference is to Babylon. Hence, a mountain is used symbolically of a great, expansionist world kingdom. In Isaiah 57:20-21, we read, "But the wicked are like the troubled sea, when it cannot rest, whose waters cast up mire and dirt. There is no peace, saith my God, to the wicked." In Jeremiah 50:41-42, we read, "Behold, a people shall come from the north, and a great nation, and many kings shall . . . roar like the sea."

Thus the sea is a symbol of the restless, warring, heaving nations of mankind.

With these clues it is easy to interpret the symbolism of Revelation 8:8. In a coming day a great nation, burning with destructive energy like a volcano, will be violently hurled into the sea of mankind. The resulting upheaval, as "the sea" tries to subdue the volcano, can well be imagined. The symbolism gives a vivid picture of a particularly widespread and violent war.

So, in handling Bible symbols we must always interpret them in the light of the Bible itself, not in terms of modern life. For example, a bear is often used these days to represent Russia. In the Bible it is used to depict Persia. The idea of the Russian bear was completely unknown to Bible writers.

Not only do symbols communicate quickly, they also communicate accurately. Words sometimes become obsolete with the passing of time or sometimes they change their meanings altogether. For instance, when the King James Version of the Bible was first published, the word *leasing* was in common use. Thus we read in Psalm 4:2, "How long will ye love vanity, and seek after leasing?" As it stands, the statement makes very little sense to twentieth-century readers because the word *leasing* (as it was used in the seventeenth century) is obsolete. When it was part of the current coinage of the English language, it meant "falsehood."

Similarly the word *prevent* as it is used in 1 Thessalonians 4:15 has changed its meaning entirely since 1611. We read: "For this we say unto you by the word of the Lord, that we which are alive and remain unto the coming of the Lord shall not prevent them which are asleep." In current usage, the word *prevent* means "to hinder." In the seventeenth century it meant "to precede." Thus the entire meaning of the passage is altered by the change in the meaning of the word in the course of time. There are not too many such drastic changes in word meanings, however, and such as there are have been corrected in revised versions of the King James text.

Now while words can and sometimes do change their meanings or drop out of circulation altogether, symbols tend to remain constant. Once the meaning, or meanings, of a symbol become established, it retains the meanings associated with it; usually some characteristic inherent in the symbol preserves its meaning. For instance, the sun is a symbol of power, authority, rule. These ideas are inherent in the sun itself which is the source of power in our solar system. God Himself uses the sun as a symbol of rule in the very first mention of it in the Bible. In Genesis 1:15-16 we read that God appointed the sun and the moon to rule ("the greater light to rule the day, and the lesser light to rule the night"). The sun and the moon are thus valid symbols of ruling powers, the sun representing supreme authority and the moon representing subordinate authority. Or, as may be required in some contexts, the sun may represent political power and the moon religious power.

A given symbol may sometimes stand for more than one concept. Water, for instance, is a symbol of the Holy Spirit, but it is also used to symbolize baptism, cleansing, and the Word of God. In speaking of the instability of his oldest son, Jacob said of Reuben that he was as weak as water. In this case water symbolizes weakness, that which always seeks its lowest level. Another symbol that stands for various concepts is the lion. It represents the Babylonian empire, Satan, and Christ.

Conversely, any given thing may be represented by more than one symbol. Satan is a lion, serpent, angel of light, dragon. The Holy Spirit is a dove, fire, water, wind, and oil.

We can take the guesswork out of interpreting Bible symbols by determining how the Bible itself employs them. This is the safe way. Giving heed to Bible clues will save the expositor from making foolish and unsupported statements which tend to bring the Bible into disrepute. In Job 41:1-34, for instance, we have a highly symbolic and poetical description of a fierce aquatic animal (probably a crocodile). Job is asked by God if he can fish this monster (leviathan) out of the deep with a hook. The whole passage is part of a lengthy exposure of Job's ignorance, limitations, and weakness. Some sensationalists have turned this passage into a description of a modern submarine to give it some sort of prophetic significance! Such handling of the Bible is not sound exposition.

Similarly, one popular author sees helicopters in Revelation 9, where we have a highly symbolic description of certain demonic and angelic powers which are to be let loose on mankind in a coming day. Such far-fetched "interpretations" may sell books but they certainly are not good exposition. The context makes clear that, whatever else these things are, they cannot be helicopters. They come out of the abyss—one of God's prisons for the incarceration of evil spirits.

A summary of the more important Bible symbols is given in Part 2 of this book.

Before leaving this subject, let us follow one trail of symbols through the Scriptures—those depicting the Holy Spirit.

As we have noted, the Holy Spirit has used various symbols to depict His own person and work. A study of these will teach us much about the various operations of the Holy Spirit.

The following list does not exhaust the subject. For instance, the Holy Spirit is sometimes symbolized by an unnamed servant. We find this in Genesis 24, where Abraham sent his servant out to find a bride for his son Isaac. If we regard this passage in its typical significance, then Abraham represents the Father, Isaac represents Christ, and the unnamed servant represents the Holy Spirit. Looked at in this way, the passage teaches us significant lessons about the Holy

Spirit's mission and method in the world today. He is here to seek a bride for Christ, sent here by the Father. The way the unnamed servant went about his task, his unobtrusiveness, and his success all highlight the Holy Spirit's way with people.

1. *The Wind: His Regenerating Power*

We first meet the Holy Spirit in the Bible in Genesis 1:2. "And the earth was without form, and void; and darkness was upon the face of the deep. And the Spirit of God moved upon the face of the waters." The New English Bible commits treason against the Word of God on the very first page and paragraph by translating that: "The earth was without form and void with darkness over the face of the abyss, and a mighty wind that swept over the surface of the waters."

The same Hebrew word *ruach* can be translated either wind or spirit. The context always determines which is the correct word to use. In actual fact the word *ruach,* which occurs 389 times in the Hebrew Old Testament, is rendered *spirit* in 237 passages and, in the remaining 152 places where it occurs, it is translated in 22 different ways in the King James Version.

It is no accident that the Hebrew word for *spirit* and for *wind* should be the same. The *wind* symbolizes the Holy Spirit. It symbolizes the Holy Spirit as the mighty, invisible, omnipresent God who manifests Himself in power and might, who goes where He wants, does what He wants, is subservient to no one, who is absolutely sovereign in His freedom of action. It was as a mighty, rushing wind that the Spirit of God came at Pentecost, to blow away the dust and cobwebs of the ages and to inaugurate a new and mighty movement in human history.

So the Holy Spirit is likened to the wind, His very name being the same word in the Hebrew tongue in which first He began to speak to man. As the wind, the Holy Spirit supremely sets forth His regenerating power. Nowhere is this more pointedly stated than in our Lord's conversation with Nicodemus. Nicodemus was a trained rabbi; a Bible scholar; a religious, good, moral, decent man. Jesus shook him out of his complacency by telling him he needed to be regenerated, needed to be born again. Moreover, apart from such a new birth he had no hope whatever of seeing the kingdom of God. It is noteworthy that the man did not argue. He did not say "Why?" he said "How"? He knew that all the years he had spent studying the rules and rites of religion had not brought the breath of divine life to his soul. In telling Nicodemus *how,* the Lord Jesus referred to the work of salvation by likening it first to *water* and then to *wind.*

"The wind," He said, "blows where it likes. You hear the sound of it but you cannot tell where it came from nor where it is going. So is every one that is born of the Spirit."

Nicodemus had experienced a physical birth—he needed to experience a spiritual birth. The physical birth resulted from fixed laws;

the spiritual birth resulted from fixed laws. He had nothing to do with the circumstances of his physical birth; he would have nothing to do with the circumstances of his spiritual birth. Just as he had some general knowledge of the laws of physical birth, so he could have some general knowledge of the laws of spiritual birth. But there was no way he could control those laws. He could take advantage of the movement of the wind, but he could not command or control the wind.

That is why it is imperative to respond to the convicting, converting power of the Holy Spirit. He is moving now. So now is the time to respond.

We know very little about the laws by which the Holy Spirit operates in regeneration, whether in the life of an individual or in the life of a nation. We do know that He passes through a meeting, and this one is saved, but that one makes no response. We know that at times He brings revival to a nation, but we cannot command a revival.

Now let us go back to Genesis 1:2. There we shall see illustrated for us the movement of the Holy Spirit as the wind. "The Spirit of God," we read, "*moved* upon the face of the waters." He brooded over the face of the deep and over the prevailing darkness, just as He broods over the darkness of a human heart.

Then He spoke. God's Word was introduced to deal with the darkness. And the entrance of God's Word brought light. Light shone upon the scene. "God, who commanded the light to shine out of darkness," says Paul, "hath shined in our hearts, to give the light of the knowledge of the glory of God in the face of Jesus Christ" (2 Corinthians 4:6).

The Spirit of God dealt first with the *darkness* and then with the *deadness* of that primeval world, just as He now deals with the darkness and deadness of a human soul.

2. *The Water: His Reviving Power*

Water is used symbolically in two ways in the Bible. Water for cleansing is a symbol of the Word of God. Water for drinking is a symbol of the Spirit of God.

The Spirit of God is like *water* to a thirsty man—it revives him. Thus we find water as a symbol of the Spirit appearing early in Israel's wilderness journey. First the *Rock* was smitten. "That Rock was Christ," Paul says. There could be no blessing apart from that. The Rock of Ages, the Lord Jesus, was smitten of God and afflicted. "He was wounded for our transgressions, He was bruised for our iniquities: the chastisement of our peace was upon Him" (Isaiah 53:5). As the hymnwriter says:

> Jehovah lifted up His rod;
>   O Christ, it fell on Thee
> Thou wast sore stricken of Thy God;
>   there's not one stroke for me;
> Thy blood beneath that rod has flowed;
>   Thy bruising healeth me.

But, once that Rock was smitten, the rivers of water flowed. The people of God were revived. When Amalek came, they were able to smite him with the edge of the sword—Amalek representing the flesh, and the sword representing the Word of God.

The classic New Testament passage on the Holy Spirit as water is found in John 7:37-39. It was the last day of the feast and Jesus stood and cried: "If any man thirst, let him come unto Me, and drink. He that believeth on Me, as the scripture hath said, out of his belly shall flow rivers of living water. (But this spake He of the Spirit. . . .)" The feast referred to was the Feast of Tabernacles, which closed the religious calendar for the year. It was the last and greatest of the feasts and, in its typology, it looked forward to the millennial reign.

In Jesus' day an interesting ritual had grown up around the feast and was always observed in Jerusalem. For seven days a procession of the priests went to the pool of Siloam or to the brook Kedron. The priests carried empty golden vessels. These they filled with water and came back to the Temple chanting parts of the Great Hallel. The Great Hallel (Israel's "Hallelujah Chorus") was made up of Psalms 113–118. Actually, the psalms were sung at Pentecost, Passover, and the Feast of Tabernacles.

So the priests came back with their golden vessels filled with water. Then, within the Temple courts, they poured out this water in a crystal stream. It was something not commanded in the Old Testament but it was a tradition of great interest and significance. The pouring out of that water signified:

(1) that God had supplied Israel's needs for water during the wilderness wanderings,

(2) that in a coming day the deserts will blossom as the rose and that rivers of water will transform the barren lands of earth into gorgeous gardens of Eden.

On the eighth day no water was poured out. On the last day, the great day of the feast, there were no golden vessels, no procession, no rivers of water. The omission was intended to show:

(1) that Israel was now in the land and there was no need for the supernatural supplies of water,

(2) that the promise of spiritual refreshment, symbolized also by the outpoured water, had not yet been fulfilled.

That was the background. On that very day, with Calvary before Him, Jesus stood and offered rivers of living water to those who would come to Him. And the Holy Spirit leaves us in no doubt about what Jesus meant. "This spake He of the Spirit," He says.

In the Bible, God the Father is likened to a fountain of living water; God the Son is likened to a well of living water; God the Holy Spirit is likened to a river of living water. The river speaks of the power of the Spirit of God to bring revival blessing when people turn to Christ.

3. *The Fire: His Refining Power*

It is significant that at Pentecost the Holy Spirit came as of cloven tongues of *fire*. Those mysterious flames sat upon each of the apostles. They were changed men from that moment. They were refined. Peter was no longer a coward. Thomas no longer doubted. Philip no longer demanded, "Show us the Father and it sufficeth us." Those men went out to set the world on fire.

4. *The Oil: His Revitalizing Power*

One of the commonest types of the Holy Spirit in the Bible is *oil*. Oil was used in the anointing of prophets, priests, and kings to symbolize the new life-transforming Holy Spirit power that was now theirs.

A great passage on the oil as a symbol of the Holy Spirit is the parable of the wise and foolish virgins (Matthew 25). In many ways the wise and foolish virgins were alike. They were all virgins; they all had lamps; they all had oil in their lamps to begin with; they all went to sleep. The difference was that the foolish virgins took no extra oil.

We have no trouble identifying the lamps. Psalm 119:105 says: "Thy word is a lamp unto my feet, and a light unto my path." A lamp is useless without oil. Apart from the energizing power of the Holy Spirit, the Word of God does not shine. The Word of God must be illuminated by the Spirit of God. That is why the Bible is a dead book to most. "The natural man receiveth not the things of the Spirit of God, neither can he know them because they are spiritually discerned" (1 Corinthians 2:14). That is why we have so many cults, all appealing to the Bible. Unenlightened people are seeking to get light from the Bible without the Holy Spirit.

The vessels represent the individual's life. David said, "I am forgotten as a dead man out of mind: I am like a broken vessel" (Psalm 31:12). Saul of Tarsus is described as a chosen vessel unto God (Acts 9:15). Husbands are to give honor to their wives "as unto the weaker vessel" (1 Peter 3:7). Concerning God's work in our lives we are told that "we have this treasure in earthen vessels, that the excellency of the power might be of God and not of us" (2 Corinthians 4:7).

The virgins, with the extra oil in their vessels, could rekindle their lamps. That is what makes the difference between those who profess to be believers and those who really are believers: True believers have oil in the vessel; they have the Holy Spirit in their lives. And therefore the Word of God, the lamp, can always be rekindled, even when it has been neglected.

5. *The Dove: His Redirecting Power*

The *dove*, too, in Scripture is a symbol of the Holy Spirit. The sacred dove of God descended from heaven and alighted on the Son of God. Now, the Holy Spirit's work in the world is to draw men and women to Jesus.

When I was a boy I used to spend an occasional hour or two on the station platform in by home town. It was a busy place, on the main line from London to South Wales and an important junction for the Valleys. It was fascinating to watch the trains, the rush and bustle, the constant ebb and flow of traffic. Fast express trains thundered past, along with long, lumbering freights. Fussy little trains left for the Valleys.

One day I saw some wicker baskets at one end of the platform. The porter explained that they contained pigeons with a well-developed homing instinct. Those birds, he said, would be put on trains going to various places, all the same distance away. At a set time the baskets would be opened and the pigeons set free. They would circle around a time or two and then head straight for home.

That is what the Holy Spirit does for us. He turns us in the direction of home.

8
The Law of Context

Always be wary of the Bible teacher who ignores the context of a verse of Scripture: "A text without a context is a pretext." Almost all false teaching is based on a disregard of context, the use of isolated, so-called "proof texts" to support an unscriptural point of view.

Tear a text out of its context and we can make the Bible say that there is no God (see Psalm 14:1). I once heard a man support the false theory of reincarnation by using the text, "Ye must be born again." Because they are ignorant of what the Bible says on the subject, many people think that the text, "Thou shalt not kill," legislates against capital punishment.

Satan took a text out of context when tempting the Lord Jesus. Having twice been foiled by the Lord's use of the Word of God, Satan used it himself, but used it deceptively. "If Thou be the Son of God," he said, "cast Thyself down: for it is written, He shall give His angels charge concerning thee: and in their hands they shall bear thee up, lest at any time thou dash thy foot against a stone" (Matthew 4:6). He was quoting from Psalm 91:11-13. What the psalmist actually said was this: "For He shall give His angels charge over thee, to keep thee in all thy ways. They shall bear thee up in their hands, lest thou dash thy foot against a stone. Thou shalt tread upon the lion and adder: the young lion and the dragon shalt thou trample under feet." The Devil conveniently ignored the context of the quotation. It spoke of his own destruction!

There are three circles of context that demand attention.

1. First, there is the *immediate context*. The verses and chapters immediately surrounding a verse should be examined to determine its significance. That context invariably sheds light on the text.

We must remember that chapter breaks and parentheses in a subject under discussion may disguise the true context. John 7:53 states, "And every man went unto his own house." There the chapter ends, and there, all too often, our reading ends. The very first verse of the next chapter reads: "Jesus went unto the Mount of Olives." Except for that regrettable chapter break we would read: "And every man went unto his own house. Jesus went unto the Mount of Olives." How much more significant that is.

The same thing occurs in Matthew 16:28 where the Lord says,

"Verily I say unto you, there be some standing here, which shall not taste of death, till they see the Son of man coming in His kingdom." There the chapter ends. If we read on, however, to the first verse of the next chapter we have an explanation of what has, to some, been a very difficult text. Chapter 17 tells the story of the transfiguration. There, Peter, James, and John saw the Lord in His glory. Moses and Elijah were present, representing the Law and the Prophets, the disciples were present representing the saints of the church age, and the whole incident prefigured the coming kingdom age when the Lord will be seen in His glory by all.

In Genesis 17 we read of a new revelation of God given to Abraham. The context is significant and, again, it is blurred by a chapter break. The last verse of the previous chapter reads: "And Abram was fourscore and six years old, when Hagar bare Ishmael to Abram." We are apt to forget that when we begin our reading again in chapter seventeen. This chapter begins: "And when Abram was ninety years old and nine, the Lord appeared to Abram and said unto him, I am the Almighty God, walk before Me, and be thou perfect." This is the first use of that lovely name, *El Shaddai*—the Omnipotent One Who Satisfies. The context shows that God had not spoken directly to Abraham for thirteen years, the fruit of his impatience in the matter of Ishmael. The time had now come, however, for Isaac to be born. Since Abraham's faith needed revitalizing, God broke the silence with a fresh revelation.

Examine the context of the three parables of Luke 15 and discover how the immediate context sheds light on the passage. The chapter begins with the words: "Then drew near unto Him all the publicans and sinners for to hear Him. And the Pharisees and scribes murmured, saying, This man receiveth sinners, and eateth with them." Evidently the stories of the lost sheep, the lost silver, and the lost son were directed especially to the publicans and sinners. But that pungent appendix to the story of the prodigal, that sketch of the elder brother—surely that was directed especially to the Pharisees and scribes. The disciples of the Lord Jesus were also present. We have, thus, three groups of people. To the disciples these were parables of faith; to the publicans and sinners they were parables of hope; to the scribes and Pharisees they were parables of love.

In some of Paul's writings, in the epistle to Hebrews, and in the book of Revelation, we find passages inserted that interrupt the flow of the narrative or argument. We must detect and mark such parentheses and take them into account when looking for the true context. The parentheses are important and are inserted where they are for adequate reasons, but they do interrupt the discussion in hand.

Take, for example, the entire passage in Hebrews from 5:12–6:20. This is a parenthesis, one of the great warning passages of the book. The writer has just introduced the subject of Melchisedec (5:5-10). His Hebrew readers are going to find that what he has to say about this king-priest is very explosive material indeed. He is forced to digress because of their dullness, but he comes back to his theme in the opening verse of chapter seven. Note how the entire digression is bracketed by the name of Melchisedec. Each of the five warning passages in Hebrews is an interruption of the book's main argument. Noting this will greatly help in reading, understanding, and interpreting the book.*

So then, the immediate context needs always to be carefully examined in interpreting a passage of Scripture.

2. Equally important is the *context of the book itself* in which any given passage is found. One great example of this is the book of Ecclesiastes, a favorite hunting ground for cultists in their search for proof texts. Any text from Ecclesiastes must be interpreted in the light of the scope and purpose of the book itself. Ecclesiastes gives us the viewpoint of man "under the sun" and underlines, by the repeated phrase "vexation of spirit," the frustrations and follies of the person whose whole life is dominated by this world.

The book was written by Solomon, probably toward the end of his misspent life. He was disillusioned and disappointed with the fruits of his carnality and backsliding. When he considered the real issues of life in the light of his own weakness and worldliness, the book of Ecclesiastes was the result. It records the perspective and the prospects of a worldly minded man. It is therefore a book inspired by the Holy Spirit to reveal the futility and short-sightedness of worldly philosophy and ambition. It records the despair and cynicism that result when life is bounded by the things of time and sense. That which is "under the sun" cannot meet our deepest needs. We must fix our sights on the next world, not this one, if we are to be truly fulfilled.

Since that is the scope and purpose of Ecclesiastes, any text taken from this book must be conditioned by its author's viewpoint and must, therefore, be handled with caution. On no account must a text from Ecclesiastes be allowed to contradict clear statements of truth found elsewhere in the Bible. Thus when Ecclesiastes 9:5 says, "the dead know not anything" (a favorite proof text of the Jehovah's Witness Cult), we must remember that this is not a true statement of fact. It is true that the worldly man says that "the dead know not anything" but what the worldly man says is not true. Luke 16:19-31 makes it clear that the dead know a great deal.

3. We must also consider the *context of the whole Bible*. Because truth has been revealed progressively, no one passage of Scripture can be considered in isolation from other passages related to it. That is why a concordance is such a valuable Bible study tool. We should use it to see what light cross-references shed on a subject. This is especially true when studying a doctrine, a topic, or an aspect of prophecy.

For instance four kinds of baptism are mentioned in the Bible:

*See the author's book, *Exploring Hebrews* (Chicago: Moody Press).

typical baptism, preparatory baptism, water baptism, and Spirit baptism. Any reference in the Bible to baptism should be examined to see just what kind of baptism is meant. Failure to differentiate between texts that refer to water baptism and texts that refer to Spirit baptism can lead to all kinds of confusion.

Leaven is mentioned in Matthew 13:33 in an important context. Some think that leaven symbolizes the gospel slowly permeating society. That this is not so can be seen by gathering together other references to leaven in Scripture. Look, for instance, at Genesis 19:3, Exodus 12:8 and 12:19, 1 Corinthians 5:6-8, Matthew 16:6,11-12, Mark 8:15 (compare Matthew 22:23,29). It is evident that leaven, in the Bible, uniformly stands for something evil; it especially stands for evil doctrine. There is no reason to make an exception in Matthew 13:33.

How often in everyday affairs we see a person's words or actions taken out of context and given an unfair and biased twist by the news media. It is possible to destroy a person's character and career in that way. Careful consideration of context will teach us to give thought to the time, place, and circumstances that give rise to a given communication. That is important in the mundane things of life and also in the Scriptures. How solemn a thing it is to misrepresent something God has said by failing to take the context of His words into consideration.

9
The Survey Principle

We must see the whole before becoming too immersed in its parts. Such a principle can be applied in many areas of study and endeavor, and it is vitally important in Bible study. Before we become too engrossed with verses and texts we need to get the broad outlines of the Bible firmly fixed in our minds. That includes the overall themes and contents of the various books, why they were written, how they relate to other books of the Bible, how they relate to history, and so on. In other words, one of the primary goals of the Bible student is to understand the whole before interpreting the parts.

The Bible contains 1,189 chapters, 23,214 verses, and 773,692 words. Taken in total they present a magnificent picture of God's dealings with humankind and with His ultimate purposes for the human race. But to those just beginning to study the Bible, the size, scope, and variety of the Scriptures can be confusing.

Think for a moment of a jigsaw puzzle with thousands of pieces all needing to be fitted together, each one with its proper place in relation to the whole. The sensible thing is to look at the overall picture on the puzzle box before trying to fit the individual pieces together. Green pieces can then be seen to belong to these trees, or this lawn, or that little girl's dress. Blue pieces can be seen to belong to a fragment of sky, or a pond, or a blue car. Red pieces evidently belong to the barn yonder, or to those flowers, or to that train on the skyline.

The sensible way to approach the Bible is similar: get its major features, book by book, well sorted out before going too far.

The casual reader of the Bible might easily think that, because the book of Jeremiah immediately follows the book of Isaiah, the two are closely related in time. In fact they are separated by about a century. When Isaiah wrote, the international scene was dominated by Assyria. When Jeremiah wrote, Assyria was just a bad memory and Babylon was the threat. The ten-tribed nation of Israel had been uprooted and its peoples scattered; only Judah remained to face the threat of Babylonian imperialism. The situation had changed significantly.

An even greater change exists between Malachi and Matthew. When Malachi wrote, the Jewish nation had been regathered from exile but the future was dark. About a century had passed since Haggai and Zechariah had preached to the returned remnant of

Israel, and a new set of sins had taken root in the land. Between Malachi and Matthew lies a gap of some 400 years. When Malachi wrote, the Persians still controlled the world. When Matthew wrote, Persia was gone, Greece was gone, the Maccabbees were gone, troublesome Egypt and Syria had been laid low, and Rome ruled the world.

In the Gospels we read of sects and parties unknown to Malachi. We read of scribes, Pharisees and Sadducees, Herodians. We read of Palestinian cities with Greek names. Hebrew has become a dead language, the language of scholars, and the Scriptures are being read in Greek. Moreover, the common language of the people is now Aramaic. We discover an Idumean on the throne of David. We are confronted by a governing religious body known as the Sanhedrin. Even the Temple is not the same one known to Malachi. In Matthew, we find public worship carried on mostly in synagogues. A vast and cumbersome collection of interpretations (both oral and written, later known as the Talmud) is growing and even replacing the Scriptures in popular and scholastic circles. Such sweeping changes must be grasped if the Bible is to be intelligible. A panoramic view of the Bible will keep students from getting lost as they approach this or that passage of Scripture.

The Lord Jesus used the Bible survey approach with those two discouraged disciples of His when He joined them (seemingly a total stranger) on the Emmaus road (Luke 24). They poured into His ears a sad story of their crucified hopes. They were so confused. They had thought that Jesus was indeed the Messiah, but Calvary had finished all that. True, stories of a resurrection had been buzzing about Jerusalem since dawn but no one surely could take them seriously.

The Lord's answer was to give them a survey of what the Scriptures actually said about Christ: "Beginning at Moses and all the prophets, He expounded unto them in all the scriptures the things concerning Himself " (Luke 24:27). In that way He gave them a proper perspective. They had thought only of a sovereign Messiah; He showed them a suffering Messiah. They had thought only of One who would be crowned; He showed them One who could also be crucified. He replaced their ignorance with truth. The larger picture revealed a Redeemer as well as a Ruler.

The survey approach to the Scriptures puts things in perspective. It saves the student from ridiculous and sometimes grave error. In Zechariah 3, for example, we read of Joshua standing before the Lord in filthy garments. One preacher expressed his astonishment that Joshua, after being such a notable leader, after having had such good training under Moses, and after having led Israel into the Promised Land, could so have allowed himself to run down as to appear before God in such a disgraceful condition. Had he known his Bible better, he would not have made such a glaring error. There are two notable Joshuas in the Old Testament: one was a soldier, the other a priest; one was a captive in Egypt, the other a captive in Babylon; one lived at the time of the exodus, the other a thousand years later at the end of the exile.

Similar mistakes can be made with the various Marys and Herods of the New Testament. There were three Marys at the cross: the Lord's mother, Mary Magdalene, and Mary the wife of Cleopas. Mary of Bethany, interestingly enough, was not there. She had already performed her burial rites (Matthew 26:7; Mark 14:3; John 11, 12:1-9), had been commended for it by the Lord, and was anticipating the resurrection. Mary the mother of Mark is not mentioned in the Gospels nor is that other Mary who resided at Rome and who befriended Paul and his companions.

As for the Herods, they were a complicated family. There was Herod the Great, who massacred the male children of Bethlehem; Herod Philip I, whose wife Herodias and whose daughter Salome left him to go off with Herod Antipas, the Herod who murdered John the Baptist and before whom Christ was sent for trial. There is Herod Agrippa I, who martyred James and planned the execution of Peter and who was eaten up of worms. There is Herod Agrippa II, the "last king of the Jews," who heard Paul's defense before Paul was packed off to Rome to appear before Nero.

Before beginning a verse-by-verse study of any passage or book of Scripture, a survey is essential. Some books of the Bible will remain a mystery unless their broad outlines are mastered first. A notable example of this is the book of Revelation. Many foolish things have been said about this book by people who have never mastered its major patterns. In the first place, the scenes alternate between heaven and earth, so it is always important to note from what position events are being observed. Then, too, the actual chronology of the book is constantly interrupted by parenthetical sections—some brief, but others extending over a whole series of chapters; some reaching back to amplify past events in the chronology and others anticipating and leaping ahead. Unless these parentheses are clearly discerned and their position in relation to the overall drama properly understood, the book of Revelation will remain confusing and unintelligible.

If a person decided to drive from Chicago to Los Angeles he would first look at a map of the United States to see which routes best suited his purpose. Next he would look at state maps to see what special problems he might meet along the way. Finally, he would examine various city maps to decide which bypasses or city highways he should take or avoid. He would thus move from the broad picture to the smaller. That is how we should proceed with Bible study: from general to the particular, from the overview to the details, from survey to analysis.

Be sure to see the summary of the books of the Bible at the end of this handbook.

10
The Importance of Structure

At one time in my life I worked in the purchasing department of a large trucking company. In the shop one of the mechanics might need a seal, perhaps, for a clutch. If the part was out of stock we in the purchasing department had to order it from the manufacturer. That would have been an impossible job for me had it not been for an all-important book supplied by the manufacturer to its customers. This book, known as the Parts Book, was an enormous volume. It contained all the information needed to order any single part of a truck. Its chief feature was the "exploded diagrams" which illustrated each part of the vehicle.

The book, for instance, provided a working illustration of the clutch for which the mechanic needed the part. Each part in the assembly was depicted in the diagram in such a way that it showed the part's exact relationship, not only to the whole assembly, but to each part with which it had contact. Looking at such a diagram it could be seen that first came this piece, then that piece, then the other piece. In addition to this helpful diagrammatic view of the assembly, showing how the whole thing fit together, each part was numbered.

As long as either the number or the exact position of the part was known, it could be found in the exploded diagram and its function understood.

In the Bible, everything has its proper place. Nothing can be more helpful, in understanding the significance of any part of the Bible, than to get at its underlying structure—to work out, so to speak, an exploded diagram.

Everything God does is perfect. In nature, for example, no two snowflakes are alike, yet each one is built on an identical six-pointed pattern. No two oak leaves are identical, yet each one can be easily recognized by its form. The same is true of God's Word. Because each part is perfectly structured, the structure of a passage will often help solve problems connected with it. For example, when we structurally analyze the difficult warning passages of Hebrews, they resolve their own difficulties. The importance of the structure of the Bible extends not only to verses and phrases but to whole chapters and entire books of the Bible. Frequently the in-wrought structure of a passage takes the form of introversion, alternation, or a combination of both.

Look at the parallelism to be seen in the story of the prodigal son (Luke 15:12-32) as indicated in *The Companion Bible* by E. W. Bullinger.

A. The younger son (12-16)
  1. His penitence (17-20A)
    2. His father's compassion (20b)
      3. The younger son's confession (21)
        4. The father's gifts (22-23)
          5. The reason—"for" (24)

B. The elder brother (25-27)
  1. His petulance (28a)
    2. His father's entreaty (28b)
      3. The elder son's complaint (29-30)
        4. The father's gifts (31-32a)
          5. The reason—"for" (32b)

The structure reveals the beauty and symmetry of the parable. It emphasizes the difference between the two brothers and brings out the two-pronged moral of the parable. The Lord's audience consisted of two classes of people, the "publicans and sinners" (verse 1) and "the Pharisees and scribes" (verse 2). The first segment of the parable is obviously addressed to the publicans and sinners, who easily identified themselves with the prodigal son; the second segment of the parable is equally clearly directed at the scribes and Pharisees, who could not fail to see themselves in the elder brother.

A different type of parallelism can be seen in the structure of the Ten Commandments (Exodus 20:2-17).

A. Commands one and two: *thought* (2-3)
  B. Command three: *word* (4-6)
    C. Commands four and five: *deed* (7-12)
    C. Commands six, seven, and eight: *deed* (13-15)
  B. Command nine: *word* (16)
A. Command ten: *thought* (17)

The structure reveals the symmetry of the decalogue. It is divided into two major segments. The first segment is controlled by the phrase "the Lord thy God," the second segment by the phrase "thou shalt not." The first five commandments are a summary of our duty to God; the second five, our duty to other human beings. In each case our duty extends through thought, word, and deed.

The Lord Jesus recognized this division of the decalogue into two major segments. When challenged by a lawyer He replied: "Thou shalt love the Lord thy God with all thy heart, and with all thy soul, and with all thy mind. This is the first and great commandment. And the second is like unto it, Thou shalt love thy neighbor as thyself. On these two commandments hang all the law and the prophets" (Matthew 22:37-40). Our inclination would be to divide the commandments into a grouping of four and six, linking parental obedience with man's duty to man. The structure shows that God links it otherwise. The phrase "the Lord thy God" ties this commandment on to the first four, about our duty to God. The reason lies in the fact that parents stand in the place of God to a child as far as obedience is concerned.

There are countless examples of the structural base of Scripture. Those interested in pursuing it through the various books of the Bible and into almost every chapter and verse should examine *The Companion Bible*. While Bullinger's ecclesiology and ultra-dispensationalism are regrettable, his handling of the structure of the Bible is fascinating.

It is not necessary, however, to restrict oneself to the introversion-alternation technique for discerning the structure of a passage of Scripture. Careful examination of any passage will yield results. Care must be taken to analyze the main thought in a passage and its subordinate thoughts. These should be tabulated and studied. Such a structural analysis can then become the basis of teaching what the Bible says. Once the structure is exposed, often all that is needed to obtain a workable outline is to put meaningful captions to the various parts of the structure.

Let us try this with Psalm 90, the famous psalm attributed to Moses.

The first thing to do is to read the psalm over and over again until its major themes are fixed firmly in the mind. Constant reading of the text is vital.

What is the writer saying here?

What is his major topic?

How is he handling his theme?

What are his arguments?

Where and why and for how long does he digress from his subject?

How is he illustrating his theme?

What supporting statements does he make?

How can I capture, in capsule form, the major divisions of this passage?

These and similar questions will soon begin to yield results.

Reading Psalm 90 in this way will show that the psalm has three main divisions: *The Right Perspective* (1-6); *The Real Problem* (7-12); *The Resulting Prayer* (13-17). The thing to do, at this point, is to mark off these divisions in the psalm itself and to write them down on a sheet of paper with their appropriate captions.

Having determined the major divisions of the structure and having given each division an appropriate title, go back and break down the first segment into its own divisions. These divisions are not to be arbitrarily imposed on the text but are to be drawn out of the text itself by paying strict attention to what is being said. Reading and rereading verses 1-6 will show that the right perspective about which Moses speaks is threefold. He is impressed by the *Sovereignty of*

God (1-2), by the *Sympathy of God* (3-4), and by the *Severity of God* (5-6). Mark these divisions and write them down under the first caption: The Right Perspective.

Each of these three subdivisions can now be examined for structure and message. We discover that, related to the sovereignty of God, Moses is awed by the fact that we have *A Tremendous God* (1a), *A Tender God* (1b), and *A Timeless God* (2). It is along those lines that he examines the sovereignty of God and adds to the perspective from which he writes the psalm.

With this start, try your own hand at breaking down each verse in the psalm into its underlying structure. Then, if you like, compare your results with the following analysis of Psalm 90 (derived from a verse-by-verse, phrase-by-phrase and, sometimes, word-by-word examination of the psalm.)*

Keep in mind that the structural approach is the exact opposite of the survey approach. In Bible survey you are looking for broad outlines, great movements, and overall themes. In structural analysis you are breaking a passage down into its parts to see how the passage is put together.

Psalm 90

I.   THE RIGHT PERSPECTIVE (90:1-6)
   A. The sovereignty of God (90:1-2)
      1. He Is a Tremendous God
      2. He Is a Tender God
      3. He Is a Timeless God
   B. The Sympathy of God (90:3-4)
      1. He Knows the Tyranny the Tomb Has over Him (90:3)
      2. He Knows the Tyranny that Time Has over Him (90:4)
   C. The Severity of God (90:5-6)

II. THE REAL PROBLEM (90:7-12)
   A. Our Lives Are so Sinful (90:7-8)
   B. Our Lives Are so Short (90:9-10)
   C. Our Lives Are so Serious (90:11-12)

III. THE RESULTING PRAYER (90:13-17)
   A. A Fresh Evidence of the Moving of God (90:13)
   B. A Fresh Enduement of the Mercy of God (90:14-15)
   C. A Fresh Expression of the Might of God (90:16)
   D. A Fresh Effulgence of the Majesty of God (90:17)

A structural analysis can be used by the Bible teacher in two ways. As it stands, it is far too detailed to try to expound to a congregation. People simple become weary and confused in trying to follow all the ins and outs of such an outline. The teacher therefore can deal only with the main topics if the structure is to become the basis for a single message. Or, if the whole psalm is to be studied, three messages can be made out of it.

---

*See John Phillips, *Exploring The Psalms*, Volume Three, (Neptune, NJ: Loizeaux Brothers).

11
The Dispensations

In studying the Bible it is of supreme importance to make a difference where God makes a difference. According to Hebrews 1:1 God not only spoke in different ways but He also spoke at different times. The time when He spoke to Abraham was much different from the time when He spoke to David. The times when He spoke by the prophets are not the same as the times when He spoke through His Son. We need to know something about these various times at which God has spoken. We call them "dispensations."

Regrettably, the word *dispensation* has become a fighting word. Some have wrongly divided the Word of truth and brought dispensational teaching into disrepute. By the time the ultra-dispensationalists have finished with the Bible they have little left for today except a handful of Pauline epistles. The other extreme, of course, is to deny that there is any dispensational teaching in the Bible. I shall try to avoid both pitfalls.

The Greek word for dispensation, *oikonomia*, refers to an act of administering. It is derived from two words, *okos* ("a house"), and *nemo* ("to dispense," "to weigh," "to deal out"—as the steward of a house would). The word *oikonomia* was used for the management or administration of a household. That Greek word is transliterated in our English word *economy*. We still use the word in its original sense when we speak of a political or a social economy. When the King James Version of the Bible was produced, the word was still commonly used to mean "administration," as it still does, of course, in the Greek New Testament. It occurs six times in the New Testament and is used either of the act of administering or of the time during which an act of administration is performed.

God has not always administered human affairs in the same way. The way He dealt with Adam before the Fall is not the same as the way He dealt with Adam after the Fall, for instance. We can detect a number of these "various times" or "dispensations" in the Bible, periods during which God has dealt with mankind in a particular way. Paul, for example, speaks of "the dispensation of the grace of God" (Ephesians 3:2). Although some difference of opinion exists about exactly how many dispensations there are, the fact that they exist is evident. We may depict them thus:

THE DISPENSATIONS

	DISPENSA-TION	CHARACTER-ISTIC	DURATION	CONCLUSION	SYMBOL
1	The Age of Innocence	Sinlessness	Creation to the Fall of Man	Expulsion from the garden	The garden of Eden
2	The Age of Conscience	Permissiveness	The Fall to the Flood	The Deluge	The mark of Cain
3	The Age of Human Government	Lawlessness	The Flood to the Tower of Babel	The confusion of tongues	The sword of the magistrate
4	The Patriarchal Age	Pilgrimage	Abraham to the bondage in Egypt	Slavery	A tent and an altar
5	The Age of the Mosaic Law	Disobedience	Moses to Christ	The crucifixion of Christ	The tables of stone
6	The Church Age	Grace	Pentecost to the Rapture	The Rapture of the Church	The cross of Christ
7	The Judgment Age	Wrath	The Rapture to the Return of Christ	The Battle of Armageddon	The mark of the Beast
8	The Millennial Age	Theocracy	Armageddon to the Great White Throne	The Final Judgment	A rod of iron
9	The Eternal State	Glory	For ever and ever	No end	The New Jerusalem

With due allowance for some variation we may say, then, that God has dealt with mankind in a state of innocence, as ruled by conscience, as curbed by government, as motivated by promise, as under the law, as under grace, as exposed to judgment, as enjoying the millennium, and as in eternity.[1]

Each of these periods (with the exception of the eternal state of those in heaven) has a beginning and an ending, and each one ends in failure and judgment. In most cases the end of one dispensation and the beginning of another are clearly marked by a catastrophe. In a few cases the two ages overlap somewhat for a brief period. We shall now summarize briefly these major time divisions in God's administration of human affairs.

We begin with *the Edenic state.* There is nothing to compare with this until we come to the eternal state at the very end. God originally placed man as a perfect, innocent creature with no knowledge of sin in a perfect environment. He was given congenial employment, a loving companion, and full fellowship with God. He was man as God intended man to be. The human spirit was indwelt by the Holy Spirit. Man was inhabited by God. Adam disobeyed God by breaking the one restriction placed on him. He was persuaded by Satan that God

---

[1] Variations arise because some expositors classify one or more of the nine divisions adopted here as subdivisions of one or other of the longer periods.

was not indispensable to him. By acting in disobedience to and in independence of God, Adam plunged the human race into sin. At once the Holy Spirit vacated the human spirit and Adam died spiritually. He was expelled from Eden and forced to face life under adverse conditions with the consequences of his sin ever afterward pursuing him and his posterity.

For the next long period God dealt with mankind as a whole. First came *the age of conscience,* a long period covering some 1,500 years of human history (four chapters in Genesis). The one legacy fallen man brought with him from Eden was a conscience, the knowledge of right and wrong. During the age of conscience every man did what was right in his own eyes. As a result the earth became wholly corrupt and filled with violence. This period of permissiveness climaxed in what Jesus called "the days of Noah" and the judgment of the Flood.

After the Flood came a change. God put the rainbow in the sky as a token that never again would He inundate the world with water. To put a curb on man's wickedness He put the sword of the magistrate into the hands of Noah and instituted capital punishment as the penalty for murder. Thus began *the period of human government.* Before long the sword of justice became the sword of the conqueror. Nimrod used the sword to enforce his will and his ideas on the rest of mankind. He became the world's first empire builder and founded the world's first League of Nations. There was to be one capital (symbolized by the great city he built), one creed (symbolized by the religious tower), and one culture (symbolized by a common language). The period ended with the building of the tower of Babel, and with a flagrant attempt to create a world society from which God was to be excluded. The result was judgment, the confounding of human language, and the consequent scattering of the nations.

God now selected one man. He no longer dealt primarily with nations as a whole but concentrated on a single individual, Abraham. To him and his descendants God made certain far-reaching commitments that instituted *the age of promise.* God's plan was to make a great nation of Abraham and his seed and to continue His plans for humankind through the Hebrew people.

The promise made to Abraham was confirmed to his son Isaac and then to his grandson Jacob. Jacob was the father of twelve sons who became patriarchs of the twelve tribes, known as the children of Israel. Jacob's sons were, for the most part, unruly and dissolute. They and their descendants needed continuous divine discipline. Thus, while waiting for Amorite iniquity to "fill full the cup of wrath," God allowed the chosen people to migrate to Egypt, there to become a populous nation under the harsh discipline of exile and oppression. During that long period, neither God nor the faithful remnant of His people in Egypt forgot the promises.

The age of promise gave way at last to the lengthy *dispensation of the law.* The nation of Israel, emancipated from Egypt, was brought to Sinai, where God gave them His commandments. There are 613 precepts in the Mosaic Law (the rabbis later taught that there were 365 negative laws, one for each day of the year and 248 positive laws, one for each bone in the body!). The Lord Jesus reduced the entire Law to two major precepts (Matthew 22:36-40).

The Law said, in effect, "This do and thou shalt live." The Old Testament prophet could properly declare, "When the wicked man turneth away from his wickedness that he hath committed, and doeth that which is lawful and right, he shall save his soul alive" (Ezekiel 18:27). Such a statement has nothing to do with the present-day believer. We are not saved by works but by grace (Titus 3:5; Romans 11:6). In actual fact the Old Testament believer was likewise saved by grace. Failure to keep the moral law necessitated the giving of the ceremonial law. The ceremonial law, for the most part, pointed forward to Calvary and to the cross.

The Law is divided into two major sections, moral and ceremonial. The moral law is repeated in the New Testament epistles. Christians keep the moral law, not because it was enjoined by Moses but because such behavior is the natural response of a regenerate human heart to the love of the Lord Jesus Christ. The ceremonial law was given exclusively to Israel. It continued in force down through the ages until the crucifixion of Christ fulfilled all that it symbolized. At that time God rent the Temple veil and rendered the whole Levitical, Mosaic system obsolete. While under the Law, the Israelites repeatedly broke it.

At Pentecost, God burst into time again with a new form of dealing with human beings. The Church was born and *the age of grace* (the church age, or the age of the Holy Spirit) began. In this age God is not dealing either with Jews or Gentiles as such. He is calling out a people for His name from all races, and the Holy Spirit is baptizing all who believe into the mystical body of Christ, the Church.

The church age was not envisioned by the Old Testament believers. It was a mystery "hid in God" (Ephesians 3:9). The present age, which began on the day of Pentecost, will end with the rapture of the Church. As in all the other dispensations, there is much failure in this one. Alongside the true Church and genuine Christianity there exists a false church and a vast system of religion we simply label "Christendom." This false, professing church will be left behind for judgment at the rapture of the true Church.

There is one basic difference between the age of grace and the age of law. In the old dispensation, righteousness was *required,* but nobody could produce the righteousness the Law demanded (except the Lord Jesus Christ). Under grace, righteousness is *received* by mankind from God. It is bestowed on the believer as a free gift by the grace of God because of the finished work of Christ.

After the rapture of the Church, an *age of judgment* will begin.

God will reinstitute direct dealings with the nation of Israel. He will set in motion events that will lead to Israel's national repentance and regeneration at the time of Christ's return to earth.

The present age (apart from God's purpose with the Church) is called *man's day*, because during this present period man is judging (1 Corinthians 1:10). The coming age is called *the Lord's day* (Revelation 1:10) or "the day of the Lord" because that will be the time when God will judge. Man's day of judging will close and God's will begin.[2]

Terrible events will transpire on the earth. God will allow the worst human passions to prevail. Jew and Gentile alike will hail the Beast as the answer to this world's woes and will worship both him and Satan. There will be a period of persecution, known as the Great Tribulation, aimed specifically at the Jews but embracing all believers. It is clear from 1 Thessalonians 5:1-5 that the Church will not be on earth during this coming time.

The tribulation period will end with the battle of Armageddon and with the personal return of the Lord Jesus to put an end to human mismanagement of the planet. He will again deal with mankind as a whole and the thousand-year reign of Christ will begin. This period is known as the *Millennium*. It will be in two stages. First, Christ will reign in His David character, putting down all His foes; then He will reign in His Solomon character, instituting a period of prosperity and peace. The curse will be almost wholly removed from the earth, Satan will be bound and the golden age will come. Like the other dispensations, however, this one will end in judgment. Satan, released from his prison, will deceive the nations for the last time and lead them in one final, futile rebellion against God. They will simply be swept away. The earth will go up in flames and the wicked will be hurled into eternity.

The final age is not really a dispensation. It is *the eternal state*. It begins with the setting up of God's great white throne and the judgment of all the wicked dead. The wicked will be forever banished to the lake of fire; the blessed will be forever with Christ in a newly created heaven and earth. Very little is told us of the eternal state. But God, who makes no two blades of grass alike and who never creates two identical snowflakes, can be trusted to make eternity as rich and as full and as wonderful as He is Himself.

These, then, in broad outline are the dispensations. Each has its special characteristics. The Lord Jesus recognized the fact of dispensational truth and forcefully demonstrated its significance in the Nazareth synagogue (Luke 4:16-20). Closing the scroll of Isaiah 61:1-2 in the middle of a sentence, He said, "This day is this

---

[2]The expression "the day of the Lord" occurs 16 times in the Hebrew Bible (Isaiah 13:6,9; Ezekiel 13:5; Joel 1:15; 2:1,11; 3:14; Amos 5:18,20; Obadiah 15; Zephaniah 1:7,14; Malachi 4:5. In the New Testament it occurs four times (1 Thessalonians 5:2; 2 Thes-salonians 2:2; 2 Peter 3:10; Revelation 1:10). The popular idea that "the Lord's day" in Revelation 1:10 refers to Sunday is inadequate. John was caught away in the Spirit to "the day of the Lord" to see those things that form the bulk of the Apocalypse.

Scripture fulfilled in your ears." He left out the last clause of Isaiah 61:2 because that clause ("and the day of vengeance of our God") was not to be fulfilled at His first coming. By closing the book when and where He did He made a dispensational distinction. There is no break or mark in the text to indicate the passage of some 2,000 years between the first clauses and the final one. Yet the break is surely there, and history proves it. In our English text there is only a comma between the two statements "the acceptable year of the LORD" and "the day of vengeance of our God." Yet the whole of the present dispensation comes between.

Dispensational truth helps explain why the Old Testament prophets, speaking and writing as they were moved by the Holy Spirit, did not understand some of their utterances (1 Peter 1:10,11). What was meant by "the sufferings of Christ and the glory that should follow"? They saw both peaks but had no concept of the valley that lay between. Numerous instances of the present dispensation being passed over in complete silence can be found in the Old Testament. "The stone which the builders refused is become the head stone of the corner" (Psalm 118:22). "Unto us a child is born, unto us a son is given: and the government shall be upon his shoulder" (Isaiah 9:6). Similarly, the angel in his annunciation to Mary passed silently over the millennia of the church age: "Thou shalt conceive in thy womb, and bring forth a son, and shalt call His name Jesus. He shall be great, and shall be called the Son of the Highest: and the Lord God shall give unto Him the throne of His father David" (Luke 1:31-32).

Because God has not always dealt with men in identical ways at all times, five principles must be kept in mind when interpreting Scripture.

1. *Truth that belongs to one part of the past must not be read into another part of the past.* We must always ascertain exactly where we are when reading a portion of the Bible. For instance, the whole period of the Gospels was a special period when the kingdom was being offered to Israel and was being rejected by Israel. Matthew 10:5-6 says: "Go not into the way of the Gentiles, and into any city of the Samaritans enter ye not: But go rather to the lost sheep of the house of Israel." According to this there could be no missionary work among Gentiles, only among Jews. Obviously there must have been a change later or else the Bible contradicts itself: Mark 16:15 says, "Go ye into all the world, and preach the gospel to every creature." The first command was given in connection with the proclamation of the King and the kingdom. When both had been rejected and the King crucified, the command was no longer appropriate and another command was given. Now it is "Go ye . . . to every creature" instead of "Go not" to the Gentiles.

2. *Truth that belongs to a past dispensation must not be used to interpret the present dispensation.* If we mix up the dispensations, we shall put ourselves under the Law. In Deuteronomy 6:25 we read, "It

shall be our righteousness, if we observe to do all these commandments before the LORD our God, as He hath commanded us." That
was law. Romans 3:20 declares, "By the deeds of the law there shall
no flesh be justified in His sight." That is grace. It is the opposite of
Deuteronomy 6:25. Both statements are true, but one was given to
Israel under a covenant of works and the other is true of Jew and
Gentile alike in this present dispensation of grace.

Some of the psalms are called "imprecatory psalms" because they
contain vigorous curses and prayers for God to pour out vengeance
and judgment on certain people. There was a time (and a time is
coming) when such language in prayer was and will be perfectly appropriate. The language of these imprecatory psalms, however, is
certainly foreign to Christians in this age of grace.

Both the past and the coming ages have to do with the kingdom;
the present age has to do with the Church. Both the former and
coming ages have to do with law; the present one has to do with
grace. Kingdom truth, therefore, has to do with a past and future
dispensation. The kingdom was foreseen by the prophets, proclaimed by John the Baptist as being "at hand" (Matthew 3:2), and
was the first subject of the Lord's ministry (Matthew 4:17). But
both the King and the kingdom were rejected. The kingdom is now
postponed. After the church age has run its course, however, the
kingdom will be set up in power and glory. The Spirit of God uses a
number of figures to depict the Church, but never once in the epistles, does He liken it to a kingdom. The Church, of course, has its
place within the vast and universal sovereign rule of God, but it is
not included for the most part in the more limited expression "the
kingdom of heaven."

3. *Truth that belongs to the present dispensation must not be read into
a past dispensation.* The present age was a secret not revealed in Old
Testament times. The "mystery" or secret of the Church was "first
made known to the sons of men" by the apostles and prophets raised
up by God for that purpose in the church age. "In other ages [it] was
not made known unto the sons of men" (Ephesians 3:5). It was no secret in the Old Testament that Gentiles would come into blessing
and be saved. But the Church was a secret. Illustrations of the
Church were buried away in the Old Testament types but we do not
go to these types for Church truth. We can recognize them as types
only because we are enlightened by New Testament truth. The Old
Testament Jew certainly did not see the Christian Church in them.

Similarly, we must not force a New Testament ethic into the Old
Testament. Such things as polygamy, slavery, divorce, and retribu-
tion are handled in a much higher way in the New Testament than in
the Old. They were all permitted in the Old Testament under the
Mosaic law but are inconsistent with the love principle that governs
the New Testament.

One of the most common mistakes is to read the Church back into the Old Testament. In some editions of the Bible, running captions are found at the head of each page. Often those who wrote the captions had no concept at all of this principle of interpretation. Over such a passage as Isaiah 29 we read, for example, a caption proclaiming: "God's Mercies to His Church." Nonetheless, the Church is not there. In providing those captions, the authors have (conveniently and inconsistently) reserved all the Old Testament blessings for "the Church" and all its judgments, warnings, and curses for "the Jews." Such comments are misleading.

4. *Truth that belongs to the future must not be read into the present.* For instance, the great tribulation is a future event. To put the Church into the tribulation is to put it where it does not belong. The great tribulation has to do with Israel and it is expressly called "the time of Jacob's trouble" (Jeremiah 30:7). Numerous passages connect this coming time of trouble with Israel: for instance, Daniel 7:8; 8:9-12,23-26.

5. Finally, *truth that belongs to one part of the future must not be read into another part.* There are advents, resurrections, and judgments all in the future and all relating to different periods. They must be properly distinguished the one from the other. The judgment that will take place at the judgment seat of Christ, the judgment of the living nations, and the judgment of the great white throne are all different. Christ's coming *for* His Church, His "appearing" (2 Thessalonians 2:1), and His coming *with* His Church, His "advent" (Isaiah 2:11; 1 Thessalonians 5:2) are totally distinct future events. The *advent* of Christ (as that advent had to do with "the day of the Lord") was a subject of extensive Old Testament prophecy but not the *appearing* (1 Thessalonians 4:13).

Do you recall Rip Van Winkle, who went to sleep in the reign of George III and awoke, some twenty years later, in the administration of George Washington? He had slept right out of one administration into another and almost lost his head shouting for the wrong George! Failure to discern changes in God's administrations will likewise lead us into difficulty. If we are not careful we will find ourselves in the doubtful company of Jehovah's Witnesses, Roman Catholics, Seventh-Day Adventists, and Mormons—all of whom have distorted Biblical truth by failing to rightly divide the word of truth and discern its dispensational base.

12

The Covenants

We see eight different covenants in the Scriptures. They are a remarkable set of contractual agreements drawn up between God and members of the human race. That is what a covenant is: a contract, a legal agreement between two or more parties. If we are to rightly divide the word of truth, we must learn to differentiate between these various contracts, their provisions, their parties, and their purposes.

Suppose a company were to draw up eight different contracts with eight customers. Each of those contracts would contain agreements, conditions, stipulations, and commitments, each designed to cover the special situations agreed upon by the company and its customers. Let us suppose the firm entering into the agreements is in the building business. In more than one case, common items could well be found in some of the contracts. Both Mr. Brown and Mr. Smith, for instance, might specify the same kind of carpet for the living room, and Mr. Jones and Mr. Wright might both want brick construction. There would also be considerable differences. Mr. Green might want a full basement whereas Mr. Black might want his house on a concrete slab. Mr. Brown might want three full bathrooms; Mr. Green might be content with two.

So the contracts, with their common and contrasting clauses, are drawn up and signed. What would happen if the business manager ignored the differences between the various contracts? He negotiates a good buy on oak flooring, so in it goes—into Mr. Smith's house, regardless of the agreement. He discovers that Green's property, just beneath the surface, is almost solid rock, so he decides to sit his house on a concrete slab and give the basement to Mr. Black instead. After all, a house is a house. The result would be total confusion.

Just so with the Scriptures. In our study of the Bible we cannot afford to neglect the covenants, nor can we afford not to differentiate between the common and different clauses in those covenants. They have been drawn up by God, in His grace, with different people, at different periods and for different purposes. First, let us lay them out for study in order. They group themselves into three categories:

1. THE PRIMEVAL COVENANTS
   a. The Edenic Covenant

Underlying theme: Goodness
b. The Adamic Covenant
Underlying theme: Guilt
c. The Noahic Covenant
Underlying theme: Government
2. THE PATRIARCHAL COVENANTS
—Dealing With the Hebrew Racial Family
a. The Abrahamic Covenant
Underlying theme: Promise (The Lord)
b. The Mosaic Covenant
Underlying theme: Precept (The Law)
c. The Palestinian Covenant
Underlying theme: Possession (The Land)
—Dealing With the Hebrew Royal Family
The Davidic Covenant
3. THE PROPHETICAL COVENANT
The New Covenant

Even a casual glance at those divisions shows some differences. Some of them, for instance, are conditional ("If you will do this or that, then . . . "). Others are wholly unconditional ("I will, I will, I will"). We have an example of a conditional covenant in Exodus 19:5 and of an unconditional covenant in Genesis 17. Be sure always to note specifically the actual beneficiary, the clauses of the agreement, and the circumstances under which it was made. Note, too, that some of the covenants have special "signs" or seals attached to them. The seal of the Abrahamic Covenant, for instance, was circumcision; the seal of the Noahic Covenant was the rainbow; the seal of the Mosaic Covenant was the Sabbath.

Here I have listed eight covenants. Others might list fewer by viewing the Mosaic Covenant as a temporary modification of the Abrahamic Covenant, the Palestinian Covenant as an appendix to the Mosaic Covenant, and the Davidic Covenant as a rider to the Abrahamic Covenant. It is simpler to study each one as a separate agreement.

THE EDENIC COVENANT
(Genesis 1:28-31; 2:8-17)

Underlying theme: *Goodness*
The Edenic Covenant, drawn up with man in a state of innocence, governed the conditions of life in the garden of Eden. Everything that the grace and goodness of God could devise for human happiness was included in this covenant, along with one simple prohibition. The terms of the covenant can be set forth in outline form:

1. THE PROVISIONS OF THE COVENANT
a. Man's Duties Explained
(1) Parental

(2) Pastoral
b. Man's Diet Explained
c. Man's Dominions Explained
2. THE PROHIBITION OF THE COVENANT

Life in Eden was idyllic. Our first parents had a perfect environment in which to live. They had congenial employment and enjoyable companionship. In the cool of the day, God Himself came down to commune with them and to crown their happiness.

Adam was to be both a gardener and a guardian. His task was "to dress" and "to keep" the garden. There was no sin and no curse. Everywhere the world displayed its beauty and its bounty in prodigal variety.

Adam was not descended from the beasts. He and Eve were made in the image and likeness of God and were indwelt by the Holy Spirit of God. They had God-given lordship over all creation (Genesis 1:28). Adam was a man of the highest intellectual ability, evidenced in his naming the animals as they were paraded before him (Genesis 2:19). To coin thousands of words for a vocabulary is no mean feat. Try it!

Adam and Eve were to "be fruitful and multiply." The human race was to rise up and spread over all the earth. They were to "subdue" the earth, that is, develop its vast resources to their fullest potential.

God gave one simple prohibition. Adam must not eat of the tree of the knowledge of good and evil, which God had reserved for Himself. Apart from that one limitation, designed as a test of Adam's love and loyalty, all else was his—richly to enjoy. That one prohibition demonstrated man's moral accountability. He was responsible for his own actions and answerable to God.

What happened in the garden of Eden disproves the popular notion that, given a perfect environment, human beings will behave in a morally acceptable way. Man began his history in a perfect environment and failed.

THE ADAMIC COVENANT
(Genesis 3:14-19)

Underlying theme: *Guilt*

The Adamic Covenant controlled man's life on earth after the Fall. Its conditions will prevail until, in the kingdom age, "the creation shall be delivered from the bondage of corruption into the glorious liberty of the children of God" (Romans 8:21). Here are the essential terms of this covenant:

1. THE REQUIREMENTS OF THE COVENANT
a. Doom Pronounced
(1) The Curse
(a) On the Serpent
(b) On the Soil

First, the serpent was cursed for its part in introducing sin into the world; a state of war was declared between the serpent's "seed" and the seed of the woman. Adam and Eve thus learned of a coming Savior, One who would be descended from the woman, before hearing God's sentence on them. The two comings of Christ were enfolded in this embryonic prophecy: His first coming, when the serpent's seed would "bruise His heel," and His second coming, when He would crush forever the serpent and all his works.

The woman was put by God in a position of subordination to the man. Adam was created first and was to be the divinely ordained head. After the Fall a firmer headship was invested in the man because of the woman's initiative in responding to the serpent. In society at large today, in many homes, and in many churches, God's order in this matter has been set aside.

The earth was cursed too, so that man's light employment became arduous toil. Adam and Eve had already experienced spiritual death; now the sentence of physical death was passed on the human race.

The Adamic Covenant, made necessary by human guilt, was not without its brighter side. Grace was already at work. The ineffective fig leaves with which Adam and Eve tried to cover their nakedness were taken away. Instead, God clothed them with skins, provided at the cost of sacrifice. Adam and Eve thus had their first view of death, and a terrible sight it must have been to them. Along with it went a sharp lesson of the severe nature of sin and the drastic measures God would eventually have to take to put it away from His sight.

An important restriction was inherent in the Adamic covenant. Cherubim, with a flaming sword, were placed at the gate of the garden of Eden to keep fallen man away from the tree of life. That, in itself, was a loving mixture of government and grace. For if man, in his fallen condition, had eaten of the tree of life he would have lived forever in his sins and no salvation would have been possible for him.

THE NOAHIC COVENANT
(Genesis 9:1-27)

Underlying theme: *Government*

When Noah and his family emerged from the ark to face a new world, and with the opportunity for the human race to make a fresh start, God at once entered into a new contractual arrangement with the human race. The Noahic Covenant was given to cover man's relationship to the world after the Flood.

Again, let us get the salient features of this covenant before us in outline form:

1. THE SOLEMN PROMISES OF THE COVENANT
   a. Regarding the Severity of God
      (1) The Pledge
      (2) The Proof
   b. Regarding the Sovereignty of Man
   c. Regarding the Stability of Nature
2. THE SIMPLE PROVISIONS OF THE COVENANT
   a. A New Diet for Man
   b. A New Discipline for Man
3. THE SUBSEQUENT PROPHECY OF THE COVENANT
   a. A Sweeping Statement
      (1) For Shem, Spiritual Preeminence
      (2) For Japheth, Secular Predominance
   b. A Significant Silence
   c. A Solemn Sentence

The sign or seal of this covenant was the rainbow, now graciously endowed by God with new significance. For the rest of time it would be His reminder that never again would He inundate the world with water. Without that pledge the race would have gazed in terror at the sky every time storm clouds began to build. Along with this, the stability of nature was restored and the promise given that henceforth the seasons would come and go undisturbed. Man's ascendency over the animal creation was reaffirmed.

The human race was given a new diet. Up until then, God had authorized only a vegetarian diet, but from now on that was to be changed. Man must eat meat but must abstain from eating blood. Although no reason is given for that change, it probably had to do with protecting mankind against demonic powers. The antedeluvian culture appears to have been a demon culture, and abstinence from eating meat is essential to spiritism and demonism.[1]

Governmental discipline was now imposed on the race to curb the violence that had been such a marked feature of the days before the Flood. From now on, society must execute a murderer. Nowhere in the Bible has God rescinded this clause of the Noahic Covenant.

This covenant has a prophetic footnote, given in the form of a special declaration made by Noah after the shameful conduct of his son Ham. Noah declared that the Messianic line would come through Shem, that world power would come to rest in the hands of Japheth, that ultimately the Japhetic peoples would become beneficiaries of

---

[1]See the author's book, *Exploring Genesis* (Chicago: Moody Press).

the spiritual blessings brought by the Semitic family to the world, and that the Canaanite races would come under the special curse of God. Noah ignored Ham altogether, passing over him in silence, bestowing neither curse nor blessing on the Hamitic peoples.

In due time all that Noah foresaw came to pass. The descendants of Shem have given the world the Bible, the Savior, and the rich spiritual blessings of the Church. The descendants of Japheth have been the world's active explorers and empire-builders. At first it must have seemed that Noah had been mistaken. The first world powers were not Japhetic at all. For centuries the nations dominating world affairs were Egypt, Assyria, and Babylon—all of Hamitic or Shemitic (later referred to as Semitic) origin. When we read, however, that "that night was Belshazzar the king of the Chaldeans slain, and Darius the Median took the kingdom" (Daniel 5:30-31), it is far more than a date mark. It marks the final passing of world power into Japhetic hands, where it has been ever since and where it will remain until Gentile world power comes in its dreadful climax under the Beast.

We come now to the greatest and most far-reaching of all the covenants of Scripture. All subsequent covenants stem from this one. God's call of Abraham marked a decisive new departure in His dealings with mankind. God delighted in Abraham and called him His friend. It seems that He could never promise Abraham enough.

THE ABRAHAMIC COVENANT
(Genesis 12:1-4; 13:14-17; 15:1-18; 17:1-8)

Underlying theme: *Promise*
Emphasis: *The Lord*

As we can see from that trail of references, God kept coming down to earth to add more and more to the initial promise. The covenant established the fact that the awaited Messiah would come through Abraham's seed, and that original agreement was embellished in God's subsequent appearings to Abraham. The Abrahamic Covenant was reconfirmed by God to Isaac (Genesis 26:2-5) and also, later, to Jacob (Genesis 28:1-4; 12-15), thus narrowing down the Messianic line. God's covenant relationship is not with the Arab peoples who descended also from Abraham (through Ishmael) but with the Hebrew people descended through Jacob.

The promises made by God to Abraham were unconditional. They will all be literally fulfilled; they are sure as the throne of God. The covenant sign, given to Abraham's natural seed, was circumcision. Let us get the main features of the Abrahamic Covenant before us in outline form:

1. THE GRACIOUS PROVISIONS OF THE COVENANT
   a. The Secular Provisions

The Abrahamic Covenant began with the promise of a Land. The actual territorial dimensions of that Land stretch from the Nile to the Euphrates and embrace most of the Middle East presently in Arab hands. Israel has never possessed more than a tithe of the land grant promised to them—yet.

Abraham's "seed" included natural descendants, the Hebrew people, but it also included a spiritual people, all those who become spiritual heirs of Abraham by exercising Abraham's kind of faith. Abraham is called "the father of all them that believe." Above all, Abraham's "seed" was Christ Himself.

Abraham was personally "counted righteous" (Genesis 15:6) because of his faith, and positionally he became the channel through whom spiritual blessings would eventually flow to all nations of the earth. This part of the promise points us directly to the Lord Jesus Christ.

Built into the Abrahamic Covenant was the promise of divine protection for the Chosen People in a hostile world. The nation of Israel is the only nation on earth with which God has entered into a treaty arrangement. Satan has always hated the Hebrew people and, from the very start of their history, has stirred up other nations against them. Hatred of the Jew is that mysterious undercurrent of evil in society which we call anti-Semitism; it is endemic among Gentile nations and at times it becomes epidemic. Historically God has visited His blessing on nations that have protected the Jewish people and visited His judgment on nations that have persecuted them.

The final aspect of this covenant was the promise to Abraham that he would be great, and so he is. He is honored worldwide by millions in the three great monotheistic faiths: Judaism, Islam, and Christianity.

It is important that we take the covenants of Scripture literally. God says what He means and He means what He says. Thus, for instance, when God promises Abraham a specified tract of territory to belong to him and to his descendants (the children of Israel), that is what He means. The fact that the Hebrew people have not, as yet, ever fully possessed that territory in no way invalidates the promise. Abraham himself never possessed in his lifetime more than the site

for a grave in Canaan and neither did Isaac or Jacob. The literal fulfillment of promises such as those made in the Abrahamic Covenant
make necessary the coming of a day when God will keep His word to
the full. We call that day the Millennium.

THE MOSAIC COVENANT
(Exodus 20)

Underlying theme: *Precept*
Emphasis: *The Law*

The Mosaic Covenant was given to Israel. It consists of the Law,
and was a temporary modification of the Abrahamic Covenant. It
contains the most remarkable legal code ever held by an ancient people. We must always distinguish between the Law as a *standard* and
the Law as a *system*. The moral laws are universal in application. It is
never right to kill, steal, lie, commit adultery, covet. The Law as a
system, as a way of life, as a religious entity, was given solely to the nation of Israel. Attempts made by various segments of Christendom
to force believers today to keep the Law as a system are misguided. It
was given to Israel, not the Church; it was never intended for us. It
was fulfilled to God's satisfaction by Christ.

1. THE SCOPE OF THE COVENANT
   a. The Basic Expression of the Law
      (1) Godward
      (2) Manward
   b. The Broad Expansion of the Law
      (1) Laws Dealing with National Righteousness
          The Moral Law
          (a) Personal Behavior
          (b) Public Behavior
          (c) Political Behavior
      (2) Laws Dealing with National Religion
          The Ceremonial Law
          (a) The Sanctuary
          (b) The Service
          (c) The Sacrifices
          (d) The Sabbaths
2. THE SOLEMNITY OF THE COVENANT
   a. Its Repeated Warnings
   b. Its Righteous Wages
3. THE SEAL OF THE COVENANT
4. THE SPIRITUALITY OF THE COVENANT

The Mosaic Covenant was summed up in the Decalogue, ten great
commandments embracing all of man's duty to God and to his fellows.
The rest of the commandments were an expansion or exposition of
the basic ten. In all there are 613 separate commandments in the

code. These probe every area of national life: matters of a personal
nature (marriage, sex, hygiene, diet) and matters of a public and a political nature (finance, welfare, government, political alliances). The
laws were simple, comprehensive, and just. They covered Israel's national life both as a pilgrim people in the wilderness and as a pastoral
people in the land. The ceremonial laws were added to teach divine
truth and make provision for covering sin as a result of failure to keep
the moral law. Jesus kept the moral law in its entirety in His life and
the ceremonial law in all its hidden depths in His death.

The Mosaic Law was given under conditions of great solemnity at
Sinai. Failure to meet its demands was met with punishments com-
mensurate with the seriousness of the transgressions. Although
severe, the punishments were never arbitrary or oppressive and
were intended to teach Israel the holiness of God and the seriousness
of sin. The death penalty was attached to a remarkably large number
of offenses. It was the penalty for murder, adultery, breaking the
Sabbath, rebellion against one's parents, witchcraft, sorcery and
spiritism, kidnapping, and sexual perversion including homosexuali-
ty and beastiality (Leviticus 20). Israel had to learn that the "wages of
sin is death."

The seal of the Mosaic Covenant was the Sabbath. This day, sanc-
tified by God at the time of the Creation, was now formally
associated by Him with the nation of Israel. It should be noted that,
although the other commandments of the Decalogue are enjoined as
binding on Christians, the one commandment *not* thus repeated is
the one to keep the Sabbath. The Sabbath was related to the nation
of Israel, not to the Church. Since the days of the apostles, Christians
have set aside the *first* day of the week for corporate worship in com-
memoration of Christ's resurrection (Acts 20:7; 1 Corinthians 16:2).
Our rest is spiritual, not physical, and is in a Person, not in a day.

The Law served one great spiritual function in Israel. Paul says it
was "our schoolmaster to bring us to Christ" (Galatians 3:24).

THE PALESTINIAN COVENANT
(Deuteronomy 27–30)

Underlying theme: *Possession*
Emphasis: *The Land*

This covenant spelled out the conditions under which Israel
would be permitted to occupy the Promised Land. It is a codicil, as it
were, to the Mosaic Covenant and an additional temporary rider to
the Abrahamic Covenant. Israel's long and sad history is one long
commentary on this covenant.[2]

Here are the essential features of this covenant:

1. LIVING UNDER GOD'S PERPETUAL CARE

---

[2]See the author's book, *Exploring the World of the Jew* (Chicago: Moody Press).

    a. Wealth
    b. Worship
    c. Witness
 2. LIVING UNDER GOD'S PERENNIAL CURSE
    a. Its Causes
    b. Its Continuance
       (1) Disease
       (2) Drought
       (3) Defeat
       (4) Deportation
       (5) Dread
 3. LIVING UNDER GOD'S PREDICTED CURE
    a. Israel Repentant
    b. Israel Regathered
    c. Israel Regenerated
    d. Israel Reigning

On the day when the people of Israel crossed over Jordan they were commanded to set up two stone pillars on which were to be engraved the words of the Law. Then the tribes were to assemble at Mount Ebal and Mount Gerizim. Half the tribes were to stand on Gerizim to recite the blessings of the Law and half the tribes were to stand on Ebal to recite the curses of the Law. There would thus be no excuse for anyone not knowing the terms of God's "land-lease agreement" with His people.

The recitation began with curses describing the causes of any future exile (Deuteronomy 28:15-26). Then came the blessings which God would shower on an obedient people (Deuteronomy 28:1-14). After this came a series of horrendous curses which would culminate in deportation and constant dread (Deuteronomy 28:15-68). These curses culminated in a prophetic picture of Israel scattered among the nations and of the Jews living in daily fear for their lives: "In the morning thou shalt say, Would God it were even! and at even thou shalt say, Would God it were morning! for the fear of thine heart wherewith thou shalt fear" (Deuteronomy 28:67).

Jewish history is one long commentary on this. Egyptian Pharaohs, Assyrian kings, Babylonian rulers, Persian satraps, Greek Hellenists, Roman Caesars, Holy Roman emperors, Roman Catholic pontiffs, Medieval monarchs, Christian crusaders, Spanish inquisitors, Nazi dictators, Communist commissars, Arab sheiks, and United Nations delegates have all turned their hands against the Jew. Yet God has preserved this people in spite of all.

The Palestinian Covenant ends with a glowing prophecy of Israel's eventual repentance, regathering, spiritual renewal, and exaltation to a place of royal power over the nations (Deuteronomy 30:1-10). Again, the literal fulfillment of these things awaits the millennial age. The fact that Israel has once more begun to return to the

Land is a harbinger of the near fulfillment of these brighter clauses of the Palestinian Covenant.

THE DAVIDIC COVENANT
(2 Samuel 7:8-19)

Underlying theme: *Messiah*

This covenant, drawn up with David, assured him that his dynasty would never end until it exhausted itself in the Person of the long-promised Messiah of Israel. Here are its main features:

1. THE SUBSTANCE OF THE COVENANT
   a. A Promised Seed
   b. A Perpetual Sovereignty
      (1) The King
          (a) His Heavenly Throne—The Throne of God
          (b) His Human Throne—The Throne of David
      (2) The Kingdom
2. THE STIPULATION OF THE COVENANT
   a. The Constant Factor
   b. The Conditional Factor

In this covenant we see, once more, how God kept narrowing down the promise of "the Seed." First it was the seed of the woman, then it was the seed of Abraham, then of Isaac, then of Jacob; after this it was narrowed down to the tribe of Judah, and now it is made to center in the family of David.

The Davidic Covenant made clear that the Messiah would be God's Son. As in so many of God's utterances, however, there is a blending of the heavenly and the human. Two of the psalms cast added light on this covenant: Psalm 45 makes clear that the promised Seed will be God and will sit on God's throne; Psalm 110 makes clear that the promised Seed will be royal in a sense that no king of David's line was ever royal: He would be a King-Priest "after the order of Melchizedek."

The Davidic Covenant was both conditional and unconditional. It was an unconditional covenant in that God Himself guaranteed that David's Son would be the Messiah. It was conditional in that misbehavior on the part of David's royal descendants would result in major modification of the covenant's prophetic fulfillment. These conditional factors are added in God's subsequent confirmation of the covenant with Solomon (1 Kings 9:1-9).

Israel's history demonstrates how both aspects of the covenant were true. The prophet Jeremiah pronounced a curse on King Jeconiah (Coniah), barring any of his direct, lineal descendants from sitting on David's throne (Jeremiah 22:30); thus the whole line through Solomon was put under interdict. God had another line in reserve, however, a line with its source in Nathan, another of David's sons. Mary, from whom the Lord Jesus was physically descended, was a direct descendant of this collateral royal line; Joseph, foster-father of Jesus, was descended from the original line through Solomon. Joseph's marriage to Mary and his God-given position of foster-father of the Lord Jesus brought both lines together in Christ.

THE NEW COVENANT
(Jeremiah 31:31; Hebrews 8:8; Matthew 26:27-28)

Theme: *Prophetic*

There remains one final covenant, in many ways the greatest of them all. It was made originally with the house of Israel, but the Lord Jesus deliberately took it up and made certain of its clauses include the Church. It is the most misunderstood of all the covenants.

1. THE BENEFACTORS OF THE COVENANT
   a. Pledged by the Word of God
   b. Procured by the Work of Christ
2. THE BENEFITS OF THE COVENANT
3. THE BENEFICIARIES OF THE COVENANT
   a. The Stated Beneficiaries
   b. The Subsequent Beneficiaries

The New Covenant was originally made with the Hebrew people in a day of national apostasy, when the Babylonian captivity was already on the horizon and when it seemed that Israel's failures had been so persistent and so dreadful that they must now become permanent. It anticipates both comings of Christ. It is an absolutely and gloriously unconditional covenant in which God pledges Himself to accomplish certain things, which things were afterward purchased and secured by the blood of Christ.

It is essential to understand one simple fact about this covenant. It contains two kinds of clause. It contains *eschatological* clauses (clauses of a prophetic nature, having to do with Israel's national future), and it contains *soteriological* clauses (clauses having to do with salvation and redemption). The eschatological clauses are *exclusive:* they belong to Israel as a nation alone. The soteriological clauses are *inclusive:* they embrace the Church in this age as well as Israel in the next. Originally, these soteriological clauses belonged to Israel and they are the basis for the coming marvelous spiritual rebirth of the Jewish nation just prior to the setting up of the millennial kingdom. However, the Lord Jesus took these soteriological clauses in the Upper Room and deliberately used them, when instituting the Lord's Supper, as an umbrella under which to include the Church. Failure to differentiate between these two different types of clause in the New Covenant leads to the confusion of equating the Church with Israel.

13
Things that Differ

It is a basic axiom of Bible interpretation that we must always make a difference where God makes a difference. Similarity does not necessarily mean identity. We shall begin with:

THE JEW, THE GENTILE, AND THE CHURCH OF GOD.

God has divided the human race into three categories: Jew, Gentile, and the Church of God (1 Corinthians 10:32). These three categories are distinct from one another; we must not mix them up. The a-millennialist, by taking prophecies from Israel and applying them to the Church, spiritualizes away much of divine truth, robbing Israel of its national future and denying the coming millennial age when Christ will reign on earth and triumph over all His foes.

A favorite Scripture with a-millennialists is Romans 11. Their error lies in reading the Church into Romans 11. The subject matter of this important chapter is not the Church but the place of Jew and Gentile in the sphere of spiritual privilege. Christians are in view in Romans 8 but in Romans 9, 10, and 11 the theme is the relation of the Jewish people to the purposes of God in light of the fact that the nation had crucified its Messiah and was now resisting the Holy Spirit. In Romans 9 Paul examines God's *past* dealings with Israel and finds the key to Hebrew history in the *sovereignty of God.* In chapter 10 he looks at God's *present* dealings with Israel and sees that it is the *salvation of God* that controls His dealings with the Jewish people in this age. There is no difference between the individual Jew and Gentile—salvation is offered to all on the same basis, faith in the Lord Jesus Christ. In Romans 11 Paul discusses God's *promised* dealings with Israel and finds the key in the *sincerity of God.* God intends to keep His pledged word with the nation of Israel.[1]

To understand Romans 11 we must see that Jews and Gentiles are the subject matter. Paul says, "I speak to you Gentiles" (verse 13). The threats and warnings that follow are not addressed to the Church, nor do they concern the Church, although they are for the Church's learning.

According to Romans 11, Israel has lost its place of religious privilege. This has now been given to the Gentiles, who have come into

---
[1] See the author's book, *Exploring Romans* (Chicago: Moody Press).

the good that Israel threw away. Today Gentiles (described as wild olive branches), through faith in Christ, are being grafted into the olive tree of religious privilege. The natural branches (the Jews) have been broken off.

Abraham is the root of the olive, since the promises were deposited with him. The tree is the race of Abraham, namely Israel. The natural branches are the Jews who first partook of the root's nourishment. The Jews have been broken off during this age, and the Gentiles have been grafted in. After the removal of the Church, however, the Jewish people will be grafted back again into the place of religious privilege. Throughout the millennial age, blessings will flow to others through the nation of Israel.

In our age the Gentiles are being grafted into the root of the olive. Gentiles do not become Jews in order to come into the spiritual blessings of Abraham—that was Galatian error. Nor do they become "of Israel." They remain Gentiles—but Gentiles occupying the position of privilege once occupied by the Jews.

Two expressions used in the New Testament help us understand what has happened. One is "the times of the Gentiles," a phrase used by the Lord Jesus (Luke 21:24); the other is "the fulness of the Gentiles," a phrase used by Paul (Romans 11:25).

The "times of the Gentiles" has to do with Israel's *political* ascendancy over the nations. This was taken away from Israel, because of its repeated apostasies, and was given to Nebuchadnezzar and his subsequent heirs to Gentile world power. The expression refers to the long period during which Jerusalem is under Gentile power. It began with Nebuchadnezzar and will end with the reign of the Beast and the battle of Armageddon.

The "fulness of the Gentiles," has to do with Israel's *religious* ascendancy over the nations. For 2,000 years, if God had anything to say, He said it in Hebrew through a Jew. He gave the nation of Israel enormous religious promises and privileges and then crowned all their other blessings by sending them His Son to be their Messiah. When Israel, however, crowned all its other apostasies by rejecting the Lord Jesus Christ, God took away from them their religious privileges and gave these over to the Gentiles as well.

In the Church, however, there is neither Jew nor Gentile as such, although, in fact, Gentiles do predominate in the Church. Gentile ascendancy began early in the book of Acts. The center of activity swung away from Jerusalem to Antioch, and then to Corinth and Ephesus and Rome. The light and energy of gospel blessing lies in Gentile hands, not Jewish. When Christ returns to set up His millennial kingdom, God's original purposes will be restored. Political power and religious privilege will be restored to a regenerated Israel. To equate the Church with Israel is to miss the whole point of Romans 11. God keeps Jew, Gentile, and the Church separate, and we must do the same.

THE CHURCH AND THE KINGDOM

We must also differentiate between the Church and the kingdom. The Church is not a continuation of the Jewish nation under another name and under spiritual means. It is a separate entity entirely. When Christ said, "Upon this rock I will build [future] My church" (Matthew 16:18), He was speaking to His disciples, Jews, citizens of the nation of Israel, but He was foretelling the coming of something new. Most of the prophetic teaching in the Old Testament and in the Gospels has to do with the kingdom. If we read "church truth" into passages which deal with "kingdom truth" we will not rightly divide the word of God.

Failure to distinguish between the kingdom and the Church has resulted in the building of magnificent cathedrals, the ordaining of ritual priests, and the introduction into Christendom of semi-Jewish ordinances called "sacraments." The visible head of the Roman Catholic Church actually claims lordship over the nations and rules in pomp and state like an emperor with all the trappings and machinery of worldly power. But the Church is not a kingdom. The Lord Jesus is the "head" of the Church (Ephesians 1:22), but He is never spoken of as its king. The Church is a "mystery" not revealed in the Old Testament, but the kingdom was no mystery. It was the subject of extensive Old Testament prophecy. God's purpose in this age is not to establish a vast, visible kingdom but to build a Church, an *ecclesia,* a company of "called-out ones." He is calling out of the world "a people for his name" (Acts 15:13-18). God is going to establish a visible kingdom on this earth but not until He has completed the Church and finished His present work. The kingdom will be established after the rapture of the Church, not before.

Three expressions are used in the New Testament to set before us truth connected with the kingdom. There is the *kingdom of God,* an expression that relates especially to salvation. "Except a man be born again, he cannot see the kingdom of God" (John 3:3). At the present time "grace [reigns] through righteousness" (Romans 5:21). At the end of the book of Acts we see Paul "preaching the kingdom of God, and teaching those things which concern the Lord Jesus Christ" (Acts 28:30-31).

There is the *kingdom of heaven,* a highly technical expression found only in the gospel of Matthew, a gospel with strong Jewish emphasis. The expression refers to the rule of heavens over the earth in answer to the Lord's prayer in Matthew 6:10. That this kingdom exists in mystery form today is clear from Matthew 13:11. It is not openly and visibly established on the earth but exists only in the willing submission of believers to the will of God. A distinction must be made between the kingdom of God and the kingdom of heaven.

Certain parables, it is true, are used in connection with both the kingdom of God and kingdom of heaven but similarity in some points does not mean identity in all points. Unsaved people are included in the kingdom of the heavens, and these will ultimately be removed (Matthew 8:12; Luke 13:28-29). There are no unsaved people in the kingdom of God (John 3:3,5). Where parables are used in relation to both kingdoms, the purpose is to draw attention, as far as the kingdom of God is concerned, to the corrupting doctrines that assail it.

The mystery parables of Matthew 13 make clear that the kingdom of heaven will not be brought in by the gradual conversion of the world to Christianity but will be established by cataclysmic judgments. It will be imposed on earth by divine power at Armageddon. During the Millennium all people will be made subjects of the kingdom (1 Corinthians 15:24-27).

As a result of the subduing of all iniquity and opposition to God, the *kingdom of the Father* will be brought in (Matthew 13:43; 1 Corinthians 15:28). This expression refers to the fixed state that will prevail in eternity when sin and sorrow will be forever banished. Thus we read of "new heavens and a new earth, wherein dwelleth righteousness" (2 Peter 3:13). In this state, righteousness will not need to be enforced; it will be the natural fruit of redemption through the regenerating power of the Holy Spirit.

The Church, unique in God's plan, is comprised of all who receive Christ as Savior between Pentecost and the rapture. All such believers are baptized by the Holy Spirit into the mystical body of Christ. In this body racial differences (such as Jew and Gentile) disappear (Ephesians 2:11-18). The preaching of the gospel today is not intended to bring men and women into the kingdom in its physical and temporal aspects; it is intended to bring men and women into the kingdom in its moral and spiritual aspects. We must leave the bringing in of the physical kingdom to the Lord who, in His own good time, will deal with all His foes and will forcibly impose His empire on the earth.

Where the gospel is heard and heeded today, it brings people into a fourfold relationship with God. They are in Christ's *Church* by means of the baptism of the Spirit (1 Corinthians 12:13). They become subjects of the *kingdom of heaven,* responsible to obey Christ's precepts. They are in the *everlasting kingdom of God* as those already possessing His life and nature (2 Peter 1:2) and as such have the blessed hope of being caught up to be forever with the Lord (1 Thessalonians 4:13-18). Also they have the assurance that the Lord will ultimately establish His rule over the earth. And, beyond all temporary dispensations, they can look forward to the *eternal state* where sin can never enter and where God will be forever enthroned among His people.

STANDING AND STATE

The believer's *standing* is "in Christ" (a favorite Pauline expression) and is therefore perfect. His *state,* however, his actual spiritual condition at any given time, may be very far from perfect. Before his conversion, the believer was a natural man with no apprehension of spiritual things at all. After accepting Christ he may be either a spiritual man or a carnal man depending on the measure of his response to the indwelling Holy Spirit.

A believer's standing results from Christ's finished work. It is perfect and entire from the moment we trust Christ. Nothing can alter that. We have our standing through faith alone. The standing of the weakest believer is as secure as that of the most illustrious apostle. "As many as received Him, to them gave He power to become the sons of God, even to them that believe on His name" (John 1:12). "Beloved, now are we the sons of God, and it doth not yet appear what we shall be: but we know that, when He shall appear, we shall be like Him" (1 John 3:2). "Therefore being justified by faith, we have peace with God through our Lord Jesus Christ: by whom also we have access by faith into this grace wherein we stand, and rejoice in the hope of the glory of God" (Romans 5:1-2).

A believer's state, on the other hand, may fluctuate from day to day and from moment to moment. "And I, brethren, could not speak unto you as unto spiritual, but as unto carnal . . . , for ye are yet carnal: for whereas there is among you envying, and strife, and divisions, are ye not carnal, and walk as men?" (1 Corinthians 3:1-3).

THE TWO RESURRECTIONS

All the dead are to be raised, but not all at the same time. There are two resurrections. Jesus declared, "Marvel not at this: for the hour is coming, in the which all that are in the graves shall hear His voice, and shall come forth; they that have done good, unto the resurrection of life; and they that have done evil, unto the resurrection of damnation" (John 5:28-29).

The first resurrection takes place in three stages. First there are the *firstfruits.* The firstfruits of the resurrection are already past. At the time of Christ's death we read that "the graves were opened; and many bodies of the saints which slept arose, and came out of the graves after His resurrection, and went into the holy city, and appeared unto many" (Matthew 27:52-53).

The second phase of this resurrection may be likened to the *harvest.* At the appearing of the Lord Jesus in the air for His saints, believers will rise to meet the Lord in the air at what is generally called "the rapture." They will then appear before the judgment seat of Christ and go on to the marriage supper of the Lamb (1 Thessalonians 4:13-17; Revelation 19:7-9).

The final phase of this resurrection may be likened to the *gleanings.* During the tribulation period many will become believers and many will be martyred for their faith in Christ (Revelation 7). These will include the two witnesses (Revelation 11:1-12) and the great host of those slain by the two beasts (Revelation 20:4). All these will be raised in their turn.

Then there is the final resurrection. After the Millennium the wicked dead of all ages will be raised for judgment. "The rest of the dead lived not again until the thousand years were finished" (Revelation 20:5). Those raised in this judgment will appear before the great white throne to be judged and damned (Revelation 20:11-15). They include all those whose names are not written in the Lamb's book of life.

THE FOUR JUDGMENTS

Four future judgments are mentioned in the Bible and need to be distinguished one from another. Always note the subjects, place, time, and results of a judgment.

1. The Bible speaks of the *judgment of sin*. The sin of the believer has already been judged at the cross. We read that the Lord Jesus "bare our sins in His own body on the tree" (1 Peter 2:24). There is "no condemnation to them which are in Christ Jesus" (Romans 8:1). The judgment of the believer is forever past, as far as sins are concerned.

2. The Bible speaks, however, of the *judgment of saints*. There is a difference, as we have seen, between the believer's standing and state. The judgment of believers has to do with their state. For saints, judgment proceeds along two lines.

First, there is judgment *as sons* of God, a judgment that needs to take place in this life. Everyone born into this world has a nature that can do nothing right in the sight of God—at least nothing that God can call "good" because the best efforts of human beings are tainted by their fallen nature. "In me, that is to say, in my flesh, there dwelleth no good thing," Paul wrote. We are born with a sin nature, an inbred tendency to do what is wrong.

When a person is born again and becomes a child of God, he or she receives a new nature. The old nature is not eradicated but a new nature is placed alongside it, a divine nature, the nature of God Himself, a nature that can do no wrong. "Whosoever is born of God doth not commit sin; for His seed remaineth in him: and he cannot sin, because he is born of God" (1 John 3:9). "Being born again, not of corruptible seed, but of incorruptible, by the word of God" (1 Peter 1:23). These two natures, in the believer, are at war—as we learn not only from Romans 7 but from bitter personal experience. Sin is the root principle within us; sins are the outward fruits of sin in the life. We must judge these sins constantly as the Holy Spirit convicts us about them. "For if we would judge ourselves, we should not be judged. But when we are judged, we are chastened of the Lord, that we should not be condemned with the world" (1 Corinthians

Hermeneutics

11:31-32). "If we confess our sins, He is faithful and just to forgive us our sins, and to cleanse us from all unrighteousness" (1 John 1:9).

Alan Redpath tells of visiting in a home where there were two young boys. One night the parents went out to special services at the church and left the two boys alone. When they returned home, the house was unnaturally quiet. Investigating, they discovered that a valuable vase had been broken and the bits and pieces gathered up and piled in a heap on the table. Along with the remains of the vase was a note. It read: "Dear Mom and Dad, we are dreadfully sorry. We broke your vase. We have put ourselves to bed without any supper. Signed, Jimmy and Joe." "Do you think," Redpath asks, "the father of those boys went upstairs, hauled the two of them out of bed, and punished them for what they had done? Of course not! They had judged themselves, and vengeance was disarmed." It is our duty to judge ourselves so that we will not have to face chastisement by our Father.

Second, along with this judgment of believers as sons of God right here and now in this life, there is a coming judgment of believers *as servants* of God. Christ died for our sins it is true, but our works as believers will be judged. The life and works of every child of God will be reviewed at the judgment seat of Christ after the rapture of the Church: "Wherefore we labor, that, whether present or absent, we may be accepted of Him. For we must all appear before the judgment seat of Christ; that every one may receive the things done in his body, according to that he hath done, whether it be good or bad" (2 Corinthians 5:9-10). "We shall all stand before the judgment seat of Christ" (Romans 14:10). "Therefore judge nothing before the time, until the Lord come, who both will bring to light the hidden things of darkness, and will make manifest the counsels of the hearts; and then shall every man have praise of God" (1 Corinthians 4:5). "Behold, I come quickly; and My reward is with Me, to give every man according as his work shall be" (Revelation 22:12; See also Matthew 16:27; Luke 14:14; 1 Corinthians 15:22-23).

The great passage on the subject, of course, is 1 Corinthians 3:11-15. There we are told that the fire will try every person's work. Some will see their works burned up as "wood, hay, and stubble." These will be "saved, so as by fire" (verse 15). Others will see their works endure the testing of the flames, revealed as "gold, silver, and precious stones" and will be rewarded by Christ. Paul looked forward to receiving a crown as part of his reward.

3. Another type of judgment mentioned in the Bible is the *judgment of states,* when all nations will be brought to judgment. Israel will be judged as a nation for its persistent rejection of Christ. This judgment will come to a head during the great tribulation. The focal point of the judgment will be Jerusalem and the land of Israel. As "the times of the Gentiles" draw to an end, the Jews will be regathered to their land. They will return in unbelief and God will

put them "under the rod" (Ezekiel 20:34-38). The partial return of Jews to the reborn state of Israel today is a harbinger of what is yet to be. The instrument God will use to chastise the Jewish people will be the Beast, whose terrible persecutions (Revelation 12:13,15,17) will be supplemented by the outpouring of the "wrath of God" on the earth (Revelation 16:1). In their extremity the Jews will at last turn to the Lord (Zechariah 12:10), and, according to Isaiah's descriptive phrase, the nation will be "born in one day" (Isaiah 66:8).

The Gentile nations are to be judged too. This judgment will take place after the battle of Armageddon, when the Lord will finally return to earth to set up His kingdom.[2] The place will be the valley of Jehoshaphat just outside Jerusalem (Joel 3:1-2, 12-14). The criteria will be how the Gentile peoples have treated the Jews (whom Christ calls "My brethren") during the great tribulation. The description of this judgment is given in Matthew 25:31-46. The resurrected saints will be associated with the Lord in this judgment (1 Corinthians 6:2; Daniel 7:22; Jude 14–15). The nations will be divided into two classes: the "sheep" (people who ministered to the Lord's brethren during the great tribulation) and the "goats" (people who refused them kindness during the great tribulation). The "sheep" will be given a place in the millennial kingdom and the "goats" will be banished to a lost eternity. The judgment of the nations will leave only a redeemed people to populate the millennial earth as the golden age begins.

4. The final judgment is the *judgment of sinners*. This judgment takes place at the end of the Millennium as the first act in eternity. The place will be the great white throne. Peter calls this judgment "the day of judgment and perdition of ungodly men" (2 Peter 3:7). Its description is given in Revelation 20:11-15. The basis of it will be the works of the unregenerate. Evidence will be taken from "the books" being kept by God. There will be no hope for those summoned to this judgment because none of their names will be found in the Lamb's book of life. All those judged at the great white throne will be cast into the lake of fire. God calls this eternal doom "the second death." The fallen angels, "reserved in chains under darkness" at the present time, will be judged at this time also. Jude calls this the judgment of "the great day" (Jude 6).

---

[2]See the author's book, *Exploring The Future* (Nashville: Thomas Nelson Publishers).

14

The Obscurity Rule

Obscure passages must always give way to clear passages. Further, we must never build a doctrine on obscure or difficult passages. Everything essential to salvation or to Christian living is clearly revealed in the Bible. We have no need to resort to obscure passages to support a Biblical belief.

One such obscure passage in the Bible is found in 1 Corinthians 15:29, where we read: "Else what shall they do which are baptized for the dead, if the dead rise not at all? why are they then baptized for the dead?" The meaning of this passage is the subject of considerable controversy.

The Mormons have formulated a doctrine of baptism for the dead based on this passage. According to them, there is no salvation except by water baptism administered by a qualified Mormon priest. They extend this teaching to include all the millions who have lived on the earth and died without a knowledge of the so-called "restored gospel" of Joseph Smith. Consequently, Mormons are constantly doing what they call "work for the dead" by compiling genealogies of their ancestors and others and being baptized for them. Joseph Smith claimed that "the books" referred to in Revelation 20:12, to be opened at the great white throne judgment, are the records of baptisms and other rites maintained by the official secretaries of the Mormon religion (*Doctrines and Covenants*, Sec. 128:6-9). One Mormon told Gordon H. Fraser (whose book *Is Mormonism Christian?* is an excellent exposure of the cult) that he himself had been baptized over 5,000 times for the dead. The Mormons have suspended this enormously heavy doctrine on a gossamer thread, their interpretation of an obscure text.

A look at the context shows, of course, that baptism was not even remotely the subject under discussion. The theme was resurrection. In actual fact, baptism for the dead was practiced historically only by heretical cults such as the Marcionites and the Montanists. Paul's reference is clearly to something abnormal. In no way does Paul imply that he approved of the practice. He simply cites it as implying a belief in the resurrection.

Paul's attitude toward the practice is indicated by his use of pronouns. He did not include himself as one of those who upheld the practice. "What shall *they* do which are baptized for the dead . . . why are *they* then baptized for the dead? And why stand *we* in jeopardy every hour? I protest by *your* rejoicing" (emphasis added). He disassociates both himself and the Corinthian believers from the *they* who were practicing this odd rite.

The doctrine of baptism for the dead soon collapses when the extensive New Testament references to baptism are examined. We may accept a doctrine as Scriptural only when it agrees with other properly exegeted references to it in the Bible. A mere passing reference, especially when it conflicts with the body of revealed truth, is no place to begin building doctrine.

15
Interpreting Types

In the Bible, a type is a species of prophecy. Some interpreters feel that only Old Testament passages specifically quoted in the New Testament as types can be legitimately regarded as such. That, I believe, is too narrow a rule. Such a rule would not allow us to regard Joseph as a type of Christ—clearly an untenable position. It can be shown that in countless ways Joseph is a deliberate and studied type of Christ, even down to the bequeathing of his body as a permanent memorial to Israel throughout their wilderness journeyings. Passages quoted in the New Testament as types do not exhaust the whole species: they are merely specimens.

Old Testament types illustrate specific Scriptural truths. They demonstrate the fact that "the Old is in the New revealed and the New is in the Old concealed." Much New Testament truth is concealed in the Old Testament in the types. For the most part the types prefigure truths connected with Christ, the Church, or the Christian. Although the Church itself is not a subject of direct Old Testament prophecy, truth concerning the Church is concealed in the Old Testament types—and, although it was not discernible in Old Testament times, we today, with New Testament revelation to enlighten us, can see it there.

Types may relate to persons, events, things, institutions, offices, actions, or rituals. Two kinds of types are found in the Bible: the innate type, one specifically declared to be such in the New Testament; and the inferred type, one recognizable as such because it conforms to the pattern seen in the innate types. The significance of any given type depends on the real grounds for similarity between the type and whatever it illustrates—the antitype. Points of difference between the type and the antitype should be carefully noted.

There are two primary rules for interpreting types. We must never attempt to prove a doctrinal position from typology. We must interpret types only on the basis of some clearly revealed New Testament truth.

The stories of many people in the Old Testament clearly foreshadow aspects of the life of Christ or the life of the Christian. Take Joseph as an example. To begin with he was the father's well-beloved son. He was set apart from his brethren, his kinsmen according to the flesh, by his coat of many colors, the garb of a chieftain or a priest. His brothers envied him and could not speak peaceably to him. They resented his favored relationship with the father. His dreams, which spoke of his coming glory and power, moved them to murderous rage. When his father sent him to his brothers, they conspired against him and sold him for the price of a slave. Handed thus over to the Gentiles, he was falsely accused and made to suffer for sins not his own.

In the prison of Pharaoh, he "preached" to others who were there awaiting their final sentence. For the chief butler he had a message of life; for the chief baker he had a message of a second and worse death. Brought out of prison, Joseph was given a position second only to that of Pharaoh, exalted to the right hand of the majesty, and thus became a ruler in the land of Egypt before whom everyone would bow.

Exalted—taken from obscurity and raised up to share his place on high—Joseph was given a Gentile bride, and thereafter began to deal faithfully with his natural brethren, the children of Israel. He brought them to the place where, in deep contrition, they confessed their long rejection of him. Finally, "all nations" came to him.

There is scarcely a point in the story of Joseph that does not parallel the story of Jesus. Joseph is one of the great life-types of the Lord Jesus Christ in the Old Testament. Moses is another and so is David. In a greater or lesser degree such men as Adam, Noah, Melchizedek, Isaac, Samson, Boaz, Joshua, Aaron, Jeremiah, and Jonah all prefigure the Lord Jesus. So do many others.

Not only persons but events in the Old Testament are frequently typical. The redemption of Israel from Egypt typifies redemption on a grand scale. Egypt represents the world; the Pharaoh is its powerful, evil king. The Hebrews, born in slavery and under the sentence of death, typify sinners and their doom. There was no help for Israel apart from God. Then came the kinsman-redeemer, Moses, whose own story is typical of Christ. The process of redemption and emancipation for Israel was centered in Moses. He shook Egypt with mighty signs and wonders and exposed Pharaoh's vaunted power as vanity. Israel was redeemed by the blood of the Passover lamb, "baptized unto Moses," and separated from the old way of life in Egypt, henceforth to walk by faith and not by sight.

Almost every incident in the wilderness experience of Israel is symbolic of experiences that come to believers today. Israel feasted on bread from heaven because the wilderness (in our case, the world) had nothing to sustain them in the way. They drank water from the riven rock (typical of the outpouring and infilling of the Holy Spirit as a result of Christ's death). They had war with Amalek and won because of the presence of Joshua—whose name means Jesus—in their midst and because of the intercessory work of Moses on high (all typical of our war with the flesh and our means of victory). They came to

Sinai to learn how believers must order their life in a way pleasing to God. They entered Canaan and learned how to live victoriously in the land (Canaan typifies "the heavenlies," a place of battles and blessings). At point after point, the story is typical.

Similarly many events in the life of David are filled with typical significance. Indeed, one of the keys to studying the lives of David's many friends and foes is to see what they did with David and what David did with them, thus to see how they illustrate what individuals do with Jesus, great David's greater Son and what, one day, He will do with them.

The book of Esther contains typical teaching as do the books of Joshua and Ruth.

In the Old Testament, a great many things are typical—the tabernacle for instance. Every part has typical significance. Henry W. Soltau's 1850 book about the tabernacle is excellent (see "Helpful Books for Study"). One of the best recent books on the tabernacle is Stephen Olford's *Camping with God* (Loizeaux Brothers). A reliable guide is essential in studying the typology of the tabernacle, because some expositors have gone to extremes and have made totally unsupported statements in their enthusiasm for tabernacle typology. Such interpretations bring typology into disrepute.

Many other things in the Old Testament also have a typical significance. Aaron's rod, Noah's ark, the various things that Jonathan gave to David, the river Jordan, leprosy, the lost axe head in the story of Elisha, honey in the carcass of the lion in the story of Samson, Gideon's lamp and pitcher, even the Tower of Babel—all have significance above and beyond the surface.

The rituals of the Old Testament were typical. All ritual connected with the offerings, the Day of Atonement, the cleansing of the leper, the Passover, the consecration of the priests, and the various annual feasts had typical significance.

Take the ritual on the Day of Atonement, for instance. On that day alone, the high priest was permitted to enter beyond the veil and minister in the holy of holies. Every facet of the elaborate ritual on that occasion was of typical significance. At the heart of the ritual were the two goats. One goat became known as the scapegoat because, symbolically and typically, all the sins of the people were ritually laid upon it. It was then delivered into the hand of a fit man and taken out of the camp into the wilderness, to "a land not inhabited." Away it went, bearing the sins of the people. The other goat was slain and its blood taken by the high priest into the holy of holies to be sprinkled on the mercy seat where God Himself was enthroned. It took the two goats to typify the work of Christ on the cross. He not only shed His blood for our sins but He bore them away. He then ascended into the holy of holies in heaven itself, as our Great High Priest, there to present before the throne the saving virtue of His blood.

A danger in handling Bible types is to strain their significance or to use artificial, overly imaginative, and Biblically unsupported methods of interpretation. If we avoid doing that, we can look to the types of the Bible for rich and rewarding teaching.

16
Interpreting the Parables

A parable has been defined as an earthly story with a heavenly meaning. Beyond the human story lies a theological truth and a spiritual lesson.

Not all parables were intended to make truth obvious to the hearer. Some, notably the parables of the kingdom of heaven in Matthew 13, were intended to conceal truth. The Lord desired that His disciples understand the stories and went so far as to interpret two of them so that they might have the key for unlocking the others. At the same time He shut up the truth from those who had rejected Him, His message, and His ministry.

A parable has three parts: the occasion that prompted it; the story itself, usually woven from some commonplace thing or event; and the moral, the spiritual lesson the parable was intended to teach.

In interpreting parables, therefore, we should pay attention to each of its parts. We begin by determining when, where, and why the story was told. The story itself is usually so obvious as to need little or no comment except where customs or practices of Bible times need to be taken into consideration. Finally we must discover how the parable relates to Christ and His kingdom.

A parable contains one central truth. It has often been said that a parable cannot be made to "run on all fours." That is, not every single item in the parable can be pressed for an underlying meaning. The aim should be to discover its main point and not insist on giving every phrase a double meaning.

Special care must be taken when using a parable to support a doctrine. It is easy to read into a parable a position we wish to defend. But our doctrinal positions must be undergirded from the plain teaching of Scripture, not from a parable.

When a parable occurs in more than one Gospel, the various accounts need to be compared. Similarity does not always mean identity.

Traits that would contradict other clear Scriptures must be regarded merely as background detail for the story and must not be rigidly interpreted. For example, to argue that, because there were five wise and five foolish virgins (Matthew 25:1-2), the number of saved and lost people must be equal would be to argue nonsense. The parable is intended to teach no such thing.

We must avoid wild and unsupported statements. St. Augustine was given to the wildest extravagances in his interpretation of parables. His handling of the parable of the good Samaritan is a case in point. To Augustine the man who went down from Jerusalem to Jericho was Adam; Jerusalem was the city of peace from which Adam fell; Jericho was the moon; the thieves were the devil and his angels; the oil poured into the victim's wounds was the comfort of hope; the wine was an exhortation to work with a fervent spirit; the beast on which the good Samaritan rode was Christ's flesh; the inn was the Church and the innkeeper the apostle Paul. With such unrestrained use of imagination, the Bible can be made to teach anything.

Let us apply proper methods of interpretation for this parable (Luke 10:25-37). We note first the occasion on which is was given. The Lord Jesus had just been challenged by a lawyer who wanted to question the Lord's knowledge and authority. As a Levite, or lawyer, this man was supposed to be an expert in the Mosaic Law and his task was to explain the Law to the people so that they could order their lives in a way pleasing to God. He asked Jesus to tell him what he must do to inherit eternal life. The Lord tossed the question right back to the lawyer. "What do you read in the Law?" He said. The lawyer responded with a summary of the Law—love for God and love for one's neighbor. Then, wishing to save face, he asked, "Who is my neighbor?" He belonged to a social class that scorned the idea that a Jew could be "neighbor" to a Gentile or to a half-breed Samaritan. The text says that he wished to "justify himself." It is possible that he had a sneaking suspicion that his Jewish exclusivism was not right. This gives the setting and occasion of the parable.

The actual story of the Good Samaritan hardly needs retelling. Jerusalem, the city where God had set His name for more than a thousand years, was the place of religious blessing and privilege, whereas Jericho was the city of the curse (Joshua 6:26). The road between Jerusalem and Jericho was infested with robbers. Josephus says that Herod had recently dismissed thousands of workmen from construction projects on the Temple. These unemployed men now swelled the brigand bands that infested the wild country between the two cities.

In the story, the traveler was accosted, molested, robbed, sorely beaten, and left for dead. Along came a priest, a representative of the Jewish religion, a religion that called for mercy to be shown to all, including animals (Exodus 23:4-5). As a man supposedly consecrated to God and occupied daily in the sacred work of the Temple, this priest surely would have compassion on the poor fellow he saw lying beside the road. But not he. He hurried past on the other side.

Then along came a Levite. (Remember that it was a Levite who here was challenging the Lord's authority.) The Levite was of the same tribe as the priest but from a lower order. He, too, was a servant of the Temple and, in addition, an expositor of the Mosaic Law. His calling was to interpret the Mosaic Law so that the people could put its tenets into practice. Surely he would help this poor man lying there on the Jericho road. But not he. He too passed by on the other side.

Jesus introduced both priest and Levite into the parable to teach the emptiness of organized religion, the heartlessness of legality, and the failure of those who profess to know God and to do good works but who are devoid of love.

Then the Lord brought the Samaritan into the story. The Jews detested the Samaritans, regarding them as half-castes. They would go miles out of their way rather than pass through Samaria. The Samaritan, in the parable, represented the Lord Jesus Himself, despised and rejected by the leaders of Israel, yet willing to help the lost, the wretched, and the fallen. Into the poor man's wounds the Samaritan poured oil and wine, oil to soothe and wine to cleanse. Then he loaded the sufferer onto his own donkey, carried him to an inn, paid his expenses, and promised to come again and settle any outstanding accounts.

Having told the story, the Lord asked, "Who was the poor man's neighbor?" The lawyer must have squirmed; there was only one answer he could give: the Samaritan. But he would not use the detested word. "He that showed mercy," he said, clinging to his prejudices. "Go thou and do likewise," Jesus said.

What was the point of the parable? It was intended to teach us our obligation to help the needy no matter who they are or in what relation they stand to us. As we go through life we constantly meet people in dire spiritual and physical need. They are our neighbors. Hasn't God shown us the way? Hasn't He made Himself the neighbor of all humankind by coming down to where we are in our sin and need? This parable can also be used as a story of the gospel, once a legitimate interpretation of it has been seen.

17
Interpreting Prophecy

More controversy rages over the interpretation of prophecy than over any other area of divine truth. At the heart of any approach to prophecy lies the imperative need to have a workable and uniform system. It is not possible to follow the golden rule of Bible interpretation—that is, to seek a literal, historical, cultural, and grammatical understanding of prophetic passages—and at the same time indulge the fancies of allegorical interpretation.

If we interpret the prophecies of Scripture according to the golden rule, we shall inevitably arrive at a dispensational view of Scripture. We cannot have a vague mix of pre-millennial, post-millennial, and a-millennial views. We must determine our viewpoint. Or, rather, we must let our viewpoint be determined by the results of our interpretation. Above all, our interpretation must be comprehensive enough to embrace all prophetic truth, and it must be consistent.

The grammatical-literal approach to prophecy will lead to balanced dispensationalism; properly developed dispensationalism will lead to a pre-millennial view of prophecy. The Old Testament prophets foretold in plain language and glowing terms a coming golden age for the earth, during which Christ will reign, Israel will be the head of the nations, Jerusalem will be the world's capital, and peace, progress, and prosperity will be the universal norm. The literal approach to the interpretation of prophecy leads directly to this view.

When approaching a Biblical prophecy it is best to get the answer to a number of questions before venturing an opinion on its meaning. Is this prophecy couched in literal, figurative, poetic, or symbolic language? What is the literal interpretation of this passage? When did the prophet live and what was his cultural and historical background? Has the prophecy been completely fulfilled, partially fulfilled, or not yet fulfilled? Has the prophecy had an immediate fulfillment relating to the prophet's own times but with residual features that demand another and more complete fulfillment at a future time? Does the prophecy relate to Jews, Gentiles, or to the Church? Is a condition attached to the prophecy as, for instance, one is attached to Jonah's prophecy concerning the doom of Nineveh? What other passages of Scripture shed light on this prophecy? Is there a mystical element in the prophecy as, for example, in Hosea's prophecy, "I . . . called my son out of Egypt" (Hosea 11:1), a prophecy that the Jews took to refer to Israel but which Matthew 2:14-15 shows actually referred to Christ? In what context was the prophecy given? In what kind of language is the prophecy couched: straightforward, symbolic, apocalyptical? (Daniel, Zechariah, and Revelation are all examples of apocalyptical prophecy.)

Nearly all prophecy relates to one of four great mountain peaks of fulfillment. Many prophecies in the Old Testament focus on *Christ's first advent.* His birth, life and ministry, sufferings and death, resurrection, ascension, and the coming of the Holy Spirit at Pentecost are all foreseen. A number of Bible prophecies relate to the *end-time events in Christendom* culminating in the rapture of the church and the general apostasy of Christendom itself. Other prophecies have to do with *Christ's final return to earth.* They speak of the coming of the Beast, of the Devil's messiah, and of the universal power he will have. They speak of the great tribulation, the battle of Armageddon, and the judgment of the nations. Other prophecies concern themselves with the *Millennium,* with the eventual establishment of Christ's literal kingdom on earth, and with the ultimate climax in the setting up of an eternal kingdom in new heavens and a new earth. Interpreting Bible prophecy will be simplified if these four chief areas of fulfillment are kept in mind.

The Bible stands apart from all other books because of its ability to foretell future events accurately and infallibly. There are certain basic requirements for genuine prophecy, and the Bible meets them all. Obviously, the prophecy must have been written before the fulfillment. It must have been beyond the possibility of human foresight alone. For instance, to foretell the visit of a comet at a specific time over a stated point on the globe is not prophecy but mathematics. The prophecy must give details. The famous utterance of the Delphic oracle that if Croesus, the rich and victorious king of Lydia, were to make war with Persia he would destroy a great nation was not a prophecy. It was a cryptic utterance which could be taken two ways. Croesus took it that he would destroy Persia and acted accordingly. But the kingdom he destroyed was his own. In true prophecy sufficient time must elapse between the giving of the prophecy and its fulfillment to make it impossible for the prophet or some other interested party to attempt a phoney fulfillment. Further, there must be a clear and evident fulfillment of the prophecy in due course. Study, for example, the prophecy of the Lord Jesus concerning His impending death. He said, "We go up to Jerusalem; and the Son of man shall be betrayed unto the chief priests and unto the scribes, and they shall condemn Him to death, and shall deliver Him to the Gentiles to mock, and to scourge, and to crucify Him: and the third day He shall rise again" (Matthew 20:18-19). There are actually twelve specific details in that prophecy, and every one of them was fulfilled.

Some principles for interpreting Scripture are of a general nature. Others have special application to prophecy. At the risk of some repetition we are going to touch lightly on a dozen basic rules.

1. The principle of *prophetic perspective*. Many Bible prophecies focus on two climactic events, the first and second comings of Christ. We can liken these focal points to two mountain peaks, one behind the other with a great valley in between. The prophets clearly saw the peaks, but could not see the valley that divided them, neither how deep nor how long it was. Thus we often find the two comings of Christ telescoped together in Old Testament prophecy. We are living today in that hidden valley so we have a perspective on both comings of Christ. We can hardly repeat too often that the Old Testament saints knew nothing of the Church Age at all, as Paul reminds us in Ephesians 3:1-6 and elsewhere. We read that the prophets themselves were curious about various aspects of their prophecies (1 Peter 1:10-12).

Psalm 22 is an example of the two comings of Christ being telescoped together. David details two things about Calvary in that great Messianic psalm. He speaks first of its terribly reality (1-21), and describes death by crucifixion with such clarity he could almost have been standing beside the cross. Then he speaks of its tremendous results (22-31), speaking first of Messiah as Priest (22-26), then as Prince (27-31). Next he leaps the ages and sees Gentile nations worshiping the Lord at the establishment of the coming kingdom. The transition from the one scene to the other is sudden, just as though no gap existed between the sufferings of Christ and the glory that was to follow. As far as David could see, there was no gap.

Understanding this principle of interpretation is a great help when interpreting the prophecies of Daniel, particularly the long and intricate prophecy of Daniel 11. The prophet sees the onward march of events from the heyday of the Persian empire right down to the death of the Syrian oppressor Antiochus Epiphanes (Daniel 11:1-35). The prophecy then takes a giant step forward and describes the coming of Antichrist (verses 36-45). Failure to see this dispensational break in the prophecy will result in confusion.

2. The principle of *panoramic reference*. Bible prophecy relates to the three classes of humankind we have already discussed, "Jews, Gentiles, and the church of God" (1 Corinthians 10:32). For the first two thousand years of human history (according to Bible chronology), God dealt with the nations, the Gentiles; from Abraham until Pentecost, God dealt with humanity through the Jews, the Hebrew people; since Pentecost, a third class has been added, the Church. All Bible prophecy relates to one or other of these classes. Many prophecies have to do with the Gentile nations and their place in God's overall plans for humankind. Hundreds of prophecies have to do with the Hebrew people, their exiles, distress, and triumph. Some

prophecies relate solely to the Church. We must keep these three great panoramic distinctions in mind.

3. The principle of *poetic utterance.* Some prophecies are couched in poetic, figurative, and symbolic language. Sometimes prophecy is given in such a way that its meaning is deliberately hidden or veiled. The mystery parables of Matthew 13 are a case in point. They were given in a form that concealed truth from the unbelieving while, at the same time, revealing it to believers (Matthew 13:10-17).

The first Biblical prophecy is poetic and cryptic in character: "And I will put enmity between thee [the serpent] and the woman, and between thy seed and her seed; it shall bruise thy head, and thou shalt bruise his heel" (Genesis 3:15). This is a prophecy about the coming of Christ. It speaks of both comings: Christ's first coming, when the serpent would "bruise his heel" (a veiled reference to the cross), and His second coming, when the woman's seed (Christ) would finally crush the serpent's head.

Interpreting Bible prophecy calls for a good working knowledge of the laws that govern symbols, figures of speech, types, parables, and allegories.

Much Bible prophecy is written in poetic form, so care must be taken to get to the literal truth behind the form. This is especially true of apocalyptic prophecy which makes extensive use of symbols. To interpret symbols properly, we need to see how the Holy Spirit handles them. It is not always easy to decide whether a given passage is to be taken literally or symbolically, since many things used as symbols in Scripture are also literal realities. When we read of a great mountain burning with fire being cast into the midst of the sea (Revelation 8:8-9), the reference could be literal. Obviously a God of omnipotent power could dig up Mount Vesuvius and cast it into the Mediterranean. The reference, however, could be a symbolic description of a coming war. The context, the general sense of the passage, and the adequacy or inadequacy of the literal interpretation must all be taken into consideration.

4. The principle of *progressive enlightenment.* Prophetic truth (like other Bible truth) was not often revealed all at once, but in stages, a little here, a little there, now a fragment to Isaiah, now a flash of insight to Jeremiah. The classic example of this principle is seen in the prophecy of the "coming seed." The truth of both the first and second comings of Christ is revealed little by little and is scattered over the entire Bible. In the same way, truth regarding the coming Antichrist is not given all at once nor in one single place in the Scriptures. It is given gradually and in various times and ways.

The fact that divine inspiration of prophetic truth has been progressive should warn us that divine illumination of such truth might be equally progressive. Daniel was told, for instance, to "shut up the words, and seal the book, even to the time of the end" (Daniel 12:4).

Some of the prophetic statements in his book would not be fully understood until near the time of their fulfillment. Today we are living on the verge of the rapture and of the fulfillment of end-time prophecies. Consequently we have much more light on the prophetic Scriptures than did devout Bible students seventy or eighty years ago. Prophecies about Israel and Russia are coming sharply into focus today, whereas two or three hundred years ago the significance of these prophecies could be discerned only dimly. Even so, it is astonishing how accurate some Bible expositors were even in their day when writing of the rebirth of Israel and the rise and fall of Russia.

Our own personal understanding of prophetic truth is also often progressive. Sometimes we have been forced to change our position on views that we once held. As we get more light, our grasp of the total prophetic picture improves.

5. The principle of *perplexing details*. The prophecy of Scripture in Hosea 11:1 illustrates the truth that sometimes a passage has a deeper meaning than appears on the surface. Israel nationally was a "son" (Exodus 4:22) and the Jews tended to treat Messianic prophecies about the son and the servant (Isaiah 53) in a national sense rather than in a personal, Messianic sense. But while Israel, as a nation, is called God's "son," the word here particularly refers to Christ. This detail concerning God's Son being called out of Egypt was literally fulfilled in the early years of Christ's life. Joseph and Mary were forced to flee to Egypt to protect the infant Christ from the rage of Herod. Matthew shows that thus, in an actual, historical, and literal way, this enigmatic prophecy was fulfilled (Matthew 2:13-15).

Interpreting prophecy is something like putting together a giant jigsaw puzzle. Often we pick up a prophetic fragment and wonder where it fits. One thing is fatal to any proper piecing together of the whole picture—we must never force a piece in where it does not naturally fit. Nor must we ignore a piece just because it is awkward, because it threatens our own scheme, or because we cannot see how or where it belongs in the completed puzzle. Sooner or later, if we are patient and honest in our handling of prophetic truth, the Holy Spirit will show us how readily the piece fits in.

There are many perplexing details in the Old Testament prophetic Scriptures dealing with Babylon, Assyria, Egypt, and other nations, details that seem to be pointing to days still future even yet. Just how and where they will all fit in is often unclear. We can be sure, however, that when the time comes for their fulfillment the solution to what puzzles us will be seen to be simple and natural after all.

6. The principle of *primary association*. The prophets were first of all preaching to their own generation. Prophets did not emerge in Israel except in times of apostasy. The prophets were primarily concerned with bringing the nation back to God. Therefore, when their messages are clearly predictive in character, we need to look at the immediate times in which the prophet lived to see if those times cast

light on the prophecy. For instance, the prophet Isaiah devotes the first five chapters of his book to denouncing Israel for its moral and spiritual wickedness. Much of what he had to say related to his own times, since on the horizon was the growing and terrifying power of Assyria. Isaiah could clearly see that the ten tribes of the northern kingdom were destined to be uprooted and scattered by the Assyrians, and that Judah, too, would feel the weight of the Assyrian arm. Many of his warnings have those things in mind.

In chapter 7 the background is the Syro-Ephraimitic alliance against Judah. Israel and Syria had joined forces against the little kingdom of Judah, whose king Ahaz was at his wits' end. The prophet was told to offer him a sign, which the apostate and stubborn king refused. He was given one anyway: "Behold, a virgin shall conceive, and bear a son, and shall call his name Immanuel" (Isaiah 7:14). Matthew 1:23 makes clear that in its broader scope, this prophecy was Messianic and foretold the virgin birth of Christ. However, the prophecy has a primary association to the prophet's own day and age and to the immediate international situation; the prophet went on to say that before this child would be grown "the land that thou abhorrest shall be forsaken of both her kings" (Isaiah 7:16). The prophecy pledged to Ahaz that, within a very short time, Pekah, king of Israel, and Rezin, king of Syria, would be swept away. One aim of the prophecy was to encourage the weak and wicked Ahaz to trust God, not to appeal to Assyria for help as he was foolishly planning to do.

In chapter 8 a further elaboration of the prophecy was given. The prophet's own wife bore a son. The prophet gave him a symbolic name, Maher-shalal-hash-baz, meaning "Haste ye, haste ye to the spoil." The prophet explained: "For before the child shall have knowledge to cry, My father, and my mother, the riches of Damascus and the spoil of Samaria shall be taken away before the king of Syria" (Isaiah 8:4). In the third year of Ahaz, Damascus was sacked, Rezin was slain, and the Assyrians were reaching for Samaria.

The primary association of a prophecy often casts light on the prophecy itself. Many Old Testament prophecies, for instance, relate to the impending Assyrian and Babylonian invasions of Israel and Judah. True, sometimes they have overtones of the end times but often much that was predicted was exhausted in the prophet's own times.

7. The principle of *partial fulfillment.* A large number of prophecies in the Bible have a near and a far fulfillment. First there was to be an initial, local, partial, and typical fulfillment, but often some of the details were not fulfilled or were only partially fulfilled. This is because there was to be a later, wider, and complete fulfillment of the prophecy. Some prophecies connected with the fall of Babylon have been only partially fulfilled in history; hence it appears that Babylon will be rebuilt in the end times so that those prophecies about Babylon

that still slumber in the womb of time can awaken to fulfillment. Revelation 18 (an additional and subsequent prophecy concerning Babylon) makes it almost certain that Babylon will be rebuilt and that it will become the financial center of the Beast's universal empire.

Joel's prophecy of the coming of the Holy Spirit had only a partial fulfillment on the day of Pentecost (Joel 2:28-32; Acts 2:16-21). Peter cited what happened as being a fulfillment of Joel's prophecy but quite evidently the judgment signs connected with the prophecy were not part of the pentecostal scene. Moreover, Joel definitely related his prophecy to "the great and terrible day of the Lord." Evidently, therefore, a second and more complete fulfillment is yet to come in the last days.

After the rapture of the Church, things will revert back to the conditions that prevailed before Pentecost. Then God will pour out His Spirit on the Jews once more. Revelation 7 shows that there will be a mighty outpouring of the Holy Spirit on the tribes of Israel and that countless millions of Gentiles will be saved. At that time the judgment signs mentioned by Joel will be present, as the Apocalypse makes clear.

8. The principle of *plain fulfillment.* We are to look for a literal fulfillment of prophecy, not take plain statements of Scripture and allegorize them. When God speaks of Israel, He means Israel; when He speaks of the Church, He means the Church. Prophecies having to do with Christ's first coming were literally fulfilled in history. Just so, prophecies that relate to His second coming will be literally fulfilled when the time comes. The literal rebirth of the State of Israel in our day heralds the approaching of the second coming of Christ.

We may not always see how certain specific promises can be fulfilled, but we can be quite sure that God will keep His word. The famine in Samaria illustrates the simple, straightforward, natural way God works things out (2 Kings 6:24–7:20).

The Syrians were besieging Samaria and the famine in the city was so great that people were eating their own children. The king heard about this particular horror and characteristically blamed the prophet Elisha. Elisha's reply was a prophecy: "Hear ye the word of the LORD; Thus saith the LORD, Tomorrow about this time shall a measure of fine flour be sold for a shekel, and two measures of barley for a shekel, in the gate of Samaria." One of the king's courtiers scoffed at Elisha: "Behold, if the LORD would make windows in heaven, might this thing be?" he said. Elisha replied, "Behold, thou shall see it with thine eyes, but shalt not eat thereof" (2 Kings 7:1-2).

The prophecy was mysterious, the fulfillment simple. During the night the Syrians heard what they took to be the noise of chariots. Concluding that the Israelites had hired Hittite and Egyptian troops, they fled in panic, leaving behind their tents, provisions, transportation, everything. Next morning, four lepers discovered the abandoned Syrian camp and reported the news to the famished people of Samaria. The king appointed the courtier who had scoffed at Elisha to supervise arrangements at the gate of the city. When people, desperate to get at the abundant Syrian provisions, mobbed the gate, the courtier was trampled to death. Thus simply, accurately, literally, and completely the prophecy was fulfilled. This is the case with all prophecy.

Numerous prophecies in the Old Testament deal with Egypt. In fact, Ezekiel has a series of seven prophecies against Egypt (chapters 29–32) and makes dozens of statements about Egypt's future. Some of these prophecies were literally fulfilled at the time of the Babylonian invasion but others have never been fulfilled. Isaiah, Jeremiah, and Joel also had much to say about the future of Egypt and that nation's enmity toward Israel. There, too, we find details that have not as yet been fulfilled. Isaiah, for instance, says, "And the Lord shall utterly destroy the tongue of the Egyptian sea" (Isaiah 11:15). The context clearly shows that the fulfillment of this particular prediction will be in the last days. At some future date the Lord is going to cut off the waters of the Nile, and that will spell disaster for Egypt which is indeed "the gift of the Nile." The details of when and where this fits into end-time events is not clear.

9. The principle of *pictorial types*. Much Old Testament biography, history, and religion are typical in character. That is, things recorded about certain people, events, and ceremonies are really a species of prophecy designed by the Holy Spirit to illustrate things God has in mind for the future.

The lives of men like David and Solomon, for instance, embody prophetic lessons. The Lord Jesus, at His return, will reign first like David, to put down all His foes, and then like Solomon, in prosperity, splendor, and peace. The "feasts of the Lord" detailed in Leviticus 23 are typical and prophetic. They were kept annually as required but each of them had a deeper significance than appeared on the surface. The feasts were divided into two groups. Four of them (Passover, Unleavened Bread, Firstfruits, and Pentecost), kept at the beginning of the year, foreshadowed events literally fulfilled in the death and resurrection of Christ, and at the coming of the Holy Spirit on the actual day of Pentecost. Then followed a gap in the Hebrew religious calendar until the seventh month, when three more feasts (Trumpets, Atonement, and Tabernacles) were kept. The calendar break between the two sets of feasts foreshadowed the present age. The remaining three feasts look forward to the final ingathering of Israel to the Land, to the cleansing of the nation and its conversion to Christ, and to the glorious and joyous millennial reign. Just as the symbolism of the first three feasts was fulfilled to the letter, so the symbolism of the remaining three feasts will be literally fulfilled as well.

Prophecy hidden in types is everywhere in the Old Testament. The story of Joseph, from beginning to end, contains an astonishing foreshadowing of the person and work of Christ. Antiochus Epiphanes (Daniel 11:21-35) is a type of Antichrist. Some things in the life of David foreshadowed things in the life of Christ. Israel's experiences from Egypt to Canaan contain hidden teaching brought to light in the New Testament. The list goes on and on.

The types, then, are a form of prophecy. They are not a good foundation upon which to build doctrinal positions. Nevertheless, they clearly illustrate New Testament truth and equally clearly illumine Bible prophecy.

10. The principle of *problem translations.* Because the Bible was not written in English, most of us have to rely on translations when reading it. No translation is accurate in every detail. Some Greek and Hebrew words simply have no equivalent in other languages. Sometimes the translator has to supply a word or even a phrase to make the sense. Rigid translations are stilted and hard to read, while freer translations include a degree of interpretation and sometimes the translator's personal bias.

In 2 Thessalonians 2:2 we read: "That ye be not soon shaken in mind, or troubled, neither by spirit, nor by word, nor by letter as from us, as that the day of Christ is at hand." The expression "the day of Christ" should be rendered "the day of the Lord." The day of the Lord is something quite different from the day of Christ. The whole sense of the passage is changed by the proper rendering.

11. The principle of *private interpretation.* No one has a monopoly of truth. We all have blind spots, yet all of us like to think that our view is the correct one. We need to be very cautious in handling prophecy. If we find ourselves holding a view that is peculiar, forced, or out of line with that held by the majority of conservative, Bible-believing scholars, especially by those who are experts in the field of eschatology, we might well be wrong. Not, of course, that the majority opinion never reflects a doctrinal or a denominational bias of which we must beware. Still, it is a good rule to proceed with caution if we find ourselves riding some kind of eschatological hobby horse or defending some prophetic oddity. We *might* have discovered an important truth, but most likely we are wrong. Crusading for an odd position is a lonely business. We need to be quite sure that our position is sound and in harmony with the rest of Scripture before we advance new ideas.

12. The principle of *perfect alignment.* We must have what theologians call "a consistent hermeneutic." That is, we must interpret the Bible evenly and uniformly, being intellectually honest with the text and with ourselves. When we find something that doesn't fit into our scheme of interpretation we need to be willing to wait for more light on the subject and, if necessary, to change our position. One cannot, for instance, take the position that the Antichrist is the first beast in Revelation 13 in one place and then identify him with the second beast in another place. Such views would be inconsistent. A good grasp of the overall prophetic picture will help us keep things in line.

18
The Laws of Mention

Even a casual glance at a concordance will show that some subjects are mentioned often in the Bible. Evidently the Spirit of God has revealed truth on a given subject in a variety of ways and over periods of time. There are three basic principles for assessing the mention of any great biblical theme.

1. *The law of first mention.* The first time any subject is introduced in the Bible is of special significance. The Holy Spirit gives the clue there to the place and significance of that subject as it relates to the whole Bible. We can see at the time of its first mention how a matter is viewed by God Himself. The best way to demonstrate this is by illustration.

Take, for instance, the first mention of kings in Genesis 14. The first king named is Amraphel of Shinar, thought to be the famous Hammurabi of Sumer. His legal code, though far inferior to the later law of Moses, was, nevertheless, an enlightened piece of legislation for his day. Ten kings are mentioned in Genesis 14, and as we might expect, they are at war. (War is also mentioned for the first time in this chapter, so we can gather important clues as to how believers should relate to this dreadful scourge of humankind.) Of the ten kings, only one is a king of righteousness, and he does not come until the end. That king is Melchizedek, who is both a king and a priest, a king of righteousness and a prince of peace. Melchizedek is one of the great types of Christ in the Old Testament. Just as Melchizedek comes in at the end of the chapter, so Christ, the true King-Priest, will come in when all other kings with their wars and wickedness have passed off the scene. There we have all of human history in embryonic form.

In that same chapter of Genesis we have also the first mention of a priest, first mention of the bread and the wine, and the first mention of tithes. From Genesis 14 we learn that God's ideal priest was not a ritual priest after the order of Aaron, even though the Aaronic priesthood dominates the entire Old Testament. God's ideal priest is a royal priest, a priest after the order of Melchizedek. The Lord Jesus could not be a priest under the Law of Moses, because that Law limited all priesthood to the tribe of Levi and the family of Aaron, whereas Jesus was born of the tribe of Judah and the family of David. The Lord's priesthood, therefore, is a superior priesthood because it derives its authority from a priesthood far older than that of Aaron's.[1]

The first mention of love is found in Genesis 22:2. "Take now thy son, thine only son Isaac, whom thou lovest." It is the love of the father for the son. The second mention of love is in Genesis 24:67. "And Isaac brought her into his mother Sarah's tent, and took Rebekah, and she became his wife; and he loved her." The second mention of love is the love of the son for his bride. Taken together, these first two mentions of love span time and eternity embracing the love of the Father for His Son and the love the Lord Jesus for His Church.

Egypt is mentioned some 600 times in the Bible and its first mention is significant. It is mentioned first in Genesis 12:10 when we read that Abraham, faced with a famine in the Promised Land, "went down into Egypt to sojourn there." Egypt, when used symbolically in the Bible, symbolizes the world: this world's system, human life, and society with God left out. In its wealth and wisdom, its politics and religion, its culture and magnificence, this world is a snare to the believer—just what Abraham found Egypt to be to him. In Egypt he denied the relationship he had with Sarah, prospered at the expense of his spiritual life, lost his testimony, and escaped covered with shame and disgrace bringing Hagar with him to be a further snare in years to come. The first mention of Egypt thus sets before us the snare and danger of the world for the believer. Abraham in Egypt out of the will of God was a curse instead of a blessing.

Likewise the first mention of Babylon is significant (Genesis 10:10). Babylon was a city built by Nimrod, the great rebel. Its early history, given in the next chapter, shows how it became the center of the world's first federation of nations, a planned society that excluded God and was essentially humanistic in character. God judged the whole thing. In miniature that first Babylon pictured Babylon as it appears in the Bible—the center of a God-defying political and religious system that will emerge at the end of the age to consummate human rebellion against God.

2. *The law of further mention.* God has evidently revealed truth progressively in the Bible, bringing men up through spiritual infancy to the advanced revelations of truth found in the New Testament. The rate of the progress of revelation varied. In the Old Testament, progress was often slow, ending with a suspension of revelation that lasted for 400 years. In the New Testament, the process of revelation was rapid, measured in years rather than centuries. The method of revelation is stated by Isaiah: "For precept must be upon precept, precept upon precept; line upon line, line upon line; here a little, and there a little" (Isaiah 28:10).

God began the process of revelation with a race so alienated,

---

[1]See the author's book, *Exploring Hebrews* (Chicago: Moody Press).

blind, and fallen that the process had to be painfully slow. For the most part, the Old Testament age was the picture-book stage of divine revelation. God taught His people, in great measure, by means of illustration, model, and type. The sacrifices, the tabernacle and Temple, the ritual priesthood, the detailed commandments of the law, the lessons from history, the countless biographies—all these were early lessons of divine truth.

There are numerous examples of the progressive nature of divine revelation. Let us return to the unfolding truth concerning the coming seed, the Messiah, which we have looked at elsewhere. To begin with, it was simply revealed that He would be "the seed of the woman" (Genesis 3:15). Embedded in that remarkable statement was the slumbering truth of the virgin birth of Christ.

It was then revealed that the Messiah was to be the seed of Abraham. Later it was revealed that "in Isaac shall thy seed be called" (Genesis 21:12), and the focus was narrowed. When twins struggled within Rebekah's womb, she was told that "the elder shall serve the younger" (Genesis 25:22-23), and it was learned that the promised line would run through Jacob, not Esau. Jacob saw that of all his sons it was through Judah that the seed would come. "The sceptre shall not depart from Judah, nor a lawgiver from between his feet, until Shiloh come" (Genesis 49:10).

In a later revelation the focus was narrowed to David: "I will set up thy seed after thee . . . , and I will establish his kingdom . . . , and I will stablish the throne of his kingdom for ever" (2 Samuel 7:12-13). Along with all these progressive revelations concerning the seed came other revelations concerning the Messiah's career, prophecies that focused on His sufferings and the glory to follow. Thus, as time went on, the Old Testament contained a vast amount of information about the coming Christ.

The fact that revelation has been progressive presents Bible interpreters with a serious challenge. Whenever approaching a passage of Scripture, they must have what has been called a sense of historical propriety. That is, they must have some idea of what could, or could not, have been believed at any given time. For example, the people of Moses' day knew that a Messiah was to come, but they certainly did not know that He would be born in Bethlehem. That truth was not revealed until much later. David did not know anything about the captivities and the return. None of the Old Testament saints knew anything at all about the Church. Thus, when one approaches an Old Testament passage in particular, a sense of historical appropriateness is needed.

The same is true in parts of the New Testament. Take for example, the classic statement of the Lord Jesus to Nicodemus, "Except a man be born of water and of the Spirit, he cannot enter into the kingdom of God" (John 3:5). People have gone to great lengths to prove the doctrine of baptismal regeneration from that verse. But the truth of Christian baptism was not even in view at the time the Lord spoke to Nicodemus. In fact it had not been revealed at all. So whatever may or may not be the meaning of the verse, it does not teach Christian baptism.

Various suggestions have been made: that the "water" is the Word of God, that the Lord was referring to Ezekiel 36:25, that it was an oblique reference to physical birth. None of these views is really satisfactory. We come back to the law of historical propriety. What would the words have meant to Nicodemus in the context in which they were spoken?

The thing uppermost in the mind of Nicodemus at that time would surely have been the ministry of John the Baptist and his water baptism at the Jordan. John's preaching had aroused the whole nation with Messianic expectation. His baptism was one of repentance, intended to prepare the hearts of the people for the coming of the Christ. The Sanhedrin had investigated the baptism of John and had rejected both him and his baptism. John had replied with a scathing denunciation of the Pharisees and their hypocrisy.

Now came this new teacher bringing the same message of repentance that John had brought to the nation. Nicodemus sought Him out and was at once confronted with the startling statement, "Except a man be born of water and of the Spirit, he cannot enter into the kingdom of God." John had baptized with water and had told of One who would baptize with the Spirit. The Lord's ringing words must have taken Nicodemus's thoughts right back to John the Baptist. After all, he was a member of that very same Sanhedrin that had rejected John. The Lord Jesus was surely saying to Nicodemus, "Unless you are born of all that John's baptism signified [that is, repentance] and of all that Spirit baptism implies [that is, regeneration] you cannot enter the kingdom of God." The law of historical propriety casts light on what the Lord's words would have meant to Nicodemus and also keeps us from reading Christian baptism into a Scripture where it is not even implied.

3. *The law of full mention.* On matters vital to the faith and spiritual life, God invariably, at some place in His Word, gathers the various threads of teaching together and gives a comprehensive statement on the matter. This is true, for example, of teaching relating to the tongue (James 3), future events (Matthew 24–25), love (1 Corinthians 13), the resurrection (1 Corinthians 15), the Church (Ephesians 2–3), the restoration of Israel (Romans 11), the nature of Christ (Hebrews 1–2), righteousness by faith (Romans 3–4), the Law (Exodus 20), and faith in action (Hebrews 11).

Look, for example, at the Lord's summary of prophecy (Matthew 24–25). Study the passage in the light of the following outline.[2]

---

[2]See the author's book, *Exploring The Future* (Nashville: Thomas Nelson Publishers), where this prophecy is explored in detail.

A. The Course of the Age—Matthew 24
  1. Events relating to the Nations 24:4-14
    a. The Difficult Problems of the Last Days 24:4-8
      (1) National disasters 24:4-5
      (2) Natural disasters 24:6-8
    b. The Dreadful Persecutions of the Last Days 24:9-10
    c. The Differing Persuasions of the Last Days 24:11-13
      (1) The false prophets 24:11-13
      (2) The faithful preachers 24:14
  2. Events relating to the Jews 24:15-39
    a. The Tenor of the Things Foretold 24:15-22
      (1) The dangers foretold 24:15-22
      (2) The deceptions foretold 24:23-26
      (3) The deliverance foretold 24:27-31
    b. The Timing of the Things Foretold 24:32-39
      (1) The fig—a parable 24:32-36
      (2) The flood—a type 24:37-39
  3. Events relating to the Church 24:40-51
    a. The Rapture of Christians Described 24:40-42
    b. The Rupture of Christendom Described 24:43-51
B. The Consummation of the Age—Matthew 25
  1. For the Jews 25:1-13
  2. For the Church 25:14-30
  3. For the Nations 25:31-46

It is evident even from this brief analysis that this statement of future events is not only comprehensive but is arranged in sermonic form, each of its three parts looking at the future from the standpoint of one of the three divisions of humankind: "Jew, Gentile, and the Church of God." It summarizes the entire scope of future events from the time of Christ's first coming until His coming again. The diligent student might like to compare the first fourteen verses of Matthew 24 with the events described under the breaking of the seals in Revelation 6. The parallel is striking. Moreover, it is evident that the Lord is drawing freely on previous prophetic revelations, especially those given in the book of Daniel.

The fact that events relating to the Church come at the end of Matthew 24 is to be understood homiletically not chronologically. Other Scriptures make it clear that the Church will not go through the great tribulation. The Lord is here dealing with end-time events in sermonic form. His first point examines the last days from the standpoint of the Gentile nations. He then drops that subject and looks at end-time events from the standpoint of the nation of Israel. Finally He looks at end-time prophecy from the point of view of the Church. Each topic is separately dealt with as in a topical sermon. There is no need to go to the extreme view of ruling the Church out of this end-time eschatology of Christ altogether, as some do. It is difficult to imagine the Lord giving His one comprehensive statement regarding the end-times and having nothing to say about that which was closest to His heart—the Church. Indeed, He keeps "the best wine until last" by following the order of history—Gentiles, Israel, the Church—as the basis for His sermon.

19

The Devotional Rule

The Bible richly repays devotional reading and meditation. This, however, is where many people let down their guard and roam at random through the Scriptures, looking for comfort and assurance, guidance and blessing. Often such devotional reading is done in an unsystematic way, with the vague hope that a verse will suddenly leap from the page in bold, brilliant emphasis and will supply the comfort and direction needed for the moment.

Of course, God knows our needs and delights to meet us in His Word. Often He will meet the sincere believer with a "promise" for the day. He is very gracious. But hopping around from chapter to chapter and from verse to verse can never really produce lasting satisfactory devotional results. Sometime, too, "guidance" derived from such a haphazard use of the Bible can be misleading.

A first rule for devotional reading of the Scriptures is that we read the Bible *methodically*. We take a book, begin at the beginning, and progress steadily through it a paragraph at a time, to the end. Or we take a theme and trace it out in a systematic way, never taking more than digestible portions at a time.

A second rule for devotional reading of the Scriptures is to read *meditatively*. Some people seem to be on a race with time in their devotions. They want to read the Bible through in a year, so off they go, day by day, at great speed, checking off the chapters like so many miles on a journey and getting frustrated if ever they fall behind. Reading through the Bible in a year or reading through a book at a sitting is doubtless a worthy goal but not if our purpose is to get a word from God in our reading.

Meditation is a lost art. Meditation actively engages the mind with the Word of God (Psalm 1:1-3). When we meditate we take a passage, preferably a paragraph or a segment, not too long or short, and turn it over and over in our mind to see what that portion contains, seeking something practical and personal for our soul. We think about a passage of Scripture, asking the Holy Spirit to open it up to our lasting good. There is nothing hurried about this process. By its very nature it takes time, patience, and thought.

A third rule for devotional reading of the Bible is to read *meaningfully*. Some have found it helpful to formulate questions, deliberately directed to the passage and preferably couched in the first person singular:

"As I read this passage, does it bring before me a sin I must avoid? a promise I can claim? a blessing I can enjoy? a command I should obey? a victory I must gain? a lesson I need to learn? Is there here a new thought about God, about the Lord Jesus, or about the Holy Spirit? is there a new thought about man or about Satan?"

As the passage yields its personal and practical message, we look for the main thought the Spirit of God is seeking to bring home to our heart. It is a good policy to keep a notebook open and to write down the thoughts and lessons the Holy Spirit is bringing to the fore.

Such devotional reading of the Scriptures does not ignore the rules of hermeneutics discussed in earlier chapters. It does, however, personalize the Scriptures.

Let us see how such a reading and meditation might work out in practice. We shall take as our portion John 12:1-11.

We can compare verse 3 with verse 5 and observe what Judas had to say about Mary. Then, in verse 7 we have a clear COMMAND to obey. "Then said Jesus, Let her alone . . ." Applied personally, that would lay upon the reader the obligation not to criticize other people.

We can focus on verses 9-11 and observe that, because of Lazarus, many people not only came to see the miracle of this life but went away believing for themselves. Here, then is a VICTORY to gain. Living on "resurrection ground" will result in a testimony for Christ that will convince unbelievers. The new life should be evident to all.

We can focus on verse 3 again and note that Mary's ointment was "very costly." When her gift was presented to Jesus "the house was filled with the odor." Here is a LESSON to learn. Worship is costly, but it results in a fragrance that not only brings joy to the Lord Jesus but also affects everyone around.

We can focus on verses 7-8 and note especially what Jesus said to Judas. Here could well arise a NEW THOUGHT ABOUT GOD THE SON. The Lord knew Mary's motives.

The Lord defends and vindicates His own. He knew the motive of Judas too, but, in grace, refrained from drawing attention to it.

We can focus on verses 10-11 and note the reaction of the chief priests. Here could well arise a NEW THOUGHT ABOUT MAN. The hatred of the unbeliever to the truth is deep-seated. It is not a case of "I *cannot* believe." The evidence of Lazarus was beyond challenge. It is a question of "I *will not* believe." Unbelief is not a matter of the mind but of the will.

In drawing together the threads of the devotional meditation it could be said that TODAY'S THOUGHT is that this passage sets forth the *work* of the believer (Martha), the *worship* of the believer (Mary), and the *witness* of the believer (Lazarus). Am I working, worshiping, witnessing?

20
Numbers in the Bible

Belief in the symbolism of numbers can be traced back to the early Egyptians. What was once perhaps a science soon degenerated into superstition and, in due course, numerology developed. The Jewish Cabalists, the Greek Pythagoreans, Philo of Alexandria, the Gnostics—all saw mystical significance in numbers. Modern numerologists have found all kinds of strange meanings in numbers.

We are not concerned with the semi-occultism of numerology. Satan always imitates God. Nor are we concerned with Biblical numerics (founded on the fact that every letter in both Hebrew and Greek is also a number), though that, too, is an area of study. Here we are concerned with the significance of Bible numbers. Although there is a diversity of opinion various numbers are generally associated with certain ideas. Nobody can have failed to notice the frequency with which the number 7 occurs in the Bible. The book of Revelation is full of 7s. The number 5 and its multiples are prominent in the tabernacle. The number 40 occurs frequently and in a way that is significant.

No scheme of Bible interpretation can afford to overlook entirely the Holy Spirit's precise use of numbers. Here we are going to examine some of the more obvious ones. Although no doctrine can be based on the significance of Bible numbers, they will give us clues to Bible truth.

God has stamped numbers on all His creation. He has also woven them into His Word. Botanists are familiar with the recurring patterns of numbers in plants. The very way leaves grow on a stem is not only according to definite law but also in strict numerical sequence. After a certain number of leaves, one will come immediately above and in direct line with the first.

The same is true elsewhere in nature. The notes on the musical scale are caused by the number of vibrations in each note. As each note climbs its way up the scale, the number of vibrations increases by eleven. Everywhere we look God has marked His handiwork this way.

In the Bible, numbers are used with great precision. They display the supernatural design in the mind of the author. Each number has its own significance, and its meaning is always in harmony with the subject matter presented.

The number 1 is a cardinal number. It is not made up of any other numbers and it is the source of all numbers. It symbolizes God, the great first cause, independent of all and the source of all. The number 1 excludes all difference; thus the great credal statement of the Jewish people was "Hear, O Israel: The Lord our God is one Lord." This does not deny the doctrine of the Trinity, but it does exclude the idea that there could possible be any other God. The Jehovah's Witnesses ridicule the doctrine of the Trinity. They attempt to express it mathematically as $1+1+1=3$. If it is to be expressed mathematically at all, it should $1\times1\times1=1$. The number 1 marks the beginning. "In the beginning God" is the way the Bible begins. We have already seen the primacy of the *first* mention of a Biblical theme.

The number 2 denotes a difference. We think of the introduction into human affairs of God's "second man" (1 Corinthians 15:47) and of how different He was from the first man. As the number 1 says that there is no other, so the number 2 affirms that there is another. The difference may be for good or for evil. Two is the first number that can be divided. We think of the two houses in the Lord's parable: one built on rock, the other on sand. We think of the man who had two sons; of the two masters it is impossible to serve; of the two gates; and of the two ways. On the second day of creation, division was made. The second book of the Bible opens with opposition. The second psalm deals with rebellion. In the epistles, the second of two epistles usually indicates the work of the enemy: 2 Corinthians, 2 Thessalonians, 2 Peter, and 2 John all illustrate this. The second of the mystery parables of Matthew 13 introduces the enemy and the tares. We think, too, of the use of the word *double* in Scripture as it is applied to the tongue, the heart, the mind.

The number 3 denotes completeness. It takes three lines to enclose a space and draw a geometric figure. It takes three dimensions to make a solid, three persons in grammar to express and include all of mankind's relationships, three divisions to express time, three kingdoms to sum up things that exist (animal, vegetable, mineral), three forms to complete the sum of human capability (thought, word, deed). Three is evidently an important number. God Himself is revealed as existing in three Persons: Father, Son, and Holy Spirit. The holy of holies in the tabernacle was a perfect cube, ten by ten by ten cubits. Christ has three offices: Prophet, Priest, and King. His resurrection took place on the third day. There are three archapostates in Scripture: Cain, Balaam, and Kore. There are three enemies of mankind: the world, the flesh, and the Devil. There are three cardinal gifts of grace: faith, hope, and love. The Lord Jesus raised three people from the dead: a young child, recently dead; a man on his way to burial; and a man dead and buried four days.

The number 4 has a special relation to things earthly, things terrestrial. It is the world number, the number of material completeness. There are four cardinal points to the compass: north, east, south, west; four divisions to the day: morning, noon, evening, and night;

four seasons of the year: spring, summer, fall, and winter. God has "four score judgments": the sword, famine, the noisome beast, and pestilence (Ezekiel 14:21). There are four women in the Lord's genealogy: Thamar, Rahab, Ruth, and Bathsheba. There are four world empires of Scripture: Babylon, Greece, Persia, and Rome. The tabernacle was God's temporary dwelling place on earth. In the tabernacle four materials were used: gold, silver, copper, and wood; and there were four coverings: seal skins, ram skins, goat skins, and fine twined linen. Four Gospels give us the story of Christ's earthly life.

The number 5 is the number of grace. It is four plus one: God adding His gracious gifts and blessing to the works of His hands. The dimensions of the tabernacle and its parts are all connected with five and its multiples. The outer court was one hundred cubits long by fifty cubits wide. Its pillars were five cubits apart. The tabernacle itself was ten cubits high, ten cubits wide, and thirty cubits long. There were twenty boards on each side of the tabernacle. On each side the boards were held together by five bars, four visible and one invisible (God, in His condescending grace, had come down to dwell among men). There were five ingredients in the holy anointing oil and five ingredients in the incense. When the Lord in grace set out to feed the hungry multitudes, five loaves fed 5,000 people. God has given five gifts to His Church: apostles, prophets, evangelists, pastors, teachers. Through them He gives expression to the gospel of His grace. When David fought Goliath, he took five smooth stones, human weakness supplemented by divine strength.

The number 6 is the number of man. Significantly, man was created on the sixth day. The hours of his day and the months of his year are multiples of six. The list of Cain's descendants is given to the sixth generation. Goliath of Gath was six cubits tall; he wore six pieces of armor; and his spear's head weighed 600 shekels of iron. Nebuchadnezzar's image was sixty cubits high and six cubits broad. Six instruments of music heralded the time to worship the image. The number of the Beast's name will be 666. Since man is by nature sinful, the number 6 is frequently connected with his sin (as can be seen from the above). He was to labor six days out of seven. The sixth commandment deals with man's most serious sin against his neighbor, murder.

The number 7 is linked with spiritual perfection. The seventh day was set apart by God for Himself and later, as the Sabbath, was given to Israel as the sign and seal of the Mosaic covenant. The Hebrew word for seven comes from a root meaning "to be full" or "satisfied." There are seven "better things" in Hebrews. Christ spoke seven words from the cross. Enoch, the first man to be translated living to heaven, was the seventh from Adam. The Day of Atonement in Israel was in the seventh month. Seven men lived more than 900 years: Adam, Seth, Enos, Cainan, Jared, Methuselah, and Noah. Noah, the seventh one, is called "perfect" by God. His father,

Lamech, lived 777 years. Naaman the leper had to dip seven times in the Jordan River for cleansing. The opening statement of Scripture, "In the beginning God created the heaven and the earth," in the Hebrew contains seven words. The closing book of the Bible is full of sevens. There are seven churches, seals, trumpets, vials, personages, dooms, and new things. In Leviticus there was to be a sevenfold sprinkling of blood. The lampstand in the holy place of the tabernacle had seven lamps.

The number 8 is associated with a new beginning and hence with resurrection. In music the eighth note is the same note as the first, lifted an octave higher to begin a new scale. The Lord made eight covenants with Abraham and the eighth was concerned with resurrection blessing (Genesis 12:1-3, 12:7, 13:14-17, 15:13-21, 17:1-22, 18:9-15, 21:12, and 22:15-18). The Feast of Tabernacles, the only feast kept for eight days (Leviticus 23:39; compare verses 34-36 and Numbers 29:39; Nehemiah 8:18), anticipated the new beginning of the Millennium. Eight people in the ark of Noah stepped out on the new earth. Christ rose from the dead on the first day of the week, the day after the Sabbath, which was, of course, an eighth day.

In the Bible the number 9 stands for finality and judgment. It has similarities to the number six (3+3=6 and 3×3=9). The sum of the twenty-two letters which make up the Hebrew alphabet is 4,995 (5×999) so that the Hebrew alphabet is thus stamped with grace and finality. When Christ took our place in judgment, He was nailed to the cross at nine o'clock in the morning. He dismissed His Spirit at three o'clock (that is to say, the ninth hour). There is a ninefold fruit of the Spirit and "against such there is no law" (Galatians 5:22-23). There are nine recorded stonings in the Bible, nine cases of leprosy, nine instances of blindness.

The number 10 is one of the perfect numbers of Scripture. It is the basis in mathematics of the decimal system. It marks completeness of order, the full round of anything. There were ten commandments containing all necessary duty. There are ten clauses in the Lord's prayer. Tithes, that is, tenths, represent what was due from man as a complete recognition of God's claims on the whole. The ten plagues on the land of Egypt signify the completeness of God's dealings with that land. The Beast's world power will be based on a ten-nation confederacy symbolized by the ten toes of the image (Daniel 2:41) and the ten horns of the beast (Daniel 7:7,20,24; Revelation 23:3, 13:1). Abraham's faith was tested and proved complete in ten trials. The ten virgins in the Lord's parable symbolize the whole nation of Israel (Matthew 25:1-13). In the Bible ten people said, "I have sinned" (Pharaoh, Balaam, Achan, Saul, David, Shimei, Hezekiah, Job, Micah, and Nehemiah), confessions that give a complete demonstration of the widespread nature of human sin. The ten words used in Psalm 119 as synonyms for the Word of God (way, testimony, commandments, sayings, law, judgment, righteousness, statutes, word, precepts) give a complete description of God's Word.

The number 12 is another of the perfect numbers of Scripture. It stands for governmental perfection. It is found either directly or in multiples with all that has to do with rule. We speak of twelve tribes of Israel; although there were, in fact, thirteen, God invariably counts only twelve in any given list. The Lord chose twelve apostles to be rulers over the affairs of the infant Church and one day to rule over the twelve tribes of Israel. The new Jerusalem, which is to be a model of perfect government, has twelve gates and twelve foundations garnished with twelve kinds of precious stones. Its length, breadth, and height will be twelve thousand furlongs. When anticipating what men would do to Him during His trials, the Lord Jesus said He could summon twelve legions of angels to His aid, did He so desire. That perfection of power would have put an instant end to man's misrule on earth. The only time the Lord is seen between His birth and His baptism is at the age of twelve, at which time He showed Himself to be perfectly ruled by God.

The number 13 is held in ill repute among men. An ill-omened number in the Bible too, it frequently stands for rebellion and apostasy. Its first occurrence is significant. "Twelve years they served Chedorlaomer, and in the thirteenth year they rebelled" (Genesis 14:4). Of the twenty successors to Solomon on the throne of David, seven were good and thirteen were given to apostasy. Ahaz, one of the worst of them all, was the thirteenth from Solomon. Uzziah, a good king at first, had reigned fifty-two years (4×13) when he rebelled and was smitten with leprosy (2 Chronicles 26:3,21). Ishmael was thirteen years old when he was circumcised. (Although he submitted to that religious rite, it did him no good since he remained a rebel at heart.) There were, in actual fact, thirteen tribes of Israel—a significant fact, since throughout their entire history the tribes were stubborn, rebellious, and often apostate. There were twelve divinely appointed judges. The detestable Abimelech, who added himself to the list, spoiled the picture by making the total thirteen. Solomon, who became a rebel against God, spent seven years building God's house but thirteen years building his own. Most of the names given to Satan have a numerical value in multiples of thirteen: dragon (75×13), tempter (81×13), Belial (6×13), serpent (60×13).

The number 40 occurs frequently in Scripture. It is the number of probation and testing. As the product of eight and five, it combines the features of grace and renewal. Israel wandered in the wilderness forty years (Deuteronomy 8:2-5; Psalm 95:10). The life of Moses is divided into three periods, each being forty years long. He spent forty years learning to be somebody in Pharaoh's courts, forty years learning to be nobody in the backside of the desert, and forty years learning that God was all in all as he guided Israel from Egypt to Canaan. Saul was given forty years to prove himself fit to be worthy to be king of Israel. In that time he sinned so frequently and with such high-handed rebellion against God that he was rejected. Jonah was to preach to Nineveh that the city had forty days to prepare itself for the coming of God's wrath. The Lord Jesus was tempted of the Devil for forty days. He tarried on earth forty days after His resurrection to prove to all that He was truly alive. Moses was on the mount forty days receiving the Law, and during that period Israel turned to idolatry.

The number 666 has ominous significance since it is the number that will identify the Antichrist. There was quite a flurry of speculation when Henry Kissinger, a Jew, became the American secretary of state. By some numerical gimmickry people were able to read the number 666 into his name. But that is nothing new. Sensationalists have been doing that kind of thing for years, with the Pope, Ellen Gould White, William Gladstone (a Victorian prime minister of England), and Adolf Hitler.

There can be no doubt that the number 666 is a curious number, quite apart from its spiritual significance in Revelation 13. With a base of 36 (6×6) a perfect triangle can be formed with 666 dots. All the digits between one and thirty-six, when added up, likewise yield the number 666. The first six Roman numerals (I, V, X, L, C, D) when written in reverse form (DCLXVI) yield the Arabic number 666.

But nobody should call that kind of thing Biblical exegesis. It savors more of numerology, one of the many pseudosciences popular in an age (like ours) that is addicted to the occult.

The number 666 will have significance to people living after the rapture of the Church. The false prophet, having created an image of the Beast, will command everyone to worship the image on pain of death. As a badge of loyalty to the empire and as a means of economic control, everyone will be required to bear the name of the Beast or the number of his name. That number is given as 666. Presumably, when the Beast's name is at last revealed and when it is written in Hebrew or Greek characters, it will yield this number.

Not many people today are familiar with the name of Ivan Panin, a scholar and literary critic in his day. In 1890 he discovered that a mathematical structure lay beneath the surface of the Biblical text, based on the simple fact that every letter in both the Hebrew and Greek languages has a numeric value. Panin used his discoveries to authenticate the Biblical text and to display the wisdom of God.

While such explorations into the original text of the Bible are beyond most of us, I believe that we can benefit from the use of numbers generally throughout the word of God.

21
Names in the Bible

The Bible is full of people and places. It is a book of names. The first person ever to live on this planet was named by God Himself (Genesis 5:2).

Adam's first recorded duty in the garden of Eden was to name the animals God brought to him for that purpose (Genesis 2:19). We can be sure that the names he gave them were significant and were based on an intelligent appraisal of their functions, appearance, peculiarities, and habits.

In Old Testament times particularly, names were not arbitrarily given. They were often associated with an event, hope, exercise of faith, or some such source of inspiration. For instance, Enoch called his son "Methuselah" (Genesis 5:21). Enoch was a prophet (Jude 14) and we can be quite sure that the name *Methuselah* was not arbitrarily given—especially since the text implies that the birth of that child had something to do with the fact that thereafter Enoch "walked with God." The name means "when he dies, it shall come." In other words, Methuselah's name was actually a prophecy and a testimony to every person who heard it: "When he dies, it [the Flood] shall come." And so it did. Methuselah lived for 969 years, almost a full millennium, longer than any other human being. God, in His mercy, thus lengthened out the "day of grace." And hard on the heels of Methuselah's death the judgment waters came surging across the world. The day of grace was over.

If prophecy inspired the naming of Methuselah, perplexity inspired the naming of Jacob. Jacob was a twin. The Bible records in some detail the circumstances surrounding his birth (Genesis 25:21-26). During her pregnancy, Rebekah was much troubled by the turmoil taking place in her womb. Then the Lord told her, "Two nations are in thy womb, and two manner of people shall be separated from thy bowels; and the one people shall be stronger than the other people; and the elder shall serve the younger." When the twins were born, "the first came out red, all over like an hairy garment; and they called his name Esau. And after that came his brother out, and his hand took hold on Esau's heel; and his name was called Jacob" (verses 25-26).

Esau means "red." And red indeed was the history of that people which came after him. The history of Edom climaxed in the person of Herod the Great, who set himself to murder the infant Christ and who, when that object was foiled, sought to accomplish it anyway by the massacre of the male children of Bethlehem.

Jacob's name means "supplanter" or, as some have suggested, "one who takes you by the heel"—"a heel," as we would say today, or "one who twists your arm." There was something prophetic about his name. Or was it, perhaps, that saddled with a name meaning "cheat," Jacob decided that he might as well live up to it?

We trace Jacob's scheming and plotting and double-dealing through chapter after chapter of his dealings with his brother, his father, and his Uncle Laban, although, in Laban, Jacob met a man who was a bigger schemer than himself. It went like that until Peniel, where God met Jacob and mastered him, broke him and blessed him, and changed his name to "Israel," which means "Prince of God."

The nation that sprang from Jacob is called by both names. The twelve tribes are characteristically called "the children of Israel," since all God's sovereign purposes for the planet are bound up with the history and destiny of this people. Yet what a stiff-necked and rebellious people it has been. Imagine the condescension, the astonishing grace, of God who said: "The Lord of hosts is with us; the God of *Jacob* is our refuge" (Psalm 46:11). Imagine God calling Himself the God of Jacob! No wonder the psalmist follows the announcement with a resounding *selah*—"There! What do you think of that?"

Scripture has so many instances of names having significance that it is no wonder we conceive the notion that perhaps *all* the names of the Bible have some kind of spiritual significance, if only we knew how to interpret them.

What is true of the names of people seems to be equally true of the names of places. We think, for instance, of Jerusalem. Its name enshrines the thought of peace. The first time the city is mentioned in Scripture it is called *Salem* (Genesis 14:18), which means "peace." The characteristic Jewish greeting to this day is "Shalom"—peace. The writer of Hebrews capitalizes on the fact that Melchisedec, the king of Salem, who met Abraham after the triumphant battle with the kings of the east, was actually king of Salem. "This Melchisedec, king of Salem . . . met Abraham . . . first being by interpretation King of righteousness, and after that also King of Salem, which is, King of peace" (Hebrews 7:1-2). The point is that Melchisedec was a type of Christ in whom "mercy and truth are met together; righteousness and peace have kissed each other" (Psalm 85:10).

The city of peace—but how little it has known peace in its stormy history. Has ever a city been so besieged, embattled, burned, and ravished? Yet one day it is to be truly the city of peace, the capital of Christ's millennial kingdom on earth.

As we might expect, the names of God in Scripture are used with great precision. In the Old Testament, God revealed Himself largely by means of His names. There are three primary names for God.

The first of these is *Elohim,* sometimes contracted to *El* or *Elah.* Its first occurrence (Genesis 1:1) links it with creation and gives it its essential meaning of creator. It is a uni-plural pronoun derived from *El* (strength) and *Alah* (to swear or to bind by oath, hence implying faithfulness). The uni-plurality of God is clearly stated in Genesis 1:26, where we read "and God said, let *us* make man. . . . " The concept of the Trinity is thus revealed in the opening revelation of God in Scripture.

The second primary name is *Jehovah.* The name means the eternal, the self-existent one. Literally, it means "He who is who He is" (as in Exodus 3:14). The word *Jehovah* (from which the word *Yahweh* is formed) means "to become," that is, "to become known," thus indicating continuous self-revelation. It is the name of God in His covenant-relationship to these He has created. Significantly the name makes its first appearance in Scripture after the creation of man (Genesis 2:4).

The third primary name for God is *Adon* or *Adonai,* generally translated "Lord." Its primary meaning is "master." *Adon* is the Lord as ruler in the earth. *Adonim* carries the thought of the Lord as owner, the ruler of His own people. *Adonai* is the Lord carrying out His purposes of blessing in the earth. Ruler, owner, and blesser are all nouns associated with this name.

Along with these primary names for God the Old Testament gives us several compound names for God, names joined either with *El* or *Jehovah.*

For instance, He is *El Shaddai* (Genesis 17:1), the strong one. But He is the strong one in the sense conveyed by the word *Shaddai* ("the breast," the common Old Testament word for a woman's breast). God is *Shaddai* because He nourishes, gives strength, satisfies, pours Himself into the life of the believer. He is God all-sufficient.

He is *El-Elyon* (Genesis 14:18). *Elyon* means highest. He is God Most High. The name is especially associated with God as "the possessor of heaven and earth." The name is appropriately associated with Christ as the Son of "the Highest" (Luke 1:35).

He is *El-Olam* (Genesis 21:33), "the everlasting God." The Hebrew word *olam* is used in connection with secret or hidden things and of ancient times. The two ideas of secret, hidden things and of matters of indefinite duration combine in the title. He is the everlasting God, the God who has control over everlasting things.

He is *Jehovah Elohim*—LORD God* (Genesis 2:4). It was God as *Elohim* who said, "Let us make man in our image" (Genesis 1:26). Once man is brought in and given his place of dominion over the earthly scene it is the LORD God (*Jehovah-Elohim*) who acts. In other

---

*In the King James text of the Bible the name LORD is printed in capital letters. It is a typographical way of telling us that the word thus rendered is the word *Jehovah.*

words God, in His Jehovah character, is especially related to man.

He is *Adonai Jehovah* (Genesis 15:2). This compound name gathers together the distinctive meanings of each, but usually the emphasis is on *Adonai*.

He is *Jehovah-jireh* (Genesis 22:14), the LORD who sees and provides. He is *Jehovah-Ropheka* (Exodus 15:26), the LORD who heals. He is *Jehovah-Mekaddishkem,* the LORD who sanctifies (Exodus 31:13; Leviticus 20:8; Ezekiel 20:12). He is *Jehovah-Shalom* (Judges 6:24), the LORD who sends peace. He is *Jehovah-Sabaoth* (1 Samuel 1:3), the LORD of hosts. He is *Jehovah-Tsidkenu* (Jeremiah 23:6; 33:16), the LORD our righteousness. He is *Jehovah-Shammah* (Ezekiel 48:35), the LORD who is there. He is *Jehovah-Elyon* (Psalm 7:17; 47:2), the LORD most high, and He is *Jehovah-Roi* (Psalm 23:1) the LORD our Shepherd.

This revelation of God by His names is inherent in the Old Testament. No scheme of Biblical interpretation that ignores it is complete. God has revealed Himself by these names in response to the needs of His people. There can be no human need not thus met by God.

Equally important are the names and titles used for God in the New Testament.

First there is the general word, God (*theos*), which corresponds more or less to the Old Testament *Elohim* and its contractions. It is used of God the Father (John 1:1; Acts 17:24), of God the Son (Matthew 1:23; John 1:1; 20:28), and of God the Holy Spirit (Acts 5:3, compare with Acts 5:4). It is even used of false gods (Acts 7:43).

The Old Testament title "I Am" is used by Christ to describe Himself (John 8:58), making direct reference to Exodus 3:14.

The name Father (*patēr*) is the name for God particularly revealed by the Lord Jesus. It is used to depict the unique relationship Jesus had with God and to describe the relationship into which we are brought when we are born into the family of God by the new birth (John 3:16, 20:17; Romans 8:15).

He is referred to as the Almighty (*pantokratōr*), a title that speaks of God as creator and Lord of all creation (2 Corinthians 6:18; Revelation 1:8, 4:8, 21:22).

The name *Potentate (dunastēs)* occurs once (1 Timothy 6:15) in relation to God. It describes Him as a mighty prince, or ruler. The word itself shows up in our English word, *dynasty.*

The name *Lord* is used frequently in the New Testament for God. It renders three words from the original, two of Greek origin and one of Aramaic. The first of these is *kurios*, which means "owner" (as in Luke 19:33). It speaks of the proprietorship and authority belonging to an owner. It is used of Jehovah (Matthew 1:22, 2:15; Luke 1:6, 10:2; John 1:23, 12:13). It is used of Christ (Matthew 21:3; Mark 2:28; Luke 1:45; John 6:34, 8:11). It is rendered "sir" six times (John 4:11,15,19,49; 5:7; 20:15).

The second word rendered "Lord" is *despotēs*. Like its companion word, this one speaks of ownership but it implies more absolute and unlimited authority and power both on earth and in heaven. It comes from *des* (to bind) *pous* (the foot). It occurs ten times in the New Testament and is translated half the time as "Master." It is used of Jehovah (Luke 2:29; Acts 4:24; Revelation 6:10) and of Christ (2 Peter 2:1; Jude 4).

The Aramaic word translated "Lord" is *rabboni* (Mark 10:51; John 20:16). It means "master" or "teacher."

The name *Emmanuel* (God with us) is used of Christ (Matthew 1:23). It is taken from Isaiah 7:14 and is a further evidence of Christ's deity.

The name *Messiah* (anointed) occurs twice (John 1:41, 4:25). It is a transliteration of the Hebrew *Māshīah,* the Greek translation of which is Christ.

Jesus (the Old Testament Jehoshua, or Joshua) means "salvation of Jehovah" and is the human name of our Lord. It conveys the relation of God to the Lord Jesus in His incarnation (Philippians 2:8). It was given to Him by divine direction (Matthew 1:21). His people never addressed Him as "Jesus" but always as "Master" (John 13:13,14; Luke 6:46). Only the demons addressed Him directly as "Jesus" (Matthew 8:29) or His enemies. It is noteworthy that He always silenced the demons when they so addressed Him.

The name *Jesus* is often associated with the title "Christ" in the New Testament. Sometimes it is Christ Jesus; sometimes it is Jesus Christ. The order of the names is always important. In the New Testament "Jesus Christ" gives primacy to the name "Jesus," the title "Christ" being subsidiary. In the Gospels it simply means "Jesus the Messiah." In the epistles the emphasis is on Jesus, who once humbled Himself but who is now exalted and glorified as God's anointed One. When the two names appear in the opposite order, priority is given to the title "Christ," the name *Jesus* being subsidiary. The thought then is always of the exalted, glorified One who once humbled Himself. The phrase "Christ the Lord" occurs only once in the New Testament (Luke 2:11). It means "Jehovah's anointed." Its companion name, "the anointed of Jehovah," occurs in Luke 2:26.

The title "Master" occurs frequently in the New Testament. It translates eight different Greek words, the first three of which are also translated "Lord." These are *kurios* (Mark 13:35; Ephesians 6:9; Colossians 4:1); *despotēs,* and *rabboni.* Other words translated "Master" are *oikodespotēs* (Matthew 10:25; Luke 13:25, 14:21), often used in the parables by the Lord to depict Himself (the word means "master of the house"); *epistatēs* (Luke 5:5; 8:24,45; 9:33,49; 17:13) which means "commander"; *didaskalos,* which occurs some fifty or sixty times and which means "teacher" or, as we would say today, "Doctor" (Matthew 8:19; Mark 4:38; 14:14; Luke 8:49; John 13:13); *kathegētes* (Matthew 23:8,10) which means "guide" or "leader"; and *rabbi* which means "teacher" (John 1:38; 3:2; 4:31; 11:8).

The title "Son of God" expresses the relationship between the Father and the Son (Matthew 1:20; Luke 1:31,35) and also speaks of our Lord as the heir of all things (Hebrews 1:2), the One who is the conqueror of the tomb (Romans 1:4).

The great title of Jesus in the Gospels is "the Son of man." It occurs 88 times and is a highly specialized title. It proclaims Him as the One who has dominion over the earth, which dominion Adam, the first man, threw away. The title first occurs in the New Testament in Matthew 8:20, where we discover that "the Son of man hath not where to lay His head." It occurs for the second time in the next chapter where we learn that He was both God and man and that as "Son of Man" He had power on earth to forgive sins (Matthew 9:6). Nearly all the references to Jesus as the Son of Man are in the Gospels. The definite article is always used with the title (to distinguish it from the Old Testament expression "son of man," used of a mere human being, especially in Ezekiel).

Elsewhere, Stephen saw Him as "the Son of man" standing at the right hand of God (Acts 7:56). He is referred to twice in the Apocalypse as "the Son of man" (Revelation 1:13; 14:14), where He is seen as coming back to claim the earth for God. What a contrast exists between the first reference to the Son of man, where He had "not where to lay His head," and the last, where He is seen with the sharp sickle in His hand and a golden crown on His head.

From this we can see how important it is to pay special attention to names and titles in the Scriptures, especially those that relate to God.

But what about the hundreds of names, both of people and places, that occur in the Bible and are not so clearly defined for us by the circumstances surrounding them? Here we must proceed with caution.

With most names we have to rely on their etymology, so most of us are driven back to concordances, Bible dictionaries, and lexicons for help. Even so we have a problem, as anyone will know who has ever tried to find out the exact meaning of a given and especially a rare name. Often the dictionary or other source will suggest a meaning for the name and then suggest alternate meanings. The problem arises from the fact that the Hebrews used only consonants when writing their language. In reconstructing words it is necessary to supply the appropriate vowels. In a sentence this is usually a mechanical procedure because the sentence itself will give clues as to which vowels to supply for a given word. But with names it is different. Names do not usually derive any meaning from the context. Therefore, where a given series of consonants can be supplied with alternative vowels, the spelling is unclear.

Because a Bible name can sometimes render a number of different meanings we must be careful when we try to build some kind of "point" around a given name. Where the meanings of names are clear and unambiguous they can often shed light on the passage under study. But where there is room for doubt we should say so.

22
Christ, the Ultimate Key

The ultimate key to all the Scriptures is Christ Himself. On the road to Emmaus the Lord Jesus warmed the hearts of two of His disciples by showing them in all the Scriptures "the things concerning Himself" (Luke 24:27). Everything centers in Him. God has no programs, no plans, no purposes for this planet, which do not ultimately come to rest in the person of His beloved Son. He is hidden in scores of Old Testament types. He is the subject of hundreds of prophecies. He is the great central figure of the Bible.

I saw once in a country novelty store a copy of the Constitution of the United States of America. It had been written longhand by an artist. The spacing of the words, however, was unusual. Some of the words and letters were cramped together. Other were spaced out, some of them quite far apart. There seemed to be no reason for the haphazard way the penman had written out the words. That is, there seemed to be little sense to it until one stood back a little way; then the artist's purpose was clear. He had so written that copy of the Constitution that the cramped areas provided shaded areas on the paper and the spaced-out words provided light areas. The result was that he had not only written out a copy of the Constitution, he had also drawn a portrait of George Washington. It was a very effective piece of work.

That is how the Spirit of God has written the Bible. Why, for example, should He dismiss the creation of all the suns and stars of space in five brief words—"He made the stars also"—yet devote about fifty chapters to telling of the tabernacle? The history of some 1,500 years is disposed of in nine verses in Genesis 4:16-24 yet a quarter of the book of Genesis is devoted to the story of Joseph, a man who was not even in the Messianic line. The rise and fall of great world empires are barely mentioned, yet God dwells long and lovingly on the stories of men like Abraham, Jacob, and Moses. The great world figures who strutted across the pages of history are mostly ignored or are mentioned in an offhand way and then only when their careers touched on the history of Israel. Yet God will spend chapter after chapter writing down the requirements of the offerings, going into the smallest detail, even saying the same thing over and over again. There has to be a reason. There is! God is writing into the pages of His Word a full-length portrait of His Son.

We will do well, when interpreting the Scriptures, to keep a sharp eye open for details that speak of Christ. We see Him in Genesis as the creator, as the seed of the woman, as the star that will rise out of Jacob, as the lion of Judah. We see Him in the story of Abel's lamb, in the ark of Noah, in what happened at Mount Moriah, in the story of Joseph. We see Him in Exodus in the Passover lamb, in every part of the tabernacle, in the Shekinah glory cloud, in the manna, and in the riven rock. We see Him in Leviticus in the offerings and as the great high priest, in the ritual for cleansing the leper, in the goats of the Day of Atonement, in all the annual feasts. We see Him in Numbers in the red heifer, in the serpent on the pole, in the parables of Balaam, in the cities of refuge.

In Deuteronomy He is the prophet like unto Moses. In Joshua He is the captain of our salvation. In Judges He is the deliverer of His own. In Ruth He is the kinsman-redeemer. In Samuel He is the ark and the rejected king brought at last to the throne. In Kings and Chronicles He reigns as Solomon in splendor and glory. In Ezra He is the ready scribe. In Nehemiah He is to be seen in every city gate. In Esther He is the One who provided the salvation.

He is to be seen in almost all the psalms. He is the blessed man of Psalm 1, the Son in Psalm 2, the shepherd in Psalm 23. He is the suffering Savior in Psalm 22 and Psalm 69. He is the King of glory in Psalm 24. He is the perfect man of Psalm 8 and the mighty God of Psalm 45. Almost every one of the psalms has a prophetic overtone, many of them plainly Messianic. In Proverbs He is wisdom incarnate. In Ecclesiastes, that sad book of worldly wisdom, He is the forgotten wise man who saved the city. In the Song of Solomon He is the shepherd who won the Shulamite's heart and who triumphs over all the blandishments of the world.

In Isaiah He is the Lamb, led to the slaughter in chapter 53 and the One who treads the winepress in chapter 63; He is the glorious Messiah of a hundred hopes and longings in stanza after stanza of the book. In Jeremiah He is the great sufferer and the Lord our righteousness. In Lamentations He is again the One acquainted with grief. In Ezekiel He sits on the throne. In Daniel He is the One cut off and the stone cut without hands.

In Hosea He is the forgiving, longsuffering husband and David's far greater king. In Joel He pours out His Spirit on all flesh. In Amos He stands on the altar, He sifts the house of Israel, and He brings in millennial blessing at last. In Obadiah He ushers in the dreaded "day of the Lord" and stands on Mount Zion. In Jonah, He is prefigured in His death, burial, and resurrection. In Micah He is seen as the One to be born at Bethlehem and as the One who will bring millennial blessing to all humankind; also He is the great shepherd and the One who pardons iniquity. In Nahum He is the great avenger before whom the mountains quake, but a stronghold and a refuge to His own. In Habakkuk He is the holy One of Israel and His people's strength and song. In Zephaniah He brings in kingdom blessing. In Haggai He builds again the Temple of the Lord, shakes the nations, is the chosen of the Lord. In Zechariah He brings in the apocalypse, is the great high priest, pours out the Spirit of the Lord upon men, is the headstone of the corner. He is the great judge. He rides into Jerusalem on a colt, is sold for the price of a slave, opens a fountain for uncleanness in Jerusalem, is the branch and the coming king of kings. In Malachi His coming is heralded by a forerunner and He is the sun of righteousness.

In Matthew He is the king of the Jews; in Mark He is the servant of Jehovah; in Luke He is the Son of man; and in John He is the Son of God. In Acts He is the ascended head of the Church. In Romans He is our righteousness; in Corinthians He is the firstfruits from the dead. In Galatians He is the end of the Law, and in Ephesians He is all in all to His Church—foundation for the building, head of the body, bridegroom of our hearts. In Philippians He is in the form of God and the One who supplies all our needs. In Colossians He is the creator, sustainer, and owner of the universe, preeminent over all. In 1 Thessalonians He comes again for His Church; in 2 Thessalonians He comes to judge the world. In 1 Timothy He is the one mediator between God and man; in 2 Timothy He is the judge of the living and the dead.

In Hebrews He is the great antitype of all the types: son, priest, sacrifice, heir, greater than Aaron or Melchisedec, greater than Moses or Joshua, greater than the angels, Son of God and Son of man. In James He is the lord of sabaoth and the One who heals. In 1 Peter He is our inheritance and the shepherd of our souls; in 2 Peter He is the One from the excellent glory. In 1 John He is the incarnate Word; in 2 John He is the One who prospers our souls and for whose name's sake the gospel goes forth. In Jude He is the preserver, the only Lord God, the only wise God, our Savior, glorious in majesty. In Revelation He is the king soon to come, who even today upholds all things by the word of His power, the One who stands astride all the factors and forces of space and time and who bends all things to His sovereign will.

We meet Him in PROPHECY. The very first prophecy in the Bible is of Him, and speaks of both His comings. The last prophecy in the Bible speaks of Him and of His coming again. The prophets spoke of His virgin birth, a scion of the royal house of David, of the tribe of Judah, in Bethlehem. They spoke of His forerunner, they spoke of His sinless life, His betrayal for thirty pieces of silver, His death by crucifixion, His burial in a rich man's tomb, His resurrection, and His coming again to reign in power and glory.

We find Him in PICTURES. In many an Old Testament story He is pictured in type and shadow. The story of Noah's ark is a case in point. God offered salvation, full and free, to all who would make the decision and enter the ark by faith. All that was required was that step of faith. The ark was to be a refuge from the wrath to come. It was the ark which bore the brunt and fury of the storm. Those who accepted the salvation God had provided were safe. Not a single drop of judgment water fell on them. The ark carried them safely to the shores of another world on the other side of judgment. All this, of course, pictures Christ as the hymn writer says:

> The tempest's awful voice was heard,
>   O Christ, it fell on Thee,
> Thine open bosom was my ward,
>   It braved the storm for me.

The Passover, the various offerings, stories from the life of David, Ruth, countless other Old Testament histories all contain these pictures of Him.

We meet Him in PERSON. We read the Gospels and trace the story of His coming, His character, His career, His cross. We see Him as God manifest in flesh—never less than God but ever and always Man as God always intended man to be: man inhabited by God. We see His miracles, listen to His parables, marvel at His goodness, thrill to His love. We see Him as Prophet, Priest, and King.

We find Him in PARABLE, in story after story He told about Himself. He is the Good Shepherd in the story of the sheep that went astray and the King in the parable of the sheep and the goats. He is the Bridegroom in the story of the wise and foolish virgins, and the Sower in the story of the seed and the soil. He is the Merchant seeking goodly pearls, the Man who found treasure hid in his field, the Son sent to negotiate with the keepers of the vineyard. He is the Good Samaritan on the Jericho road, and the King who went to a distant shore to receive a kingdom.

We meet Him in the PREACHING of Peter, James, and John, in the preaching of John the Baptist, in the preaching of the apostle Paul, and in His own preaching. He is the true Vine, the Door, the Way, the Truth, and the Life. He is the Light of the world, the Bread from heaven. His is the only name under heaven given among men whereby we must be saved. He is the stone rejected by the builders. He is the lamb led to the slaughter, the One who so intrigued the Ethiopian eunuch. He is the unknown God of the Athenians. He is the Lord from heaven who met Paul on the Damascus road, and the One on whom the Philippian jailor believed.

We meet Him in POWER in the Apocalypse which from first to last is "the revelation of Jesus Christ" (Revelation 1:1). He is seen standing in the midst of the lampstands, stepping into the spotlight of eternity to receive the seven-sealed scroll. He it is who rides the star-strewn pathways of the sky on a great white horse to make man meet his Maker at Megiddo. He it is who sits on the Great White Throne and holds the Last Assize. He is the Lamb who is all the glory of Immanuel's land. He is the root and offspring of David, the bright and morning star.

Turn where you will in the sacred library, and the Holy Spirit will point you to Jesus. So look for Christ in the Bible. To meet Him when striding down one of the broad, well-beaten highways of the Word, to come across Him while exploring a seldom-traveled path of truth, will be the most rewarding experience of all.

Part 2

Helps

1
A Survey of the Bible

An overall survey of the Bible is vital to a proper understanding of it, so here is a brief summary of the various books. A swift-paced tour shows how each book is put together and how each relates to the whole.

THE OLD TESTAMENT

PATRIARCHS

Genesis

Genesis is a book of genealogies and biographies. After a brief introduction in which *the creation* and *the curse* are described, the book gets down to its major theme, the story of the patriarchs: the fathers of the human race and the fathers of the Hebrew race. The names and stories of these people take up most of this book.
—*Fathers of the Human Race* The human race has two sets of fathers, those who rose to prominence *after the Fall* and those who rose to prominence *after the Flood*.
    After the Fall, two great civilizations developed on earth.
    We are introduced first to the Cainite civilization, which centered around Cain and Lamech. It was a godless, lawless civilization, one that produced a brilliant social and scientific culture, but ruled out God. It eventually ended in such a violent and vice-ridden civilization that God had to wipe out the whole thing.
    Side by side with Cainite culture a Sethite civilization developed, one that centered around Seth, Enoch, Methuselah, and Noah—godly men, saints and seers, who sought to walk with God amid surrounding gloom.
    After the Flood a new generation of fathers arose. Noah's three sons, Shem, Ham, and Japheth, became the progenitors of a new race. From the Hamitic race came Nimrod, a great rebel, founder of the tower of Babel and leader in lawless plans that brought further judgment from God: the confounding of human language and the dispersal of mankind into ethnic groups. From the Semitic race came Terah, Haran, and, finally, Abraham, the man chosen by God to be "the father of all them that believe."

—*Fathers of the Hebrew Race*   The Hebrew race was chosen by God to be His instrument for giving the world the Word of God and the Son of God. The Hebrew people had three *titular heads*: Abraham, Isaac, and Jacob. About half of the book of Genesis is concerned with the story of these three men to whom God gave the promises that underlie the formation of the Hebrew nation.

There were also twelve *tribal heads*, the sons of Jacob. For the most part, the stories of these men are woven into the story of Joseph. A quarter of the book of Genesis is concerned with him, one who as a youth was detested by his brothers, was sold as a slave into Egypt, and then was remarkably raised up by God to become a ruler of Egypt and to settle the tribes in Egypt until the purposes of God matured.

PROTECTORS

Exodus

The Israelites remained in Egypt for about 400 years. During those centuries they multiplied so rapidly that the Pharaohs came to fear them. In time there came a Pharaoh who transformed their Egyptian asylum into a ghetto and who planned the gradual extermination of the entire Hebrew people. Exodus is the story of how God used Moses and Aaron not only to foil Pharaoh's plots but to bring the Hebrews out of Egypt and on to Mount Sinai in the Arabian peninsula.

The story is in three parts. We see God *saving* His people by sending Moses, armed with a mandate and with mighty power, to break Pharaoh's hold on the children of Israel. Salvation itself ultimately hinged on the slaying of the Passover lamb. Then we see God *separating* His people by taking them out of Egypt and across the Red Sea into the wilderness. Finally we see God *sanctifying* His people by giving them the Law and teaching them how His people should behave. The Law He gave them covered all that was needful for their walk through and worship in the wilderness.

PRIESTS

Leviticus

Leviticus, primarily a priestly book, has four major themes. The first, dealing with *the way to God*, describes the five offerings and their laws. Next *the walk with God* is detailed in a series of laws about social life. Then truth concerning *the worship of God* is revealed, special attention being paid to the priestly family and to the prophetically significant annual feasts of the Lord. In closing, the book concentrates on *the witness to God*. Special attention is paid to the conditions under which Israel would be allowed to enter the Promised Land of Canaan. The important lesson of Leviticus is that God insists on holiness in even the smallest details of life.

PILGRIMS

Numbers

This book records two numberings, or censuses, of Israel. The first was at the outset of their pilgrimage, when the people who came out of Egypt were numbered. The second was just prior to the entrance into Canaan, when a new generation was numbered in anticipation of that event. The book is largely concerned with *Israel in the wilderness.* Special attention is focused on the events leading up to the rebellion at Kadesh-Barnea and to the wilderness wanderings that resulted. The people who trusted God to bring them *out* of Egypt failed to trust Him to get them *into* Canaan. The later chapters show *Israel on the way.* The new generation was counted and prepared for the coming conquest of Canaan.

PEOPLE

Deuteronomy

This book consists of ten addresses made by Moses prior to his death. A more picturesque title for it might be "The Memoirs of Moses." It contains four "looks": looks backward, inward, forward, and upward. In *the backward look* the people are reminded of recent victories over the giants Sihon and Og. They were to face many more such giants in Canaan but they were not to fear them. *The inward look* rehearses God's holy laws. *The forward look* lays special emphasis on the land laws of Israel. Finally there is *the upward look,* pictured in the death and supernatural burial of Moses. The key phrase in Deuteronomy is the phase "beware lest ye forget" and its kindred expression "thou shalt remember."

PATRIOTS

Joshua, Judges, Ruth

The book of *Joshua* tells *how the land was conquered* in a series of dramatic victories. Joshua completely overthrew the foes in Canaan. First he drove a wedge into the center of the country by taking the key fortress of Jericho. Then, after a setback at Ai, he overwhelmed a coalition forming against him in the south. Next he wheeled his army north and crushed a massive coalition formed against him there. Joshua, however, made three political mistakes, which led to disaster in Israel's later history. He failed to take the coastline from the Philistines and Phoenicians, he made a fatal league with Gibea, and he did not complete mopping-up operations against his defeated foes. As a result, the Canaanite tribes were able to recover to a large extent and became a constant moral, political, and religious thorn in the flesh to Israel.

Judges tells *how the land was contested*. The resurgent Canaanite tribes brought Israel constantly into bondage. Again and again God raised up deliverers, who were called judges, to bring the oppressed people relief and a measure of revival. The more prominent judges were Othniel, Gideon, Barak, Deborah, Jephthah, and Samson. The book records a repeating cycle: sin, followed by servitude, followed by sorrow, followed by salvation, followed by sin, and so on. God used the Mesopotamians, Moabites, Ammonites, Amalekites, Canaanites, and Philistines to oppress and scourge Israel for its repeated apostasy during this period. There were few days darker in Israel's history than the days of the judges.

The book of *Ruth* tells *how the land was conserved*. It forms one of three appendices to the book of Judges, the other two being found at the end of Judges itself. It demonstrates that God had a believing, godly remnant in the land even though the days were dark and apostate. The central character is Boaz, a lord of the house of Judah, who in accordance with the demands of the Mosaic law, married Ruth, a Moabite woman who had accepted the God of Israel. This union involved the Messianic line; the great grandson of Boaz and Ruth was David. The book is the story of redemption. It tells how God "devised a means whereby His banished be not expelled from Him." The goodness, grace, and godliness of Boaz are a reminder that God has His people in key places, through whom He can pursue His purposes.

PRINCES

Samuel, Kings, Chronicles

This long section tells of the march of empire, the rise and fall of nations, the ebb and flow of dynasties. The story is in two parts.

The books of Samuel and Kings set before us *the march of history*.

In *1 Samuel* we have the story of *Israel's first king*. The book is taken up with three themes: the failure of the priestly office in Eli, the founding of the prophetic office in Samuel, and the forming of the princely office in Saul. Failure is everywhere in the book. Eli failed both as a priest and as a parent. Samuel failed with his sons, who did not have the same spiritual integrity as their godly father. We see the failure of Saul, Israel's first king. Samuel is the hero of the book, a gentle, faithful servant of God who first began to draw the tribes together in national unity. The saddest character in the book is Saul who, despite early promise, degenerated into a savage, vengeful, demon-haunted man obsessed with determination to get rid of David in whom he rightly discerned God's heir-apparent to the throne.

In *2 Samuel* we have the story of *Israel's finest king.* He found the nation torn by civil war and a prey to its enemies. He left it united, respected, courted, and feared. He put its archives in order, wrote half its hymnbook, organized its religious life, and left it a dynasty that would last until the coming of Christ. The book of 2 Samuel tells of *the patient years* in David's life, the time of waiting for the final dissolution of the house of Saul. Then come *the prosperous years* when David could seemingly do no wrong. The book closes with *the perilous years* during which David paid in full for his seduction of Bathsheba and for his murder of Uriah. The book is crowded with characters, all of whom need to be studied in relationship with David.

The two books of *Kings* deal with the history of *Israel's further kings.* Considerable space is devoted to the *Davidic kingdom,* focusing on the story of Solomon, his glory and his tragic mistakes. His serious backslidings led to the prophetic announcement that his kingdom would be broken in two when he died. The books of Kings go on to chronicle the story of the *divided kingdoms.* Ten of the tribes rebelled and set up a rival kingdom in the north ruled from Samaria; the two remaining tribes, Judah and Benjamin, remained loyal to the throne of David, and were ruled from Jerusalem. The ten tribes were known as Israel, the other two as Judah. The history seesaws back and forth between Israel in the north and Judah in the south.

All the kings of Israel were bad. Some were great, but none paid heed to the true worship of God centered in the Temple in Jerusalem. The first of the three great kings of the north was Jeroboam, who founded the cult of calf-worship which remained a constant religious snare to the tribes. The next prominent king was Ahab, who married a Phoenician princess and allowed her to debauch his people with Baal worship. The only other great northern king was Jeroboam II, the last of the northern kings to reign with any semblance of divine authority.

The kingdom of Israel came to an end when the Assyrians invaded the land and captured Samaria.

Judah continued for another 136 years until the Babylonian invasion. The same number of kings ruled over both the north and the south, but Judah's kings reigned longer on the average than Israel's kings, perhaps because a number of Judah's kings were good. Two of them, Hezekiah and Josiah, were outstanding. Both sought to bring the nation back to God, Hezekiah under the influence of the prophet Isaiah, and Josiah under the influence of the prophet Jeremiah.

The two books of *Chronicles* set before us *the moral of history.* They cover much the same historical ground as the other books of royal history, but they were written *after* the Babylonian captivity and they concentrate mostly on Judah. The two books of Chronicles present the history from the viewpoint of the priests rather than the prophets. They were written primarily to interpret to the returned remnant the significance of their history and to show that, although the throne of David was gone, the royal line remained.

PIONEERS

Ezra, Nehemiah, Esther

Ezra, Nehemiah, and Esther close the historical section of the Old Testament. Ezra and Nehemiah are concerned with *the conclusion of the captivity.*

The seventy years of exile came and went and the Babylonian empire gave place to the Persian empire. Cyrus, the Persian, magnanimously freed all captives in his realm so that the Jews were able to go home.

That historical development gave rise to the pioneers. As the captivity had taken place in three stages, so did the return. Only a small number of Jews responded, however; the majority enjoyed life in Babylon. Led by three men, Zerubbabel, Nehemiah, and Ezra, a remnant of the Jews chose to return to their ancestral homeland and to rebuild the wastes.

Ezra was a *scribe,* a priest of the family of Aaron. His book records (1) the rebuilding of the Temple walls, a work entrusted to Zerubbabel, a prince of the royal family of David, and (2) the rebuilding of Temple worship, a work pioneered by Ezra himself.

Nehemiah was a *statesman.* It took Zerubbabel twenty years to get the Temple finished. Sixty years later, Ezra arrived to spur religious revival. Twelve years later, Nehemiah, a highly placed court Jew in Persia, came to rebuild Jerusalem's walls. He finished this almost impossible task in just seven weeks.

The book of *Esther* is concerned with *the character of the captivity.* The Jews were so well treated in Babylon that many rose to high office. Most of them became wealthy, or at least well-to-do.

After the exile ended, the vast majority of Jews chose to remain in their comfortable homes in Babylonia. Not for them the hardships and dangers of pioneering in Palestine! Yet they lived in danger. At the whim of a despotic king their position could change overnight from prosperity to peril.

The book of Esther reminds us of this. The name of God does not appear in the book, although it is cryptically hidden there. In this book God works behind the scenes and in the shadows, overruling in human affairs and working out His sovereign will.

Rather than allow Israel to be assimilated, He sent persecution to prevent it. Nor would He allow the Jews to be exterminated; He acted providentially to hinder that. The book of Esther is a fascinating study in God's sovereign, secret rule over the nations of mankind in general and over the destiny of the Hebrew people in particular.

POETS

Job, Psalms, Song of Solomon, Proverbs, Ecclesiastes

These five books give us the distilled wisdom of the Hebrew people.

The book of *Job* was written by an unknown *saint*. And if ever there was a suffering saint on earth, that saint was Job. The book is a detailed study of the problem of pain. Job is seen in three ways: first, in the hands of Satan; then, in the hands of men; and finally, in the hands of God. We see him facing calamity, facing criticism, and facing conviction. Nothing ever written gives such insight into the causes and consequences of suffering as this book.

The book of *Psalms* was written by a *singer*; David, who wrote half the collection, is called "the sweet singer of Israel." Other psalms were written by Moses, Solomon, Hezekiah, and others, and a number of psalms are anonymous. All were written out of deep emotional experiences. Joy and sorrow, despair and triumph, hope and fear, love and hate, peace and unrest—the lows and highs of human experience can be found in the psalms. Further, all the psalms contain a prophetic element, and some are clearly Messianic.

Three of the books of poetry were written by a *sage*. One deals with love, one with learning, and one with life. The *Song of Solomon* was probably written when Solomon was young. It is a love song, written to commemorate Solomon's encounter with a Shulamite shepherdess. *Proverbs* contains Solomon's epigrammatical sayings on nature, religion, psychology, human relations, government, parental authority, and similar themes. *Ecclesiastes* was probably written toward the end of Solomon's misspent life. It gives the perspectives and prospects of a worldly minded man and, as such, is full of cynicism, despondency, and discontent. It shows that this world is simply not satisfying enough to fill the restless hunger of the human heart. Only God can do that.

PROPHETS

Isaiah to Malachi

The prophetic books are usually divided into two categories: the major prophets and the minor prophets. Since the division is made, for the most part, on the length of the books of these prophets, it is a convenient, if somewhat arbitrary, division.

—*Major Prophets* There are four major prophets. Three of them focused on *the Hebrew nations*. Daniel had a much broader view.

We begin with *Isaiah*. His vision may, perhaps, be summed up in the word *Jesus*. His name can be freely translated "Jesus saves." He prophesied to Israel and Judah, lived through the stormy era of the Assyrian invasions, and saw his prophecies against Israel fulfilled when "the Assyrian came down like a wolf on the fold." He lived, too, to see the threat against Judah melt away, but could clearly see that the threat from Assyria would be replaced by one from the emerging empire of Babylon. But always his gaze comes back to the Messiah. No other prophet had such a clear vision of both Golgotha and the Millennium.

Next comes *Jeremiah* with his *Lamentations*. One word that summarizes his visions is *Judah*. He preached to that tiny kingdom, shaken and stripped as it was by the Assyrian incursions. In his day the Babylonians were the world super-power, and his task was to preach to the Jews the coming collapse of Judah and the inevitable Babylonian captivity. He wept to his people, was ignored by most, and was denounced at last as a traitor. He saw his writings torn up in contempt, and he himself was the object of persistent persecution.

The third of the trio is *Ezekiel*. A word that sums up his prophecies is *Jerusalem*. Ezekiel was one of the exiles of Babylon. He was deported to Babylonia at the time of the second of Nebuchadnezzar's three invasions of Judea. His task was to tell the Jews still left in Jerusalem that, far from being heaven's favorites, their turn was coming. Jersusalem and the Temple would be destroyed; their captivity was sure. To his fellow exiles he also preached, at times finding it necessary to act out his prophecies in order to gain their attention. After the final fall of Jerusalem, he told his compatriots that their city would rise again and would one day become the capital of the world.

Although Isaiah, Jeremiah, and Ezekiel all mentioned other nations in their prophecies, they preached primarily to the two Hebrew nations. *Daniel* had most to say about the *heathen nations*.

Like Ezekiel, Daniel lived as an exile in Babylon. He rose to a position of power not only in the empire of the Babylonians but also in that of the Persians. He lived nearly all his long life in Babylonia. His visions and prophecies were concerned largely with the great empires of Bible history: Babylon, Persia, Greece, and Rome. He foretold Christ's triumphal entry into Jerusalem, detailed key events to transpire during the four silent centuries between the Testaments, and depicted matters still awaiting fulfillment in the coming days of Antichrist.

—*Minor Prophets* There are twelve minor prophets. For convenience we divide them into nine *pre-exile* (who delivered their messages prior to the Babylonian captivity) and three *post-exile* prophets.

Of the nine pre-exilic prophets, six addressed themselves to *national problems*, problems confronting the Hebrew nation.

The six minor prophets who spoke to national problems focused on three specific eras. Amos, Hosea, and Micah are related to the time of *the first upheaval*, the upheaval caused by the Assyrian invasions. *Amos* was a *scornful farmer*, a plain countryman sent to prophesy against the royal court of Israel's kings in Samaria. Popular at first because he denounced some of the petty neighboring states, including Judah, he was hated soon enough for thoroughly denouncing sinful Samaria. *Micah* was a *simple frontiersman* who lashed out at both Jerusalem and Samaria denouncing prophets, people, priests, and princes alike for their sins, which made judgment imperative. *Hosea* was a *sorrowful father* whose domestic woes were God-ordained so that they might illustrate to Israel the nation's woes.

Two of the prophets, Zephaniah and Habakkuk, are connected with the time of *the further upheaval*, the upheaval caused by Babylon. Their words were directed against Judah. *Zephaniah*, the great-great grandson of godly King Hezekiah, was the *princely prophet*. He preached during the time of good King Josiah and helped promote the religious revival that took place in that reign. However, neither he nor his contemporary, Jeremiah, was able to restrain for long the national apostasy and decline. *Habakkuk* was the *puzzled prophet*. He saw the impending and inevitable Babylonian invasion and understood that Judah's sins had to be punished. But how could God punish an unrighteous nation using as His instrument an even more unrighteous nation? In wrestling with that problem, Habakkuk made it quite clear to the Jews that their doom was not far off.

One of the pre-exile minor prophets focused on *the final upheaval*, the upheaval yet to take place at the end of time. This was the prophet *Joel*. His burden was "the day of the Lord." While his visions had a partial fulfillment at the time of the Assyrian invasion of Israel, his vision goes far beyond that event to events even yet not transpired.

Of the nine pre-exilic minor prophets, three were concerned with *neighboring powers*.

Two of them preached concerning a *seemingly invincible city*, the dread city of Ninevah. *Jonah* preached against this city first, but the judgment he predicted was *forestalled* by the repentance of the Ninevites. *Nahum* preached against it some 200 years later, and his predictions were *fulfilled* literally.

The remaining pre-exilic minor prophet was *Obadiah*. He preached against a *supposedly invulnerable city*, Seir (now called Petra), the stronghold of the Edomites. As there had been enmity between the twin brothers Esau and Jacob, so there was an age-long enmity between the nations (Edom and Israel) that sprang from them. When Nebuchadnezzar razed Jerusalem, the Edomites were delighted. they even captured fleeing Jews and handed them over to Nebuchadnezzar's army. Obadiah foretold Edom's inevitable doom.

The remaining three minor prophets were post-exilic—that is, they prophesied after the Babylonian captivity was over. These three are Haggai, Zechariah, and Malachi.

Two of these prophets, Haggai and Zechariah, are concerned with *Israel's return to the land.* They stood with the pioneers who dared the difficulties in the land in order to rebuild a nation for God.

Haggai was concerned with *the Temple of God.* As a result of his passionate preaching, the long-neglected Temple, begun years before, was finally finished and dedicated. *Zechariah* was more concerned about *the truth of God.* He was a prophet given to apocalyptic vision. Some of his visions dealt with things that will not be fulfilled until the time of Christ's return. He also foresaw the criminal folly of his people in their rejection and crucifixion of the Messiah.

The last of the prophets, *Malachi,* was concerned with *Israel's relapse in the land.* The Jews returned from Babylonia cured of idolatry. As time went on, however, they substituted different sins— sacrilege, profanity, witchcraft, adultery, fraud, oppression—with which to provoke God. The formalism of Malachi's day was to come to full fruit in the Pharisaism and Sadduceeism of Matthew's day. Thus, as the Old Testament books are arranged in our Bible, Malachi closes the Old Testament canon. The book of Genesis begins with blessing; Malachi ends with a curse.

The New Testament

It is astonishing that the priceless teaching of the New Testament is contained in four biographical sketches, one brief historical abstract, twenty-one letters (some of them little more than memo-length), and one short prophetic digest. For the most part, the New Testament was committed to writing in the form of letters. One of them, the most important letter ever written (Paul's epistle to the Romans) was carried by a courageous woman over many dangerous miles.

Letter-writing seems like an inadequate way to commit such weighty documents to posterity, but there was a reason for it. The Christian faith is not something to be merely studied in a theological seminary; it is something to be experienced and lived out everyday. Hence the communication of these great truths by letters.

One way to survey the books of the New Testament is to group them according to their major emphases. Doing this, we discover that they concern themselves with the Christian's beliefs, brethren, and behavior.

CHRISTIAN BELIEFS

What are the cardinal, essential, imperishable truths of the New Testament? What makes up the imperatives of the faith? Of the fourteen writings that deal with the essentials, some are concerned with what is fundamental, others with what is false, and a few with what is future.

THE FUNDAMENTAL

Matthew, Mark, Luke, John, Romans

The basic truths of the New Testament are contained in the books of Matthew, Mark, Luke, John, and Romans. Take away other New Testament writings, and Christianity would be impoverished; take away these, and Christianity would be impossible.

In the four Gospels we have the facts; in Romans we have the faith. In the Gospels the life is exemplified; in Romans the logic is explained. In the Gospels we have the person of Christ; in Romans we have the principles of Christianity. In the Gospels we discover in whom we must believe; in Romans we learn what we must believe.

Matthew, Mark, Luke, and *John* set before us the *person of Christ.* A tax collector, a nobody, a physician, and a fisherman. Who would have chosen such an odd assortment of men to pen the most valuable books in the world? The four Gospels themselves were not written as biographies of Christ; they are more like memoirs.

Matthew wrote primarily for the Jews, Mark for the Romans, Luke for the Greeks, and John for the Church. They present Christ as Sovereign, Servant, Savior, and Son of God. Matthew and Mark present Christ in His official capacity as Sovereign and Servant; Luke and John present Christ in His personal character as Son of Man and Son of God. The first three Gospels are called *synoptic* Gospels because they present the truth about Christ from a similar point of view. John is a *supplementary* Gospel because it presents Christ from a different point of view. In the synoptic Gospels we have the earthly and the outward, the Galilean and the public ministry of Christ, and the humanity of the Lord Jesus. In the Gospel of John we have the heavenly and the inward, the Judean and the private ministry of Christ, and the deity of the Lord Jesus.

The four Gospels tell of the matchless Person: His virgin birth, sinless life, countless miracles, magnificent teachings, atoning death, triumphant resurrection, and glorious ascension.

Romans sets before us *the principles of Christianity.* It is "the gospel according to Paul." In this book he takes the facts of the gospel and transforms them into the faith of the gospel. The four Gospels tell how Christ long ago gave His life for us; Romans tells how He now gives His life to us. It deals with the doctrines of sin, salvation, sanctification, sovereignty, and service. Its key word is "righteousness," a word occurring sixty-six times. Romans tells how righteousness is required, received, and reproduced.

These books, then, deal with what is fundamental. Obviously Satan could not leave such books unchallenged. Within the life span of the first generation of Christians, he threw at the Church every heresy he could invent. In the wisdom of God this concentrated attack took place during the lifetime of the apostles so that error could be dealt with apostolically and recorded in the Bible in the next six books of the New Testament.

THE FALSE

Galatians, Colossians, Hebrews, 2 Corinthians, 2 Timothy, 2 Peter, Jude

That attack on the truth can be considered under two major topics: antagonism to the truth and apostasy from the truth. One was bad; the other was worse. Four of the letters dealt with *antagonism to the truth.*

Of the four letters dealing with antagonism to the truth, Galatians, Colossians, and Hebrews deal with antagonism toward *the principal teachings of Christianity.* The moment these books are opened, the atmosphere of controversy is felt. Vital truths have been assailed. Errors have surfaced which, if not dealt with competently and completely, will destroy Christianity. The three errors involved were legalism, gnosticism, and Judaism. Galatians deals with the first, Colossians with the second, and Hebrews with the third.

Legalism was an attack on *the liberty of the Christian,* and it is answered in *Galatians.* Many people in the early Church thought that Gentiles should become Jews in order to become Christians, that Gentiles should be forced to keep the law of Moses, submit to the right of circumcision, observe the Sabbath, and adopt the Levitical dietary code. Such a requirement would have made Jerusalem the Mother Church and Christianity a Jewish sect. It would have stifled the faith by making its rituals and rules repulsive to the majority of Gentiles. Moreover, legalism was wholly contrary to the mind of the Holy Spirit. Galatians deals with that error in no uncertain terms.

Gnosticism was an attack on *the lordship of the Christ,* and it is answered in *Colossians.* Gnosticism was one of the most dangerous, subtle, and far-reaching heresies of the early church. It combined a vaunted mysticism with elements of Judaism, intellectualism, and ritualism. The result was a particularly pernicious attack on the person and work of Christ. The Gnostics, believing that matter was evil, denied Christ's humanity. They believed that He was a form of angelic being sufficiently removed from God for Him to be able to adopt a material body without contaminating the deity. Colossians tells the truth about Christ, about the cult, and about the Christian. It begins with a magnificent declaration of the absolute deity of Christ as creator, sustainer, and owner of the universe.

Judaism was an attack on *the legitimacy of the Church,* and it is answered in *Hebrews.* The first Christians were all Jews. It was very difficult for them to see that Judaism was obsolete, that the Church was not merely an extension of Judaism but a totally new departure in God's dealings with humankind. There was no way the Church could function within the confining enclosures of the Temple and synagogue. The book of Hebrews examines the Old Testament in the light of Calvary and shows the impossibility of trying to perform a balancing act between Judaism and Christianity. The book sets forth the superior Person of Christ, the superior provisions of Calvary, and the superior principles of Christianity.

Thus three of the letters, dealing with antagonism toward the truth, focus on antagonism toward the principal teachings of Christianity. The fourth letter, *2 Corinthians,* deals with antagonism toward *the principal teacher of Christianity,* the apostle Paul. It was given to Paul to set down the great truths of Christianity in permanent written form. Paul was thoroughly disliked by many in the Jewish Christian community. He was detested and persecuted by unbelieving Jews because he so thoroughly espoused the cause of the Gentiles. Galatians takes care of their attacks on his principles; 2 Corinthians takes care of their attack on his person. In this, the most autobiographical of his writings, he talks about his commission, converts, and critics. His critics had accused him of being fickle, proud, boastful, dishonest, even insane. The attack on the man was an attack on the message. Therefore Paul defended himself with vigor, bluntness, and skill.

So then, four of these letters deal with antagonism to the truth; the remaining three deal with *apostasy from the truth.* Antagonism could be dealt with by a good dose of medicine; apostasy called for major surgery.

Of the three epistles dealing with apostasy, *2 Timothy,* the last of Paul's writings, deals with *the development of apostasy.* This was a pastoral letter written from Rome, where Paul was expecting momentary execution. Its purpose was to warn Timothy not to succumb to the many forces that might pull him away. Its central passage deals with the final apostasy that will overtake Christendom in the end times. Paul clearly saw that this coming apostasy would manifest itself in a growing disobedience to parents, a lack of natural affection, the dawning of "perilous times," and the unrestrained wickedness of evil men and seducers.

The other two epistles, *2 Peter* and *Jude,* deal with *the dangers of apostasy.* Both treat the subject in similar ways. Both go back into history to cite proof that God abhors apostasy, to point out the filthy sins it spawns, and to show its corruption of society at large. Both demonstrate that God always overwhelms an apostate people with catastrophic judgment.

THE FUTURE

1 Thessalonians, 2 Thessalonians, Revelation

Eschatology, the study of the end times, is an important part of Christian doctrine. Three New Testament writings deal with it.

1 Thessalonians deals primarily with *the rapture of the Church.* The second coming of Christ for His own is mentioned in every chapter, but its central theme is the calling away of the Church to meet the Lord in the air. That event, we are assured, will take place before the coming of the day of wrath.

2 Thessalonians deals primarily with *the ruin of the world.* Its central passage deals with the coming of the Beast, the Devil's messiah, and with his seduction of mankind by means of the strong delusion, the ultimate lie.

Revelation deals with *the return of the Lord.* Four visions dominate the book: visions of God, grace, government, and glory. The action is carried by the various series that are conspicuous in the book: the seven seals, seven trumpets, and seven vials. We glimpse, in succession, a world ruined by men, ruled by Satan, and rescued by God. Much of the rest of the book is a commentary on the action disclosed under these series.

CHRISTIAN BRETHREN

God's great instrument for accomplishing His purposes in this age is the Church. It is not surprising, therefore, that five New Testament writings concern themselves with this subject. One book deals with its origins, two with its operation, and two with its officers.

ORIGINS OF THE CHURCH

Acts

This book is largely historical and transitional in character. It bridges the gap between the Gospels and the epistles. Much that is in the epistles would be unintelligible apart from the book of Acts. But, because it is transitional rather than doctrinal, we go to the Acts for information rather than for doctrine. We obtain our doctrine from the epistles.

Acts revolves around three men: Simon, Stephen, and Saul. The foundation emphasis of the Church is associated with Simon (Peter), the forward emphasis with Stephen, and the foreign emphasis with Saul (Paul). The book begins in Jerusalem and ends in Rome; it begins with Jews and ends with Gentiles; it begins in a narrow upper room and ends reaching out to the whole world. It records Paul's three missionary journeys. It covers a period of about thirty years, the life span of a generation. In that time, tens of thousands were converted. The secret, of course, lies in the emphasis on the Holy Spirit in the book. He is mentioned fifty-eight times in twenty-eight chapters.

OPERATION OF THE CHURCH

1 Corinthians, Ephesians

First Corinthians and Ephesians deal with the Church in both its local and universal aspects. In *1 Corinthians* we have *the community church*, the church as it is to be found in any given community. The local church at Corinth was an assembly of gifted believers. Yet it was the most worldly and carnal of all Paul's churches. There were *divisions* in the church at Corinth that Paul had to deal with. There were serious *disorders* in the church, some relating to moral issues and some relating to monetary issues. There were *difficulties* in this church. Paul had to deal with matters relating to the personal walk of believers, especially to matters relating to marriage and to meats, and matters relating to the public witness of believers (notably with the abuse of grace at the table and with the abuse of the gift of tongues). Then, too, there was *disbelief* in this church. Paul had to emphasize the importance of belief in the resurrection. By the time he had finished dealing with all that was wrong at Corinth, he had produced a letter showing how to do things right in the local church for all the rest of time.

In contrast to 1 Corinthians, Paul's letter to the *Ephesians* deals with the Church in its *catholic* or universal aspect. The local church is intended to be a miniature of the universal Church. Nobody has ever seen the universal Church and nobody ever will until, at the rapture, the entire Church is caught up. Even the gifts mentioned in Ephesians are universal gifts—apostles, prophets, evangelists, pastors, teachers—gifts given for the building up of the Church as a whole. The illustrations used are likewise universal. The Church is a building, a body, a bride.

OFFICERS OF THE CHURCH

1 Timothy, Titus

First Timothy and Titus give instructions about leadership in the

local church. Two classes of leaders are envisioned, and the qualifications for both are set very high. They are spiritual qualifications.
The elders are to be responsible for the *spiritual* affairs of the local
church and the deacons for the *secular* matters.

CHRISTIAN BEHAVIOR

If there is one thing we learn from the New Testament it is that
Christianity is practical. If we do not have a "belief that behaves,"
then our belief is almost worthless. The seven remaining New Testament epistles all deal with aspects of this truth. All the epistles have a
practical thrust to them, but the ones listed here seem to place special
emphasis on behavior.

DEALING WITH SITUATIONS

Philippians

Four basic situations are dealt with in this letter: suffering, sacrifice,
service, and sickness. Four examples are given: Paul, Christ, Timothy,
and Epaphroditus. Paul's Philippian letter resounds with joy, even
though he was writing from prison in Rome. At Philippi he had been
severely beaten for preaching the gospel, yet he and his co-worker
Silas had sung in prison! (And at least one man in the Philippian assembly would shout a loud "Amen" as Paul wrote about his bonds in the
same paragraph he mentioned his joy. That man was the jailer.) The
Lord Jesus was Paul's example of sacrifice; he takes us to Calvary for
the greatest declaration concerning the sufferings and consequent
glory of Christ found anywhere in the Bible. Timothy exemplified
service. Paul's own convert Timothy was also Paul's most faithful
helper. Epaphroditus exemplified the fact that not all sicknesses are
healed and that healing is not an essential part of the atonement in this
age. Paul pays Epaphroditus high tribute when he says of him that he
did not regard his life, so eager was he to be of help.

DEALING WITH SLAVERY

Philemon

The greatest social problem of Paul's day was slavery. Philemon
was a slave owner and Onesimus was his runaway slave who had met
Paul in Rome. There, he was won to Christ and sent back to face the
consequences of his behavior. Paul's response here to the issue of
slavery was not social but spiritual. He instructed Philemon to regard Onesimus as a brother in Christ and to treat him as he would
treat Paul himself. Certainly, however, such an attitude would have
social consequences.

James

Of all the epistles, the one written by James is most like the Sermon on the Mount. James was the Lord's half-brother, His sibling, and a late convert. He was an austere man with rigid, almost pharisaical views. His letter was probably the first of the New Testament writings, his audience primarily Jewish. He demands that any profession of Christianity be proven by an evident practice of Christianity: "Faith without works is dead." It is not that James did not appreciate the doctrine of salvation by faith alone. James makes the point that while we are justified by faith in the sight of God, we are justified by works in the sight of other people. In other words, he demands evidence of the believer's conversion.

1 Peter

The Lord Jesus suffered. The Bible does not exempt believers from suffering. In fact, those who live godly lives can expect suffering. Christians, however, must not bring suffering on themselves by sinful or silly behavior. This is Peter's great theme. His letter was probably written about the time of the Neronic persecution.

1 John

All of John's writings were penned toward the close of the first century of the Christian era. An old man when he wrote, he had long pondered the significance of those wonderful years he had spent with Jesus and the significance of all that had happened since. In his day, heresy had made deep inroads; gnosticism was an undeniable problem. The keynotes running through John's first letter are those of the new birth and Christian fellowship. Paul's characteristic words are faith, hope, and love; John's are light, love, and life. As John sees it, being born into the family of God is not merely a theological proposition; it is serious business. It is either Christ or Antichrist, salvation or damnation.

2 John

Second John was addressed to an unknown Christian lady (some think the Church) to congratulate her on the exemplary behavior of her children. John cautions this excellent woman not to entertain in her home those who bring divisive and devilish doctrines. Christian charity does not include extending a helping hand to heresy.

3 John

Three people are addressed in 3 John. Set forth are the prosperity of Gaius, the praise of Demetrius, and the pride of Diotrephes. This latter person evidently regarded himself as a person of importance in the local assembly. He even ranted against the beloved apostle himself. John promises to deal with him the next time they meet. The epistle was thus written to warn against strife and the haughty spirit from which it grows.

2

A Harmony of the Gospels

	Matthew	Mark	Luke	John
I. Preparation 5 B.C. — A.D. 26				
Prologue to John's Gospel				1:1-18
Introduction to Luke's Gospel			1:1-4	
Ancestry of Jesus	1:1-17		3:23-38	
A. Birth of Jesus				
Annunciation to Zacharias			1:5-25	
Annunciation to Mary			1:26-38	
Annunciation to Joseph	1:18-25			
Mary's visit to Elisabeth			1:39-56	
Birth of John the Baptist			1:57-80	
Birth of Jesus			2:1-7	
Annunciation to the shepherds			2:8-20	
Circumcision and presentation in the Temple			2:21-38	
Wise Men	2:1-12			
Sojourn in Egypt	2:13-18			
Return and settling in Nazareth	2:19-23		2:39	
B. Boyhood of Jesus				
At Nazareth for thirty years	2:23		2:39-40	
Visit to Jerusalem at the age of twelve			2:41-50	
Back to Nazareth			2:51-52	
C. Baptism of Jesus A.D. 27				
John the Baptist's ministry	3:1-12	1:1-8	3:1-18	
Baptism of Jesus by John in Jordan	3:13-17	1:9-11	3:21-23	
Temptation of Jesus	4:1-11	1:12-13	4:1-13	
John's testimony about Jesus				1:19-28
John the Baptist publicly identifies Jesus as Messiah.				1:29-34

	Matthew	Mark	Luke	John
II. Proclamation A.D. 27-30				
A. Preliminary Activities in Galilee				
John, Andrew, and Peter called to be disciples				1:35-42
Philip and Nathanael called to be disciples				1:43-51
First miracle: water to wine at Cana				2:1-11
Christ goes to Capernaum.				2:12
B. Early Ministry in Judea A.D. 27 (8 months)				
Jerusalem: The First Passover				
Cleansing of the Temple				2:13-25
Talk with Nicodemus				3:1-21
Judea: Jesus baptizes His disciples.				3:22-24
John the Baptist's loyalty to Jesus				3:25-36
C. Visit to Samaria A.D. 27 (a few days)				
Jesus leaves Judea.	4:12	1:14	4:14	4:1-3
Woman at the well				4:4-26
Rebuking the surprise of the disciples				4:27-38
Ministry in Sychar				4:39-42
D. Early Ministry in Galilee A.D. 27-28 (22 months)				
Imprisonment of John the Baptist			3:19-20	
Jesus arrives in Galilee.	4:12	1:14	4:14	4:1-3
Galilean ministry begins.	4:12-17	1:14-15	4:14-15	4:43-45
Nobleman's son healed at Cana				4:46-54
Nazareth synagogue; Christ's claims rejected			4:16-30	
Christ goes to Capernaum.	4:13-16		4:31	
— First Circuit of Galilee				
Miraculous catch of Fish —Simon, Peter, Andrew James, and John called to full-time service	4:18-22	1:16-20	5:1-11	

	Matthew	Mark	Luke	John
Cure of demoniac in the Capernaum synagogue		1:21-28	4:31-37	
Healing of Peter's mother-in-law at Capernaum	8:14-17	1:29-34	4:38-41	
Preaching and miracle-working in Galilee	4:23-25	1:35-39	4:24-44	
Cleansing of a leper	8:2-4	1:40-45	5:12-16	
Paralytic man healed at Capernaum; Pharisees mentally accuse Christ of blasphemy.	9:1-8	2:1-12	5:17-26	
Matthew called; makes a feast for Jesus.	9:9-13	2:13-17	5:27-32	
E. Visit to Jerusalem A.D. 28 (Second Passover)				
Jesus heals a man at Bethesda on the Sabbath: controversy.				5:1-47
F. Back in Galilee A.D. 28-29 (about twelve months)				
Pharisees ask why Jesus' disciples do not fast.	9:14-17	2:18-22	5:33-39	
Pharisees criticize Christ's disciples for plucking corn on the Sabbath.	12:1-8	2:23-28	6:1-5	
Jesus heals a man with a withered hand in the Capernaum synagogue on the Sabbath: controversy.	12:9-14	3:1-6	6:6-11	
Fame of Jesus spreads; multitudes healed; plots against Jesus	12:15-21	3:7-12		
Jesus selects His twelve disciples.		3:13-19		
Jesus delivers the Sermon on the Mount.	5:1-8:1			
— Second Circuit of Galilee				
A centurion's servant healed at Capernaum	8:5-13		7:1-10	
A widow's son raised at Nain			7:11-17	
John the Baptist sends his disciples to question Jesus; Jesus testifies to John's greatness.	11:2-19		7:18-35	

	Matthew	Mark	Luke	John
Chorazin, Bethsaida, and Capernaum denounced	11:20-24			
Jesus prays and calls all to Himself.	11:25-30			
Simon the Pharisee criticizes Jesus because a sinful woman anointed His feet.			7:36-50	
Galilean woman who ministered to Jesus			8:1-3	
Cure of a demoniac at Capernaum; blasphemy against the Holy Spirit rebuked by Jesus	12:22-37	3:19-30	11:14-23	
Scribes and Pharisees demand a sign	12:38-42		11:29-54	
Parable of the swept house	12:43-45		11:24-28	
Jesus' mother and brothers come to Capernaum and desire to see Him.	12:46-50	3:31-35	8:19	
Christ delivers the parables of the kingdom.	13:1-53	4:1-34	8:4-18	
Jesus stills the storm on the sea of Galilee.	8:23-27	4:35-41	8:22-25	
Gadarene demoniac healed	8:28-34	5:1-20	8:26-39	
Jairus' daughter raised at Capernaum	9:18-19 23-26	5:21-24 35-43	8:40-42 49-56	
Woman with the issue of blood healed	9:20-22	5:25-34	8:43-48	
Two blind men cured at Capernaum	9:27-31			
A dumb demoniac healed at Capernaum	9:32-34			
— Third Circuit of Galilee				
Jesus rejected at Nazareth again	13:54-58	6:1-6		
Journeys throughout Galilee	9:35	6:6		
The Twelve sent out to minister	9:36—11:1	6:7-13	9:1-6	
John the Baptist murdered	14:1-12	6:14-29	9:7-9	
The Twelve return to Jesus at Capernaum		6:30-32	9:10	

	Matthew	Mark	Luke	John
The five thousand miraculously fed	14:13-20	6:33-44	9:11-17	6:1-13
The multitudes sent away	14:22-23	6:45-46		6:14-15
Jesus walks on the water.	14:24-33	6:47-52		6:16-21
Triumphant tour of Gennesaret	14:34-36	6:53-56		
Discourse on the bread of life (at the time of the third Passover)				6:22-71
Pharisaic tradition denounced at Capernaum	15:1-20	7:1-23		
G. Later Ministry in Galilee A.D. 29 (6 months)				
Healing of the Syro-Phoenician woman's daughter	15:21-28	7:24-30		
Deaf and dumb man and others healed in Decapolis	15:29-31	7:31-37		
Four thousand miraculously fed in Decapolis	15:32-38	8:1-9		
Pharisees and Sadducees demand a sign.	15:39—16:4	8:10-12		
Warnings against leaven and materialism	16:5-12	8:13-21	12:1-21	
Blind man healed near Bethsaida		8:22-26		
Peter's great confession near Caesarea Philippi	16:13-20	8:27-30	9:18-21	
Christ foretells His death and resurrection.	16:21-26	8:31-37	9:22-25	
Christ tells of the coming of His kingdom.	16:27-28	8:38—9:1	9:26-27	
Transfiguration in the region of Caesarea Philippi	17:1-8	9:2-8	9:28-36	
Coming down from the Mount	17:9-13	9:9-13		
Demon-possessed boy healed	17:14-21	9:14-29	9:37-43	
Christ again foretells His death and resurrection.	17:22-23	9:30-32	9:44-45	
Payment of the Temple tax	17:24-27			
Sermon on the child-text	18:1-5	9:33-37	9:46-48	
Beware of stumbling others	18:6-14	9:38-50	9:49-50	

	Matthew	Mark	Luke	John
Sermon on forgiveness	18:15-35			
Jesus tarries in Galilee.				7:1-9
H. Later Ministry in Judea A.D. 29 (3 months)				
Jesus leaves Galilee.	19:1-2	10:1		7:10
Jesus rejected by the Samaritans			9:51-56	
Discourse on true discipleship	8:19-22		9:57-62	
— In Jerusalem				
Feast of Tabernacles				7:11-52
Woman taken in adultery				7:53—8:11
Conflict with Pharisees at the feast: the light of the world				8:12-59
Man born blind healed; conflict				9:1-41
The good shepherd				10:1-21
— In Judea				
The seventy sent out and return			10:1-24	
Parable of the good Samaritan			10:25-37	
At Bethany in Martha's and Mary's home			10:38-42	
The disciples taught to pray			11:1-13	
The disciples warned against worldliness			12:22-34	
Warnings in view of the second coming			12:35-48	
Christ to be a divider of families			12:49-59	
Remarks on the slaughter of the Galileans			13:1-5	
Parable of the barren fig tree			13:6-9	
Bound woman loosed in a synagogue on the Sabbath; rulers of synagogue rebuked			13:10-17	
Parables of mustard seed and leaven			13:18-21	
Feast of Dedication				10:22-39
III. Peraea Ministry in A.D. 29-30 (3½ months)				
Jesus goes to Bethany beyond Jordan.				10:40-42
Warnings about salvation			13:22-30	

	Matthew	Mark	Luke	John
Jesus warned against Herod			13:31-35	
Jesus heals a man in a Pharisee's house on the Sabbath.			14:1-6	
Parable of the ambitious guest			14:7-15	
Parable of the great supper			14:16-24	
Parables to the multitudes about discipleship			14:25-35	
Parables of the lost sheep, silver, and son			15:1-32	
Parable of the unjust steward			16:1-13	
Pharisees rebuked			16:14-17	
Teaching on divorce			16:18	
The rich man and Lazarus			16:19-31	
Teaching on forbearance, faith, and humility			17:1-10	
Ten lepers cleansed (somewhere between Samaria and Galilee)			17:11-19	
Teaching on the suddenness of the second coming			17:20-37	
Parable of the importunate widow			18:1-8	
Parable of the Pharisee and publican			18:9-14	
Raising of Lazarus at Bethany				11:1-46
Caiaphas counsels that Jesus be slain: Jesus returns to Peraea.				11:47-54
Teaching about divorce	19:1-12	10:1-12		
Christ blesses the little children	19:13-15	10:13-16	18:15-17	
Rich young ruler	19:16-30	10:17-31	18:18-30	
Parable of the laborers and the vineyard	20:1-16			
Third prediction by Christ of His death and resurrection	20:17-19	10:32-34	18:31-34	
Request of James and John rebuked	20:20-28	10:35-45		
Two blind men healed near Jericho	20:29-34	10:46-52	18:35-43	

	Matthew	Mark	Luke	John
IV. Persecution A.D. 30*				
A. *Sixth Day before Passover (9th of Nisan) (Thursday sunset to Friday sunset)*				
The Lord approaches Jerusalem from Jericho.			19:1-10	
He spends Thursday night at Zacchaeus' house.			19:5	
He delivers the parable of the pounds.			19:11-27	
He continues toward Jerusalem.			19:28	
He sends two disciples for the colt.	21:1-7			
He enters Jerusalem from Bethphage.	21:8-9			
People ask who He is.	21:10-11			
He cleanses the Temple.	21:12-16			
He returns to Bethany.	21:17			12:1
B. *Fifth Day before Passover (10th of Nisan) (Friday sunset to Saturday sunset)*				
He spends the Sabbath at Bethany.				
A supper is made, likely at the home of Lazarus				12:2
He is anointed. Judas challenges the act.				12:3-11
C. *Fourth Day before Passover (11th of Nisan) (Saturday sunset to Sunday sunset: Palm Sunday)*				
Triumphal entry into Jerusalem; the Lord sends to fetch the colt.		11:1-7	19:24-35	12:12
He starts from Bethany and is met by the crowds from Jerusalem.		11:8-10	19:36-40	12:12-19
He foretells the doom of Jerusalem.			19:41-44	
He enters the Temple and observes.		11:11		
He returns to Bethany.		11:11		

---

*The position is taken here that the traditional view does not sufficiently allow for all the facts. If the crucifixion took place on Good Friday, then Christ could not possibly have been in the tomb three days and three nights. Moreover, all the events said to have taken place between the death and burial of Christ could not have been squeezed into the brief space of time allowed. By placing the crucifixion on a Wednesday, allowance is made for the full length of time in the tomb and for the various coincidental events to take place. (Times are from sunset to sunset.)

		Matthew	Mark	Luke	John
D.	*Third Day before Passover (12th of Nisan) (Sunday sunset to Monday sunset)*				
	Monday morning He returns to Jerusalem.	21:18	11:12		
	He curses the fig tree.	21:19-22	11:13-14		
	He cleanses the Temple one more time.		11:15-17	19:45-46	
	Teaching in the Temple			19:47	
	He is opposed by the rulers.		11:18	19:47-48	
	He goes back to Bethany.		11:19		
E.	*Second Day before Passover (13th of Nisan) (Monday sunset to Tuesday sunset)*				
	Tuesday morning, going to Jerusalem the disciples comment on the withered fig tree.		11:20-26		
	Back in Jerusalem and the Temple	21:23-27	11:27-33	20:1	
	Teaching by parables and questions in Jerusalem	21:28— 23:29	12:1-44	21:4	
	The question of tribute to Caesar	22:15-22	12:13-17	20:20-26	
	The Sadducees and the resurrection	22:23-33	12:18-27	20:27-40	
	The lawyer and the great commandment	22:34-40	12:28-34		
	Christ's question about David's Lord	22:41-46	12:35-37	20:41-44	
	Denunciation of the scribes and Pharisees	23:1-39	12:38-40	20:45-47	
	The Temple treasure and the widow's mites		12:41-44	21:1-4	
	The Jews reject Christ.				12:20-36
	The Greeks desire to see Him.				12:37-50
	The great prophecy in the Temple			21:5-36	
	Christ's practice during the feast period			21:37-38	
	Olivet Discourse	24:1-51	13:1-37		
	Olivet parables	25:1-46			
	Jesus says: "After two days is the Passover."	26:1-5	14:1		
	He returns to Bethany. The supper in the house of Simon the leper. The second anointing. The disciples are indignant.	26:6-13	14:3-9		

	Matthew	Mark	Luke	John
F. *The Day before Passover* *(14th of Nisan)* *The "Preparation Day" (1st day* *of unleavened bread)* *The Day of the Crucifixion* *(Tuesday sunset to* *Wednesday sunset)*				
The plot of Judas Iscariot to betray the Lord	26:14-16	14:10-11	22:1-6	
The preparation for the Last Passover	26:17-19	14:12-16	22:7-13	
Tuesday evening. The betrayal ripens.	26:20	14:17		
The Last Supper commences. Jesus washes the disciples' feet.				13:1-20
Jesus reveals the betrayer.	26:21-25	14:18-21		13:21-30
The Lord's Supper instituted	26:26-29	14:22-25	22:14-23	
The Lord foretells Peter's denials. Peter's boast				13:31-38
Strife as to who should be greatest			22:24-30	
Peter's denials again foretold			22:31-34	
The Lord comments on the disciples' first commission			22:35-38	
The Upper Room discourse				14:1-31
The last talk to the disciples on the way to Gethsemane				15:1— 16:33
Christ's intercessory prayer				17:1-26
The Lord and His disciples go to Gethsemane.	26:30-36	14:26-29	22:39	18:1
Peter's denials foretold yet again		14:30-31		
The Lord's agony in Gethsemane	26:37-46	14:32-42	22:40-46	
The betrayal and arrest	26:47-56	14:43-50	22:47-54	18:2-11
The escape of the unknown disciple		14:51-52		
The night trial by the Jews before Annas				18:12– 19:23
The trail before Caiaphas and the Sanhedrin: Christ mocked	26:57-68	14:53-56	22:54-65	18:14,19-24
Peter denies the Lord	26:58,69-75	14:54,66-72	22:54-62	18:15-18, 25-27
Christ condemned to death by the Sanhedrin	27:1	15:1	22:66-71	
Judas commits suicide.	27:3-10			
Christ tried before Pilate	27:2,11-14	15:1-5	23:1-5	18:28-38

	Matthew	Mark	Luke	John
Christ before Herod Antipas			23:6-12	
Christ back before Pilate	27:15-26	15:6-15	23:13-25	18:39—
				19:16
The soldiers mock Christ.	27:27-30	15:16-19		
Tuesday midnight (sixth hour) Pilate said: "Behold the Man"				19:14-15
Jesus led away to be crucified	27:31-34	15:20-23	23:26-31	19:16-17
The malefactors led away			23:32-33	19:18
The inscription				19:19-22
Gambling for the Lord's clothes	27:35-37	15:24	23:34	19:23-24
The time of the crucifixion: Wednesday at 9 A.M. "The third hour"		15:25-26		
The two thieves crucified	27:38	15:27-28		
The Lord reviled by the rulers and thieves	27:39-44	15:29-32	23:35-43	
Jesus commits His mother to John's care.				19:25-27
Wednesday noon: the darkness begins (sixth hour)	27:45-49	15:33	23:44-45	
Wednesday, 3 P.M. (ninth hour) The Lord's dying shout	27:50	15:34-37	23:46	19:28-30
The Calvary miracles. The breaking of the thieves' legs	27:51-56	15:38-41	23:47-49	19:31-37
Sunset Wednesday (about 6 P.M.) Christ buried in haste before "the high day" (the first day of the feast) began.	27:57-66	15:42-47	23:50-56	19:38-42

G. *The First Day of the Feast*
  (15th of Nisan)
  The "high day"
  (Wednesday sunset to
    Thursday sunset)
  First night and day in the tomb
  The Second Day of the Feast
  (16th of Nisan)
  (Thursday sunset to
    Friday sunset)
  Second night and day in the
  tomb
  The Third Day of the Feast
  (17th of Nisan)
  The Weekly Sabbath
  (Friday sunset to Satur-
    day sunset)
  Third night and day in the tomb

	Matthew	Mark	Luke	John
H. *The First Day of the Week* (*18th of Nisan*)				
Saturday sunset. The third day (Matt. 16:21)	28:1-19	16:1-18	24:1-49	20:1-23
V. Preeminence				
The women observe where the body was laid.	27:61	15:47	23:55	
They prepare spices for the burial on the eve of the High Sabbath.			23:56	
They rest in keeping with the Law (Lev. 23:7)			23:56	
They visit the tomb at the close of the weekly Sabbath (first day of the week).	28:1	16:1-2	24:1	20:1
They wonder how to move the stone.		16:3		
They discover the stone already moved.	28:2-4	16:4-5	24:2	20:1
They are spoken to by the angel.	28:5-7	16:6-7	24:3-7	
They leave the tomb.	28:8	16:8	24:8-9	
They meet the risen Lord.	28:9-10			
They tell Peter and the disciples.		16:9-11	24:10-11	20:2
The guard makes their report.	28:11-15			
Peter and John visit the tomb.			24:12	20:3-10
Mary visits the tomb.				20:11-18
The Lord appears on the Emmaus road.		16:12	24:13-32	
The Emmaus disciples return to the eleven.		16:13	24:33-35	
The Lord's first appearance in the Upper Room			24:36-44	20:19-23
The great commission given			24:45-49	
The second appearing in the Upper Room: Thomas challenged		16:14		20:24-29
The great commission given again		16:15-18		
John's comment about Christ's signs				20:30-31
The eleven depart for Galilee.	28:16-18			
The great commission given again	28:19-20			
The Lord appears to the seven in Galilee.				21:1-23
The Lord's ascension		16:19-20	24:50-53	
John's closing statement				21:24-25

3
A Summary of Bible History

Adam created
Eve created
The temptation
The curse and expulsion from Eden
Cain born
Abel born
Abel murdered
Cain branded
Seth born
Enos born
Cainan born
Mahalaleel born
Jared born
Enoch born (seventh from Adam)
Methuselah born
Lamech born
Adam died (930 years)
Enoch translated (365 years)
Seth died (912 years)
Noah born
Enos died (905 years)
Cainan died (910 years)
Mahalaleel died (895 years)
Jared died (962 years)
Japhet born
Ham born
Shem born
Lamech died (777 years)
Methuselah died (969 years)
The Flood (Noah 600 years old)
Arphaxed born
Salah born
Eber born
Peleg born (Earth divided)
Reu born
Serug born
Nahor born

---

*NOTE: The dates given in this summary are sometimes given only approximately. Scholars differ widely on some of them. The date of the Exodus, for instance, is hotly debated. The dates of some of the prophets and of some of the epistles are also uncertain.

Date B.C.	Biblical Event	Other Events
	Terah born	
	Peleg died (239 years)	
	Nahor died (148 years)	
2165	Abraham born	
	Reu died (239 years)	
	Serug died (230 years)	
	Abraham's first call	
2090	Terah died (205 years)	
	Abraham entered Canaan	
2089	Abraham went to Egypt	11th dynasty in Egypt
	Abraham returned from Egypt	
	Abraham married Hagar	
2079	Ishmael born (Abraham 86 years old)	
2066	Covenant of circumcision	
	Sodom and Gomorrah destroyed	
2065	Isaac born (Abraham 100 years old)	
2062	Ishmael and Hagar cast out	
2050	Isaac offered on Mt. Moriah	
2028	Death of Sarah (127 years)	
2025	Isaac married Rebekah	
	Abraham married Keturah	
	Esau and Jacob born	
		Middle Kingdom (12th dynasty) in Egypt
1990	Abraham died (Isaac 75, Jacob 15)	
	Esau married Hittite wives	
1942	Ishmael died (137 years)	
1928	Jacob received the patriarchal blessing	
	Jacob fled to Haran	
1921	Jacob's marriages	
	Reuben born	
	Simeon born	
1919	Levi and Dan born	
	Judah and Naphtali born	
	Gad born	
	Asher and Issachar born	
	Zebulun born	
	Dinah born	
1914	Joseph born	
	Jacob arrived back in Canaan	
	Jacob met Esau	
1908	Jacob at Shechem	
1898	Jacob at Bethel	
	Rachel died	

Date B.C.	Biblical Event	Other Events
	Benjamin born	
1897	Joseph sold into Egypt	
1885	Isaac died (180 years)	
1884	Joseph exalted in Egypt	
1858	Jacob died after 17 years in Egypt	
1804	Joseph died (110 years)	
1730	Hebrew bondage in Egypt began	Hyksos invasion of Egypt
1570		Hyksos rulers expelled from Egypt
1528	Aaron born	Thutmose I, pharaoh of Egypt
1525	Moses born, reared in pharaoh's court	
1508		Thutmose II, pharaoh of Egypt
1504		Hatshepsut and Thutmose III ruled Egypt
1485	Moses in exile in Midian	
1483		Thutmose III, sole ruler of Egypt Oppression
1450		Amenhotep II, pharaoh of Egypt
1445	The Exodus	
1444	Tabernacle completed	
1410		Amenhotep III, pharaoh of Egypt
1405	Moses died, Joshua assumed command	
1398	Conquest of Canaan completed	
1381	First oppression of book of Judges	Chushan-rishathaim, oppressor
1373	Othniel became judge	
1334	Second oppression	Eglon of Moab oppressor
1318		Rameses I, pharaoh of Egypt
1316	Ehud became Judge	

Date B.C.	Biblical Event	Other Events
1301		Rameses II, pharaoh of Egypt
	Shamgar became judge	
1257	Third oppression	Jabin and Canaanites oppressors
1237	Deborah and Barak became judges	
1198	Fourth oppression	Midianites oppressors
1191	Gideon became judge	
1190		Philistine settlement of Canaan coastline
1165	Eli born (a descendant of Aaron through Ithamar)	
1151	Abimelech usurped power	
1149	Tola became judge	
1126	Jair became judge	
	Marriage of Ruth and Boaz	
1107	Eli priest of Shiloh	
1105	Fifth oppression	Ammonites oppressors in the east
	Birth of Samuel	
1087	Jephthah became judge in east	
	Sixth oppression	Philistines oppressors in the west
1081	Ibzan became judge in east	
1075	Elon became judge in east	
1069	Samson became judge in west	
1067	Samuel began his ministry	
1065	Abdon became judge in east	
1043	Saul became king	
1011	Death of Saul	
	Abner made Ishbosheth king	
	David crowned king over Judah	
1004	David became king of all Israel	
971	Solomon became king of all Israel	
996	Temple started	
		Sheshonk (Shishak), pharaoh of Egypt
931	Death of Solomon, division of kingdom	
	Rehoboam became king of Judah	
	Jeroboam became king of Israel	
913	Abijam became king of Judah	

Date B.C.	Biblical Event	Other Events
911	Asa became king of Judah	
910	Nadab became king of Israel	
909	Baasha became king of Israel	
886	Elah became king of Israel	
885	Zimri became king of Israel	Benhadad I, king of Syria
	Tibni seized half of Israel	
	Omri seized half of Israel	
	Civil war in Israel	
883		Ashurnasirpal, king of Assyria
880	Omri became king of all Israel	
874	Ahab became king of Israel	
859		Shalmaneser III, king of Assyria
857	Elijah ministered in Israel	
853	Ahaziah became king of Israel	
852	Joram became king of Israel	
	Elisha ministered in Israel	
850	Jehoram became king of Judah	
841	Jehu became king of Israel	Hazael, king of Syria
	Ahaziah became king of Judah	
	Athaliah seized throne of Judah	
835	Joash became king of Judah	
830	Joel ministered	
814	Jehoahaz became king of Israel	
798	Jehoash became king of Israel	Benhadad II, king of Syria
796	Amaziah became king of Judah	
787	Jeroboam II became king of Israel	
	Jonah ministered	
783	Uzziah (Azariah) became king of Judah	
765	Amos began to minister	
753	Zechariah became king of Israel	
752	Shallum became king of Israel	
	Hosea began to minister	
	Menahem became king of Israel	
750	Jotham became co-regent of Judah	Rezin, king of Syria
745		Tiglath-pileser III, king of Assyria
742	Pekahiah became king of Israel	

Date B.C.	Biblical Event	Other Events
740	Pekah became king of Israel	
739	Jotham became full king of Judah	
	Isaiah began to minister	
736	Micah began to minister	
735	Ahaz became king of Judah	
732	Hoshea became last king of Israel	
727		Shalmaneser V, king of Assyria
722	Fall of Samaria	Sargon II, king of Assyria
	Ten tribes of Israel into captivity	
715	Hezekiah became king of Judah	
705		Sennacherib, king of Assyria
701	Judah invaded by Assyria	
687	Manasseh became king of Judah	
681		Esarhaddon, king of Assyria
669		Ashurbanipal, king of Assyria
645	Nahum prophesied about this time	
642	Amon became king of Judah	
640	Josiah became king of Judah	
635	Zephaniah ministered	
627	Jeremiah began to minister	
626		New Babylonian empire founded
622	Book of the Law discovered	
620	Habakkuk ministered	
612		Fall of Nineveh
609	Jehoahaz became king	Pharaoh Neco II on throne of Egypt
	Jehoiakim became king	
605	Johoiakim became subject to Babylon	Nebuchadnezzar, king of Babylon
	Seventy-year captivity began	First Babylonian invasion
	Daniel taken to Babylon to minister	

Date B.C.	Biblical Event	Other Events
604	Jehoiakim cut Jeremiah's scroll	
602	Jehoiakim rebelled against Nebuchadnezzar	
598	Some 3,000 taken to Babylon	Second Babylonian invasion: beginning campaign
	Jehoiakim died, given contemptuous burial	
597	Jehoiachin became king of Judah	
	Jehoiachin taken to Babylon	
	Ezekiel and others taken to Babylon	
	Zedekiah became last king of Judah	
593	Ezekiel began to minister in Babylon	
586	Jerusalem taken by Babylonians	Final Babylonian invasion
	Zedekiah blinded and taken to Babylon	
	Jeremiah carried to Egypt by Jewish rebels	
582	Further small deportation of Jews	
556		Nabonidus, king of Babylon
		Belshazzar, coregent in Babylon
546		Cyrus of Persia defeated Croesus of Lydia
539		Babylon captured by Cyrus; Belshazzar slain
538	Daniel's vision of the seventy weeks	
	Return from captivity under Zerubbabel	
537	Altar set up in Jerusalem	
536	Foundation of Temple laid	
530		Cambyses, king of Persia
522		Pseudo Smerdes, king of Persia

Date B.C.	Biblical Event	Other Events
521		Darius Hystaspes (the Great), king of Persia
520	Haggai began to minister Work resumed on the Temple Zechariah began to minister	
519	Work on Temple challenged	Darius confirmed the decree of Cyrus
516	Temple completed	
486		Xerxes, king of Persia
478	Esther became queen of Xerxes	
465		Artaxerxes I Longimanus, king of Persia
459	Ezra commissioned to go to Jerusalem	
446	Nehemiah cupbearer of Artaxerxes Nehemiah led another group back	
445	Nehemiah rebuilt walls of Jerusalem	
432	Malachi began to minister	
359		Artaxerxes III, king of Persia Philip became king of Macedonia
336		Darius III Codomannus, king of Persia Alexander the Great, king of Greece
323		Death of Alexander; division of his empire
223		Antiochus III (the Great), king of Syria
175		Antiochus IV Epiphanes, king of Syria
133		Attalus III king of Pergamum bequeathed his kingdom to Rome

Date B.C.	Biblical Event	Other Events
63		Pompey captured Jerusalem
48		Julius Caesar in Rome
30		Augustus became Caesar in Rome
Date A.D.		
4	Birth of Christ	Death of Herod the Great
9	Jesus visited Jerusalem as a boy	
14		Tiberius became Caesar (14-37)
26	John the Baptist began his ministry	
27	Jesus baptized	Pilate became procurator of Judea (27-36)
	His early moves in Galilee	
	He called His first disciples	
	His first miracle	
	His early Judean ministry (8 months)	
	Jerusalem: the first Passover	
	The Temple cleansed	
	Nicodemus and Jesus	
	Judea and Samaria	
	The woman at the well	
27	Early Galilean ministry (22 months)	
28	John imprisoned	
	The Nazareth synagogue. Rejected	
	He goes to Capernaum	
	First Galilean circuit	
	Miracles, preaching, calling disciples	
	Jerusalem: the second Passover	
	Sabbath healing at pool of Bethesda	
28	Back in Galilee (12 months)	
29	Criticism by Pharisees	
	Christ's fame spreads	
	Plots against Him	
	Sermon on the Mount	

Date A.D.	Biblical Event	Other Events
	Second Galilean circuit	
	Miracles. Growing opposition	
	The mystery parables given	
	More miracles	
	Third Galilean circuit	
	Christ again rejected at Nazareth	
	The Twelve sent out to preach	
	John the Baptist murdered	
	Feeding of the 5,000	
29	Final Galilean ministry (6 months)	
	Miracles. Increasing opposition	
	Peter's great confession at Caesarea Philippi	
	Christ foretells His death and resurrection	
	The transfiguration	
	More teaching	
	Back to Judea (3 months)	
48	Peter visits Antioch	
	Judaizers visit Antioch	
	Dispute over the law	
	Paul wrote GALATIANS (to churches founded on his first missionary journey)	
49	Paul's third visit to Jerusalem— with Barnabas, to attend the council	Jews expelled from Rome
	Paul and Barnabas return to Antioch	
50	Dispute over John Mark	
	Paul's second missionary journey	
51	Paul's "Macedonian call" to Europe	Gallio becomes proconsul of Achaia (51)
	Paul preaches at Philippi, Thessalonica, and Berea	
	Paul preaches at Athens	
52	Paul at Corinth	Felix becomes procurator of Judea (52-59)
	Paul writes 1 THESSALONIANS	
53	Paul visits Ephesus on his way to Jerusalem	

Date A.D.	Biblical Event	Other Events
	Paul writes 2 THESSALONIANS	
54	Paul's fourth visit to Jerusalem	Nero becomes emperor (54-68) and for five years, influenced by his tutor Seneca and Africanus Burrus, the honest prefect of the praetorian guard, Rome enjoyed a miniature golden age (54-59)
	Paul's goes to Antioch	
	Paul's third missionary journey	
55	Paul's two-year ministry at Ephesus	
	Mark writes his Gospel?	
57	Paul writes 1 and 2 CORINTHIANS Paul goes to Corinth for three months	
58	Paul writes ROMANS Paul's last visit to Jerusalem Paul arrested and sent to Caesarea Paul's defense before Felix MATTHEW writes his Gospel (58?) LUKE writes his Gospel (58-60?) while Paul was at Caesarea ACTS written (58-62)	
59	Paul imprisoned at Caesarea	
60	Paul's defense before Festus Paul's defense before Agrippa Paul sent to Rome (Sept. Oct.) Paul shipwrecked at Malta (Winter)	
61	Paul arrives at Rome	Burrus died, Tigellinus replaced, Seneca retired, Octavia divorced, and Nero shows signs of degeneration (61).
	Paul under house arrest at Rome for about two years.	
	Paul writes his prison epistles: EPHESIANS, PHILIPPIANS, COLOSSIANS, PHILEMON.	
62	Death of James in Jerusalem	Nero married Poppaea who was

Date A.D.	Biblical Event	Other Events
	Paul released from prison	friendly to the Jews and perhaps a "God-fearer." (62)
64	Hebrews written (?) in view of the impending war with Rome	The great fire of Rome Nero persecutes the Christians
65	Paul visits Spain? 1 and 2 PETER written?	
66	Paul visits Asia minor? Outbreak of Jewish war Paul back in prison at Rome	
67	Paul writes 1 and 2 TIMOTHY and TITUS	
68	Paul martyred at Rome	Nero committed suicide Galba emperor 68-69 Vitellius emperor 69 Vespasian emperor 69-79
70	Destruction of Jerusalem; twenty-five years of silence	
81		Domitian becomes emperor (81-96) Begins to perse-cute Christians (81)
95	John in Asia Writes his Gospel and 1, 2, 3 JOHN	
96	John writes REVELATION	
98	John martyred	
100	Death of Herod Agrippa II (the last "King" of the Jews) at Rome	

4
Symbols in the Bible

Given below is a glossary of the major symbols used in Scripture, together with some of the references where they are found and also their suggested meanings. The significance of any given symbol is always determined ultimately by the context in which it is employed.

Abomination: Word is used to epitomize all kinds of idolatrous worship. The "abomination of desolation" is the great image of the Beast (the Devil's messiah), which will be set up, by instigation of the false prophet, in the rebuilt Jewish temple in Jerusalem (1 Kings 11:5-7; Ezekiel 8:5-6; Daniel 9:27; 11:31; Matthew 24:15).

Adamant: Fixed hardness toward God. We use the word in everyday speech to symbolize hardness when we say, for example, "He was adamant in his decision" (compare Ezekiel 3:9).

Adder: Spiritual and moral evil. Like the serpent it is often outwardly attractive and fascinating, but it is swift, secret, and deadly when it strikes (Genesis 49:17; Psalm 140:3; Proverbs 23:32).

Adultery: Marital unfaithfulness. Used symbolically, it represents spiritual unfaithfulness to God. It is used especially to symbolize Israel's unfaithfulness to Jehovah when the nation became involved in idolatry. It is also used to depict worldliness in the Christian (Jeremiah 3:8-9; Ezekiel 23:36-37; James 4:4).

Air: Moral and spiritual influences that act on mankind. It is Satan's sphere of operation as "the prince of the power of the air" (Ephesians 2:2; Revelation 9:2; 16:17).

Almonds: Early blooming tree. Aaron's rod, when laid up before the Lord, bore miraculous almonds as proof of his position as Israel's high priest. Almonds symbolize fruitfulness, but particularly that fruitfulness which is the result of our new life in Christ—fruitfulness because of resurrection, the fruit of the Spirit (Exodus 25:33-34; Numbers 17:8).

Altar, brazen: Jewish altar in the outer court of the tabernacle and Temple. Sacred fires continually burned on this altar and many of the sacrifices were offered there. It symbolizes judgment on sin and particularly speaks of Christ taking the place of judgment on the sinner's behalf (Exodus 27:1-8).

Altar, golden: Altar by the veil in the holy place of the tabernacle and Temple. Incense was burned on this altar. It symbolizes worship and speaks particularly of Christ in His perfect humanity and deity as the One who upholds the believer's worship (Exodus 30:1-10).

Anchor: Security. It symbolizes confidence because it is linked with the finished work of Christ. Our hope is said to be anchored within the veil. That is, it derives its strength from Christ Himself in the glory (Hebrews 6:19).

Angel: A messenger. A divine or Satanic representative of great influence and power (the context determines which is meant). Usually angels are referred to in a literal rather than a symbolic sense (Matthew 18:10). Some think they are mentioned symbolically in the letters to the seven churches (Revelation 2, 3).

Anoint: To consecrate and thus bestow power (Exodus 29:7; Leviticus 8:10-12; Acts 10:38; 2 Corinthians 1:21; 1 John 2:27).

Apples: Fruit of divine righteousness. The apple as a symbol of temptation is unscriptural. It assumes that in the garden of Eden it was an apple that Eve gave to Adam to eat. "Apples of gold in pictures of silver" represent something rare and costly—divine righteousness (gold) enhanced by the atonement (silver) (Proverbs 25:11).

Apple trees: Christ as the bridegroom. The apple tree stands in contrast with the forest trees, which bear no edible fruit (Song of Solomon 2:3; 8:5).

Ark, Noah's: Salvation provided for mankind through the atoning work of Christ. The ark is usually mentioned literally in Scripture. There may be a symbolic reference in 1 Peter 3:19-21.

Arm: Connotes strength and power, either human or divine. A similar thought is connected with the finger and the hand. The creation of the universe is attributed to God's fingers. How much power is implied then in His hand and in His arm (Psalm 10:15; Isaiah 53:10).

Ark of the covenant: Sacred chest kept in the holy of holies. It contained Aaron's rod that budded, a pot of manna miraculously preserved from decay, and the tables of stone on which were engraved the Mosaic law. The ark symbolizes Christ in His human (acacia wood) and divine (gold) nature; Christ, in whose heart ever resided God's unbroken law; Christ, who meets all His people's needs. The ark is also a symbol for God's throne, since the Shekinah glory cloud rested on the mercy seat which covered the ark (Exodus 25:10-12; Psalm 132:8, Revelation 11:19).

Arrows: Judgment, chastening, war (Job 6:4; Psalm 7:13).

Ashes: Indication of a spent fire. Ashes cannot be rekindled into flame. They symbolize sin judged. They also symbolize deep humiliation and thorough self-judgment (Numbers 19:9-19; Job 42:6).

Ass: Common beast of burden. The firstborn colt of the ass had to be redeemed with a lamb or else slain. It symbolizes man as he is by nature, stubborn and ungovernable as well as unclean (Exodus 13:13; Job 11:12).

Babe: Term for spiritual immaturity in a Christian. Undeveloped and therefore unhealthy (1 Corinthians 3:1; Hebrews 5:12-14).

Babylon: Human rebellion against God, first organized at Babylon. Idolatry originated there. All human history will again focus in Babylon. The rebuilt city will become the Beast's capital. It is used symbolically to represent ecclesiastical apostasy (Revelation 17:18).

Badgers' skins: Outer covering of the tabernacle. In actual fact this covering was made of seal skins, the rendering "badgers' skins" in the King James text being poor. There was nothing attractive about this skin to the eye, although it both concealed and protected. It symbolized defense against various forms of evil. It also depicts Christ (Ezekiel 16:10; Exodus 26:14).

Balances: Man measured and weighed by God. A time of famine (Daniel 5:27; Revelation 6:5-6).

Bear: Powerful and destructive foe. It particularly symbolizes the Persian empire. The bear raised up on one side symbolizes the lopsided Medo-Persian alliance in which the Persian predominated (Daniel 7:5).

Beard: Male facial hair, symbolizing human energy displayed (Leviticus 14:9; 2 Samuel 10:5).

Beast: Man acting in carnal energy and in independence of God. Imperial power acting in independence of God. Gentile world power. The coming Antichrist (Daniel 4:16; Daniel 7; Revelation 13). In Peter's vision (Acts 10:9-16) the unclean beasts represented the Gentiles whom religious Jews regarded as ceremonially unclean and whose company they avoided.

Bees: Numerous enemies. The Assyrian (sometimes a symbol of the coming world Gentile power) in a future judgment of Israel (Deuteronomy 1:44; Psalm 118:12; Isaiah 7:18).

Bells: Worn on the edge of the high priestly robe of the ephod. They symbolize the Holy Spirit's testimony to Christ's acceptance within the veil. When the high priest of Israel entered into the holy of holies on the Day of Atonement the people waiting outside knew he was still alive (and therefore was accepted by God on Israel's behalf) by the tinkling of the bells on his ephod (Exodus 28:33-34; 39:25-26).

Belly: Physical appetite. In Nebuchadnezzar's dream, the belly of the image represented the coming Grecian empire (Daniel 2:32, 39; Romans 16:18).

Billows: Overwhelming sorrows, especially those brought on by God's judgment (Psalm 42:7; Jonah 2:3).

Birds: Agents for good or evil. Demons, Satan, spiritual wickedness (Isaiah 31:5; Matthew 13:4,19; Revelation 18:2).

Black: Mourning. Moral evil. Famine (Jeremiah 4:28; Revelation 6:5).

Blindness: Inability to see spiritual truth (2 Corinthians 4:4; Revelation 3:17).

Blood: Life forfeited by sin but claimed by God. In the Levitical sacrifices, the blood of the animal symbolized Christ's blood shed on the cross. The pollutions of human nature. Fearful slaughter. Divine judgment (Genesis 4:10; Leviticus 17:10-14; Revelation 14:20).

Blue: Heavenly character. Blue was the predominant color in the coverings and curtains of the tabernacle (Exodus 26:1,31).

Book: Record of judgment. Record of Christian behavior. Register of true believers in eternity. Title deeds of earth (Revelation 3:5; 10:2; 13:8).

Bosom: Place of affection and rest. "Abraham's bosom" was the Hebrew expression for the place where the blessed dead resided (Luke 16:23; John 1:18).

Bow: Far-reaching conflict. Deceit and falsehood (Jeremiah 9:3; Revelation 6:2).

Brass: Used in the brazen altar (which symbolizes Christ's bearing the fires of God's wrath in judgment at Calvary). Hence, symbolically, brass stands for judgment. It also symbolizes strength and endurance. The Greek empire of Alexander was symbolized by brass. The word rendered "brass" should probably be translated "copper" (Exodus 36:38; Psalm 107:16; Daniel 2:39; Zechariah 6:1; Micah 4:13).

Bread: The incarnate Son of God. Sustenance. Christ as the means of communion for His people (i.e., the one loaf), or Jehovah as the means of communion for Israel (the twelve loaves on the table in the tabernacle). All kinds of food (Leviticus 24:5-9; John 6; 1 Corinthians 10:17).

Breasts: Fruitfulness (Genesis 49:25; Isaiah 66:11).

Breastplate: Shield for the heart. Hence it symbolizes one's moral state (Ephesians 6:14; 1 Thessalonians 5:8).

Bridle: Divine or moral restraint imposed on human nature (Psalm 32:9; Isaiah 30:28; James 3:2).

Brimstone: Divine wrath and judgment (Job 18:15; Revelation 14:10).

Buckler (shield): Protection, especially that given by God (Psalm 18:2).

Bullock: Christ as a sacrifice offered to God in all the strength and power of His perfect humanity. A bullock was the biggest and most expensive of the sacrifices which could be brought for the burnt offering (Leviticus 7). As such it symbolizes the believer's mature appreciation, apprehension, and appropriation of the work of Christ (Leviticus 1:1-5; 16:3).

Bulls: Unfeeling, powerful enemies (Psalm 22:12; Jeremiah 50:11).

Camp: Judaism. The rules, rites, and regulations of religion from which the believer is to separate himself (Hebrews 13:13).

Candle: Artificial light (Revelation 22:5). The seven candlesticks (Revelation 1:12-20) symbolized seven local churches.

Candlestick, golden: One of the pieces in the holy place of the tabernacle and the Temple. It symbolized the beauty of Christ illuminated by the Holy Spirit (Exodus 26:35; 37:17).

Carpenters: God's agents for the judgment of the Gentile nations which oppress Israel (Zechariah 1:20,21).

Caterpillars: Numerous destructive enemies (Jeremiah 51:14; Joel 1:4).

Cedar: Human greatness. It speaks of man as displayed to his best advantage and in his fairest, most impressive form. Greatness (Leviticus 14:4-6; Numbers 19:6; Ezekiel 17:1-10; 31:1-18).

Chariots: Imperial or divine powers (2 Kings 6:16-17; Psalm 68-17; Isaiah 66:15).

Cherubim: Supernatural beings associated with God's creatorial and redemptive rights. They symbolize the moral character of God's government administered in justice and in judgment (Genesis 3:24; Exodus 37:7; 1 Kings 6:28; Ezekiel 10:5).

Cisterns: Human or divine resources (Jeremiah 2:13; Isaiah 36:16).

City: Often symbolizes mankind gathered in corporate defiance of God. Cain built the first city (Genesis 4:17) and named it after his son Enoch ("Initiated"). The builders of Babel expressed their defiance of God by building a city and a tower (Genesis 11:4). They wished to build a world society from which God was excluded. Cities in the Bible sometimes symbolize refuge. In the Apocalypse a city symbolizes the capital of the revived Roman empire and also the Church in both its glorified and apostate forms (Proverbs 18:11; Revelation 16:19; 17:5; 21:2).

Clay: Human mortality. The brittleness of human empire apart from God (Psalm 40:2; Daniel 2:33,41; Romans 9:21).

Clouds: The presence of God with His glory veiled (Exodus 24:15-18; Luke 9:35).

Colors: Various glories. The tabernacle colors symbolize Christ: the blue depicts Him as Son of God, the scarlet as Son of man (He was the "last Adam"; the name Adam means "red"). The purple was a perfect blend of blue and scarlet and thus symbolized the nature of Christ in which both humanity and deity are perfectly mixed (Exodus 26:31).

Cords: Restraint, human or divine. The drawing power of love (Psalm 2:3; Hosea 11:4).

Corn, old: Christ in all His fullness enjoyed by His people (Joshua 5:11).

Crown: Sovereignty, power, kingly authority. Delegated authority. The believer's rewards for faithful service (the crown of gold for all the redeemed; also the martyr's crown of life, the crown of righteousness for faithful service and witness, the crown of glory for the faithful shepherd) (Ezekiel 16:12; 2 Timothy 4:8; 1 Peter 5:4; Revelation 2:10; 4:4-10; 9:7; 19:12).

Cup: Symbol of God's wrath, to be given to the sinner to drink. Thus the Lord prayed that "the cup" might pass from Him. It can also be a symbol of God's favor given to the believer to enjoy (Psalm 75:8; 23:5).

Curtains: Symbol of those beauties and glories of Christ not seen by the outsider. The curtains of the tabernacle were of rich colors and made of fine linen (Exodus 26:1). They hung inside the tabernacle and were not visible from the outside. The unbeliever's view of Christ is stated in Isaiah 53:2: "There is no beauty [in him] that we should desire him." Believers see Christ quite differently, especially when they have learned the inner secrets of true worship.

Darts, fiery: Sharp and sudden temptations (Ephesians 6:16).

Death: God's judgment on fallen man (Revelation 6:7-8).

Dog: An expression of contempt. An epithet often reserved by the Jews for Gentiles. Uncleanness. Persons without either feeling or conscience. Satan (Psalm 22:16; Proverbs 26:11; Matthew 15:27; Philippians 3:2).

Door: A means of access. God-given opportunity and opening for service. That which keeps Christ out of the life (1 Corinthians 16:9; Revelation 3:8,20).

Dove: Harmlessness, spotlessness. The Holy Spirit (Psalm 68:13; Matthew 3:16; 10:16).

Dragon: Egyptian power expressing itself in cruelty. Satan (Ezekiel 29:2-3; Revelation 12:13).

Drunkenness: Insensibility to moral responsibility and divine judgment. Carnal excitement. Surrender to an influence opposite to that of the Holy Spirit (Isaiah 29:9; Ephesians 5:18).

Dung: Complete contempt and abhorrence. Jezebel's name means "dunghill" (Malachi 2:3; Philippians 3:8).

Dust: Total humiliation. Nothingness. Human mortality (Psalm 22:15; Daniel 12:2).

Eagle: The symbol of strength, safety, tenderness, and care. Heavenly power and dignity. Judgment from on high. The king of Babylon. The king of Egypt (Exodus 19:4; Deuteronomy 32:11; Job 39:27-30; Ezekiel 17:3,7, Luke 17:37).

Ear: Human or divine attention. The pierced ear of the Hebrew slave pictured devoted surrender and obedience (Exodus 21:1-6; Psalm 34:15; Revelation 2, 3).

Earth: The nation of Israel (Revelation 10:2; 13:11).

Earthquake: Social and political upheavals among the nations (Isaiah 29:6; Revelation 6:12; 16:18).

Eating: Communion and fellowship. The personal appropriation of Christ (Matthew 26:26; Acts 11:3-9; 1 Corinthians 10:16).

Eyes: Intelligence, perception, direction, or guidance (Numbers

10:31; 2 Chronicles 16:9; Psalm 123:2). The seven eyes of the Lamb speak of Christ's omniscience (Revelation 5).

Face: Intelligence. God's presence (Exodus 33:13-23; Ezekiel 1:10; Revelation 9:7).

Fat: Fruitfulness, plenty, abundance (Numbers 13:20; Psalm 63:5; 119:70; Isaiah 6:10). The fat of the sacrifices was always given to God. It symbolizes Christ's inner excellence which led Him to the cross in obedience to God (Leviticus 1:8). Since *fatness* pictures self-indulgence run to excess, fat is oftentimes used in the Bible as a symbol of complete insensibility toward God.

Feet: The walk and ways of the believer. To be put under the feet symbolizes total subjection (John 13:1-10; Romans 16:20; 1 Corinthians 15:27).

Fig tree: Security, prosperity, and blessing. The fig tree is one of the symbols of the nation of Israel. It stands for the condition of Israel between the time of Christ's rejection by the nation and His return (Judges 9:10-11; Hosea 9:10; Matthew 24:32).

Fire: Judgment. Purification. The Holy Spirit. God's word in action (Malachi 3:2; Jeremiah 23:29; Matthew 25:41; Acts 2:3).

Firstborn: Rank or dignity. The position of the firstborn did not always go to the one born first (e.g., Ishmael and Isaac, Esau and Jacob, Ephraim and Manasseh). As it applies to Christ, the symbol speaks of His preeminence (Psalm 89:27; Colossians 1:15).

Fish: Symbol of the Church among the early Christians, although not so used in Scripture except by vague inference (from John 21:11 or Matthew 4:19). Fish also symbolize the scattered Jewish people in the last days (Jeremiah 16:16; Ezekiel 29:4-5).

Flame: Hell. The severity of God's judgment (Isaiah 29:6; Luke 16:24).

Flesh: Human nature, principle in man that is essentially and determinedly opposed to God. Sometimes the flesh is used to symbolize human life as such. It also symbolizes humankind in general (Genesis 6:3; Luke 3:6; Romans 7:5; Galatians 5:16-19; Philippians 1:22).

Forehead, marked: Symbolizes the setting apart or dedication of an individual for God or for some evil purpose. The mark of the Beast will be stamped either on the hand or the forehead. The mark on the hand may symbolize the working classes whereas the mark on the forehead may symbolize the world's intelligentsia (Ezekiel 9:4; Revelation 14:9; 13:16).

Forest: Kingdom, or the great ones of the earth (Isaiah 10:18-19; Jeremiah 21:14; Ezekiel 20:46).

Fornication: Worldliness, spiritual wickedness (Revelation 2:20-21; 17:2).

Foundation: Something permanent and secure. Christ as the One upon whom His people rest and upon whom they build for eternity (Isaiah 28:16; 1 Corinthians 3:11-12; 2 Timothy 2:19).

Fountains: Sources of life or refreshment. Resurrection life (Isaiah 41:18; Revelation 8:10).

Fowls: The great ones of earth. Instruments of destruction. Evil spirits (Isaiah 18:6; Ezekiel 31:6; Matthew 13:32).

Fox: Crafty or cunning people. Christ called Herod a fox (Ezekiel 13:4; Luke 13:32).

Frankincense: Speaks of fragrance, particularly of the Lord Jesus Christ in the fragrance of His life as that fragrance was known and appreciated by God Himself. Not to be confused with the incense from which frank*incense* was an ingredient. Scripture does not tell us how the frankincense was derived. It was added to the offerings (Exodus 30:34; Leviticus 2:2).

Furnace: Deep trial and suffering. Affliction. Divine judgment (Deuteronomy 4:20; Isaiah 48:10; Matthew 13:42; Revelation 1:15).

Garden: Paradise. The kingdoms and powers of this world. Something set apart for private enjoyment (Song of Solomon 4:12; Ezekiel 36:35; 31:8-9).

Garments: Personal and practical holiness (Exodus 28:40-43; Revelation 3:4; 16:15).

Gate: In Bible times the seat of government. A symbol of security, access (Genesis 19:1; Revelation 21:12-13).

Girdle: Readiness for service. Also a symbol of restraint (Exodus 29:9; Psalm 109:19; Revelation 1:13; 15:6).

Goat: Alexander the Great, the Grecian conqueror. The great sin offering used especially on the Day of Atonement. Those alive at Christ's return who will be banished eternally from His presence because of their treatment of the Jews (Leviticus 16:7; Daniel 8:21; Matthew 25:32-33).

Goat's hair: One of the outer coverings of the tabernacle. It symbolizes Christ's ability to separate from evil (Exodus 25:4; 26:7; 35:6).

Gog and Magog: The future Russian leader and his country, thus named in Ezekiel 38 and 39. The expression is used symbolically in the Apocalypse to depict those who will join Satan in his last rebellion against Christ. Russia's defiance of God and consequent aggression against Israel and her utter defeat will doubtless be remembered long afterward; the expression "Gog and Magog" will become synonymous with anti-Semitism, God-hate, and disaster.

Gold: Widely used in the construction of both the tabernacle and the Temple. It symbolizes Christ. Also it stands for divine righteousness, for deity, for the Lord's divine nature (Exodus 25:11,18,24).

Grapes, ripe: Apostates ripe for judgment. Fruit for God (Isaiah 5:1-7; Revelation 14:18).

Grass: The masses of mankind. Prosperity of a fleeting kind (James 1:10-11; Revelation 8:7).

Grasshoppers: Personal insignificance. Numerous enemies (Numbers 13:33; Judges 6:5; Isaiah 40:22).

Hailstones: Severe judgment from on high (Isaiah 30:30).

Hair, long: Subjection, glory. The woman's glory and attractiveness. In the case of the Nazarite it symbolized subjection to God. Once his Nazarite vow expired, the Jew had to cut off his distinguishing hair and burn it. He was not to glory in a past dedication (1 Corinthians 11:15; Revelation 9:8).

Hand, right: The place of power and privilege. Security. Judgment (Exodus 15:6; Psalm 45:4-5; Mark 16:19; Hebrews 10:12).

Hands: Actions. Service. Human or divine work (Psalms 90:17; 73:13).

Harlot: A depraved and corrupting religious system or people (Ezekiel 16:1-63; Hosea 3:1-5; Revelation 17:5).

Harvest: The outcome of earlier actions. Discriminating judgment (Matthew 13:30; Revelation 14:15).

Head: Supreme authority. Christ as the One who controls the Church. Nebuchadnezzar. The seat of government, intelligence, and power in man (Isaiah 7:8-9; Zechariah 6:11; 1 Corinthians 11:3-10; Colossians 1:18).

Heart: The seat of feelings and emotions (Proverbs 6:18; Luke 6:45; 24:25; John 12:40).

Heaven: God's home. The abode of the redeemed (Matthew 24:29; Revelation 6:13; 8:10).

Heavenly places: The "heavenlies." Realm where the Christian's battles and blessings are located and where Satan and his hosts hold sway (Ephesians 1:3; 6:12).

Helmet: Assurance of salvation (Ephesians 6:17; 1 Thessalonians 5:8).

Herbs: Bitter herbs, used in connection with the Passover. They symbolize judgment of evil and its bitterness (Exodus 12:8; Deuteronomy 11:10).

Hill: Seat of royal or divine government. Something that cannot be moved apart from God's power (Psalm 2:6; 24:3).

Hind: Agility. Liberty. Affection (2 Samuel 22:34; Psalm 18:33; Song of Solomon 2:7; 3:5).

Honey: Natural sweetness. It was not to be included in the offerings. Natural affection (Leviticus 2:11; Psalm 119:103; Revelation 10:10).

Hooks (taches): Hardware connected with the tabernacle and made of gold and silver. They symbolize security. The security of the believer is linked to the person of Christ (gold) and the finished work of Christ (silver, always a symbol of redemption). (See Exodus 26:6, 36:13,18).

Horns: Kings. Two "little horns" are mentioned in Daniel. One symbolizes Antiochus Epiphanes and the other Antichrist, both kings of great power. Horns symbolize power, strength, and glory (Psalm 75:10; Daniel 7:8; 8:9; Revelation 5:6; 13:1).

Horses: War. Successful power in war (Zechariah 6:1-8; Revelation 6:1-8).

Hunger, thirst: Intense desire, either spiritual or physical (Psalm 42:2; Matthew 5:6; John 6:35).

Hyssop: Bushy herb common in the East. It was used to apply the blood of the Passover lamb to the door posts of the Hebrew homes in Egypt. It was also used in connection with the cleansing of the leper. It therefore is associated with man in his worst condition (Leviticus 14:4; Numbers 19:6; Psalm 51:7).

Idolatry: Anything that takes precedence over God in a person's life (1 Corinthians 10:14; compare Philippians 3:19; Colossians 3:5; 1 John 5:21).

Image, graven: Idol, made to represent either the true or a false God (Genesis 1:26; Acts 19:35; Colossians 1:15).

Incense: Prayer ascending to God. Christ in the fragrance of His person as He offered Himself to God (Leviticus 16:13; Revelation 5:8).

Indignation: The coming time of Israel's judicial punishment at God's hand (Isaiah 10:25; 26:20).

Iron: The Roman empire. Strength, irresistible power. A hardened conscience. One day the Lord is to rule the nations with a rod of iron, symbolic of His inflexible righteousness and suppression of evil (Job 40:18; Psalm 2:9; Daniel 2:40; 1 Timothy 4:2).

Jasper: Precious stone. It signifies the display of God's glory (Revelation 4:3; 21:11,18).

Jewels: The preciousness of the believer to God. Marks of God's favor (Isaiah 61:10; Ezekiel 16:17; Malachi 3:17).

Key: Authority. The right to exercise divine authority. Government (Isaiah 22:22; Matthew 16:19; Revelation 1:18).

Kidneys: Considered by the Hebrews to be the seat of feeling and affection (Leviticus 9:10,19).

Kings: Government. Power. The royal dignity of the Lord's people (Revelation 1:6; 5:10; 17:12).

Kiss: Human or divine expression of love (Luke 15:20; 1 Corinthians 16:20; 1 Peter 5:14).

Knee, bended: Submission. Reverence (Ephesians 3:14; Philippians 2:10).

Ladder: Christ, the one link between earth and heaven (Genesis 28:12; John 1:51).

Lamb: Gentleness, meekness, tenderness, yieldedness. Sacrifice. Supremely the lamb symbolizes the Lord Jesus in His sufferings and glory. The expression "little lamb" occurs twenty-eight times in the Apocalypse in connection with the glorified and mighty Lord Jesus. It is preeminently His apocalyptical title (Isaiah 53:7; Luke 10:3; Acts 8:32; Revelation 5:6-7).

Laver: Large wash basin. The brazen altar stood for a radicial cleansing from sin: cleansing by blood. The laver stood for a recurrent cleansing from sin: cleansing by the washing of water of the Word (as in Psalm 119:9). No measurements were given for the laver; there is no limit or measure to our need for daily and continual cleansing. There is no laver in the heavenly temple. Instead, there is a sea of glass, depicting fixed holiness. Christ is symbolized by the laver and the Word of God by the water (Ephesians 5:26).

Lead: Judgment of evil (Exodus 15:10; Zechariah 5:7-8).

Leaf: Empty profession of spiritual things. The fig tree brought forth only leaves, no fruit. Leaves also symbolize spiritual freshness and life. They likewise symbolize millennial blessing and healing (Psalm 1:3; Matthew 21:19; Revelation 22:2).

Leaven: In Scripture, uniformly a symbol of a secret, active, corrupting evil. Moral and doctrinal evil. Some have wrongly taken the leaven in the parable of Matthew 13:33-35 to symbolize the gospel. (Matthew 16:6; 1 Corinthians 5:5-8; Galatians 5:9).

Legs: The Roman empire, especially after its east-west division. Stability. Strength (Psalm 147:10; Song of Solomon 5:15; Daniel 2:33).

Leopard: The Grecian empire and its swift, powerful conquests (Daniel 7:6).

Leprosy: Sin. The stroke of God. The Hebrews regarded leprosy as a special manifestation of God's displeasure. King Uzziah was smitten with this disease for his presumption in seeking to unite in his person the offices of priest and king. Symbolically, leprosy stands for uncleanness in heart and life (Leviticus 13:14).

Lightning: God's presence in power and judgment. Obedience. The coming of Christ (Ezekiel 1:13; Daniel 10:6; Zechariah 9:14; Matthew 24:27; Revelation 4:5; 8:5).

Lily: Loveliness. Virgin purity (Matthew 6:28; Song of Solomon 2:1-2).

Linen: Christ in all His personal purity. The personal purity and righteousness of believers (Revelation 15:6; 19:5-14).

Lion: The Babylonian empire. Christ. Satan. Majesty and royal power (Daniel 7:4; 1 Peter 5:8; Revelation 5:5).

Loaves: Symbol of the Church as it actually is. On the day of Pentecost, Israel annually took two loaves and presented them to the Lord. These contained leaven. In its actual state, the Church on earth has never been entirely free from sin. It took two loaves to symbolize what happened when the day of Pentecost fully came: the Church formed on the day of Pentecost consisted solely of Jews, but later the Gentiles were brought in. Now there is but one loaf (1 Corinthians 10:17).

Locusts: Numerous foes. Total and far-reaching destruction. Demonic hordes (Psalm 78:46; Joel 1:4; Revelation 9:3-7).

Loins: Inner strength. Loins girt symbolize resolution of soul (Luke 12:35; Ephesians 6:14).

Manna: Christ, especially in His humility. Christ as food for His people during their sojourn in this world (Exodus 16:15; John 6:31,49).

Measuring: Appropriation. Possession (Zechariah 2:2; Ezekiel 40; Revelation 11:1; 21:15).

Meal offering: Symbol of Christ in the perfection and evenness of His human nature as it was offered up to God. The translation "meat offering" is faulty. (Exodus 29:41; Leviticus 2:1).

Meat: Christ in His strength and fullness as food for the believer's new nature. The carnal and spiritually underdeveloped Christian cannot appropriate Christ in this way (John 6:27,55; 1 Corinthians 10:3).

Mercy seat: Golden covering of the sacred ark of the covenant. It was fashioned of one solid piece of gold together with likenesses of the cherubim. It was sprinkled with blood on the Day of Atonement. The cherubim gazed inward and downward on the blood and thus, symbolically, were occupied with the finished work of Christ. The Shekinah glory cloud rested on the mercy seat, which symbolizes God's throne. It also stands for Christ, the true mercy seat today (Exodus 25:21,22; Leviticus 16:15; compare Romans 3:24,25).

Mire: Pollutions of this world. Total moral degradation (Isaiah 10:6; 2 Peter 2:22).

Milk: Elementary truth for babes in Christ (immature Christians), in contrast to "meat" (1 Corinthians 3:1,2; Hebrews 5:12).

Moon: Delegated authority. Ruling, possibly religious, powers. The Church. The moon has no light of its own. It shines by reflecting the light of the sun. The new moon symbolizes Israel's reappearance in a coming day and her assumption of rule (Genesis 1:16; Song of Solomon 6:10; Revelation 8:12; 12:1).

Mother: Religion. A source of either religious corruption or blessing (Galatians 4:22-31; Revelation 2:20; 17:5).

Mountain: National power. The great mountain burning with fire of Revelation 8:8 symbolizes a nation consumed with fierce and militant energy. A mountain generally symbolizes political or moral stability or greatness, especially as those qualities are expressed nationally (Daniel 2:35; Jeremiah 51:25; Psalm 125:1-2).

Mustard seed: Something small and insignificant in itself. The parable of the mustard seed in Matthew 13:31,32 derives its force from the fact that such a small seed grows into a tree-size herb. (compare Matthew 17:20).

Nail: Something steadfast and firmly fixed (Isaiah 22:23-25; Zechariah 10:4).

Nakedness: Spiritual poverty. It also signifies the state of those without Christ (2 Corinthians 5:3; Revelation 3:17-18).

Net: A trap (Psalm 9:15; Proverbs 1:17; Habakkuk 1:16).

Nurse: Affection (1 Thessalonians 2:7).

Oak: Power and prosperity (Isaiah 1:30; Amos 2:9).

Oil: The Holy Spirit (Matthew 25:4).

Olive tree: The nation of Israel in its greatness after the return of Christ. Abundant fruitfulness for God (Judges 9:8-9; Jeremiah 11:16; Romans 11:17-24).

Ostrich: Parental neglect. Cruelty (Job 39:13-17; Lamentations 4:3).

Oven: Fierce judgment (Psalm 21:9; Malachi 4:1).

Owl: In the Bible, a symbol of solitariness in suffering. The popular notion of an owl as a wise bird is not found in Scripture (Psalm 102:6; Micah 1:8).

Oxen: Patience. Strength and ability to labor for others (Psalm 144:14; 1 Corinthians 9:9; 1 Timothy 5:18). The ox is a symbol for Christ.

Palm tree: Victory. Palms were used to celebrate Christ's triumphant entrance into Jerusalem. Palms also symbolize the righteous, especially in their spiritual growth and health. (Psalm 92:12; John 12:13; Revelation 7:9).

Paradise: A pleasure garden, Persian in etymology. In Ecclesiastes 2:5 the word *orchards* is *paradesim,* i.e., "parks" or "pleasure grounds." Such paradises were made by oriental monarchs. The garden of Eden is thus commonly called "Paradise." It symbolizes heaven, God's home (Luke 23:43; 2 Corinthians 12:4).

Pearl: Symbolizes Christ in His sufferings; pearl-formation is the oyster's response to injury. The gates of pearl in the celestial city show the vastness of Christ's sufferings, which alone give access to Glory. Pearl also stands for the Church in all its preciousness and beauty (Matthew 13:46; Revelation 21:21).

Pillars: Strength and stability. The ability to support and uphold (Galatians 2:9; 1 Timothy 3:15; Revelation 3:12).

Plow, plowing: Spiritual labor. Work calling for patience, skill, and concentration. To ensure a straight furrow, the plowman fixes his gaze on an object at the opposite side of the field and never takes his eye off it while making a furrow. (Luke 9:62; 1 Corinthians 9:10).

Plumbline: Judgment (Amos 7:7-8).

Pomegranates: A fruit full of seeds and therefore a symbol of fruitfulness. Artificial pomegranates were attached to the garment of the high priest of Israel to remind him that his life was to be fruitful for God (Exodus 28:33-34; Song of Solomon 4:13).

Potter: God as sovereign over human beings and their circumstances (Psalm 2:9; Jeremiah 18:1-10; Romans 9:21).

Pounds: Divinely bestowed gifts to be used for others (Luke 19:13).

Pricks: A goad. Sharp troubles, adverse circumstances (Numbers 33:55; Acts 9:5).

Purple: Royalty. In the veil of the tabernacle and the Temple the colors scarlet, blue, and purple were used to depict the person of Christ. The harlot is shown wearing purple to depict the assumption of worldly, regal power by the false church (Exodus 26:36; John 19:2; Revelation 18:16).

Race: The Christian life. A race must be run according to the rules; otherwise, all the energy expended is invalidated (1 Corinthians 9:24; Hebrews 12:1).

Rain: Revival. Blessing from on high. Times of refreshing brought by the Holy Spirit (Deuteronomy 32:2; Psalm 84:6; Hebrews 6:7).

Ram: The Medo-Persian empire. Christ offering Himself in consecration to God in all His maturity and strength. Consecration (Leviticus 8:22; Daniel 8:6).

Rams' skins: Dyed red, used as one of the coverings of the tabernacle. They symbolize Christ's death as the covering for His people (Exodus 25:5; 26:14).

Red: The color of blood, symbolizing bloodshed and judgment. It also symbolizes man's sin as seen by God (Isaiah 1:18; Revelation 6:4).

Reed: Weakness, fragility, worthlessness, especially a broken reed (Isaiah 36:6; Matthew 11:7). It is said of the Lord Jesus that He will not crush a broken reed nor quench a smoking flax (used as a wick in a lamp). The smoking flax symbolizes something once useful but now impaired; a broken reed symbolizes something that never was of any use. Thus the Lord shows His mercy to the backslider and sinner alike.

Reins: Kidneys. The Hebrews ascribed knowledge, joy, pain, and pleasure to the reins. They therefore symbolize our inward thoughts and feelings (Psalm 26:2; Jeremiah 11:20; Revelation 2:23).

Ring: Authority. Love. The eternal. Honor (Genesis 41:42; Esther 8:8; Luke 15:22).

River: Spiritual blessing. Also the Holy Spirit (Psalm 1:3; John 7:38; Revelation 22:1-2).

Robe: Righteousness (Jeremiah 51:10; Luke 15:22; Revelation 6:11).

Rock: Christ. Something firm and immovable. A foundation. Some interpreters take the rock in Matthew 16:18 to refer to Peter's confession, although others think it to be Christ Himself in contrast with Peter, whose name means "pebble" (Deuteronomy 8:15; 32:31; Matthew 7:24). What the Lord said to Peter was: "Thou art Peter (*petros,* a pebble); on this rock (petra) I will build my church." The word *petra* is also the name of an ancient rock city in Edom.

Rod: Power and authority. Chastisement or judgment. A tribe or people (Psalm 2:9; 23:4; Hebrews 9:4).

Rose: Israel. The Church. Beauty and fragrance (Song of Solomon 2:1).

Salt: An agent for arresting corruption. Before the days of refrigeration, meat was preserved with salt. Salt also symbolizes sound speech. It stands for what is enduring (Matthew 5:13; Colossians 4:6).

Sand: An innumerable multitude. Abraham's seed was compared with the sand of the seashore (Genesis 22:17; Revelation 20:8).

Sapphire: Blue gemstone, symbolizing the glory of God's throne (Exodus 24:10; Ezekiel 1:26).

Scarlet: Man's sin as seen by God. Human pomp and glory (Numbers 4:8; Revelation 17:3-4; 18:16).

Sceptre: Sovereignty, power, authority, whether human or divine. Israel in her tribal condition (Genesis 49:10; Psalm 45:6; Amos 1:5).

Scorpion: Something that causes anguish and torment. The locust-scorpions of Revelation are evidently evil spirits that inflict intense mental and spiritual anguish on their victims (Revelation 9:3-10).

Scourge, overflowing scourge: One of the terrors Israel can anticipate in the last days. Symbolic reference to a great enemy that will threaten Israel from the north, attacking the nation with all its strength at that time (Isaiah 28:15,18). Probably Russia (Ezekiel 38,39).

Sea: The Gentile nations. The first beast of Revelation 13 comes up out of the sea and is therefore probably a Gentile. This is in contrast with the second beast who comes up out of the earth and is therefore probably a Jew. He is called "the false prophet." Wicked people in their unrest and unruliness and uncleanness (Isaiah 57:20; Revelation 8:8; 13:1).

Seal: Ownership. Security. Something that restrains (1 Corinthians 9:2; Ephesians 4:30; 2 Timothy 2:19; Revelation 5:1; 7:2).

Serpent: Satan. Subtlety. Satanic or worldly wisdom (Isaiah 27:1; Revelation 12:9; 20:2).

Sheep: Lost people, a graphic symbol of the sinner. Sheep are not strong, swift, or smart. They easily stray from the fold and are incapable of finding their own way back. They are defenseless against their enemies. Sheep also symbolize the Lord Jesus Himself as well as the Lord's people in their relation to Christ. Many animals have characteristics that illustrate traits of human nature and are introduced as such into the Scriptures (Isaiah 53:6; John 10:3).

Shepherd: Christ. Civil or religious overseers or pastors (Nahum 3:18; Psalm 23:1; Zechariah 13:7, John 10:14; Hebrews 13:20).

Shoes: Walk and witness (Ephesians 6:15). Shoes removed symbolize reverence (Exodus 3:5). In the story of the prodigal son (Luke 15) the father put shoes on his son's feet. Shoes were removed in the Old Testament to depict humility; they are put on in the New Testament to depict position in the family.

Shoulder: The place of strength. Christ needs but one shoulder for the government of the world but two for the lost sheep. The work of redemption is far more weighty than the work of world government (Isaiah 9:6; Luke 15:5).

Silver: The price of redemption. Hence it symbolizes the precious blood of Christ. Silver is also a symbol of the Medo-Persian empire (Daniel 2:32). It stands, too, for human wealth (Proverbs 8:19).

Skin: Outward appearance. In the Old Testament offerings, the skin was given to the priest. It symbolizes Christ in His outward glories, which man can see and appreciate, in contrast with His inner and hidden perfections, which only God could appreciate (Leviticus 7:8).

Sleep: Death. Used symbolically, it refers to the body. Sleep never refers to the soul; the soul never sleeps (1 Corinthians 11:30; 1 Thessalonians 4:14).

Smoke: Judgment. Smoke darkens, blinds, and suffocates. It also indicates the presence of fire (Isaiah 14:31; Revelation 9:2-3; 19:3).

Snow: Purity (Isaiah 1:18; Lamentations 4:7).

Sparrow: God's love for even the humblest creature (Matthew 10:29).

Spices: The attractiveness and fragrance of divine and moral perfections (Exodus 30:23-38; Song of Solomon 4:14).

Staff: Support. Pilgrimage. Power and judgment (Psalm 23:4; Isaiah 14:5; Hebrews 11:21).

Stars: Angelic hosts. Both the stars and the angels are referred to as the hosts of heaven. Stars also symbolize lesser rulers. They stand, too, for guidance (Isaiah 14:13; Revelation 8:12). Christ is "the bright and morning star" (Revelation 8:10; 9:1; 22:16).

Sun: Christ. A supreme ruling power (Malachi 4:2; Revelation 1:16; 8:12).

Supper: The final occasion for fellowship, refreshment, and communion before midnight comes. It can symbolize either grace or judgment (Luke 14:16-24; Revelation 19:9,17).

Swallow: Restlessness, as suggested by the darting flight of the swallow (Psalm 84:3; Proverbs 26:2).

Swine: Uncleanness both in essential character and in practice (Deuteronomy 14:8; 2 Peter 2:22).

Sword: The word of God in its power to penetrate and expose man's innermost thoughts and intentions. War. Judgment. The power of civil rule. The death penalty (Genesis 3:24; Romans 13:4; Hebrews 4:12; Revelation 6:4; 19:15).

Table: Communion and fellowship (Psalm 23:5; 1 Corinthians 10:21).

Tail: False prophets or their teachings (Isaiah 9:14-15; Revelation 9:10).

Talents: Gifts or abilities bestowed for the service of others (Matthew 25:14-30).

Tares: Satan's religious counterfeits (Matthew 13:25).

Teeth: Cruelty. Power (Daniel 7:5-19; Proverbs 30:14; Revelation 9:8).

Tempest: Judgment. Affliction (Job 9:17; Psalm 11:6).

Thighs: Strength. After Jacob's thigh was out of joint, he could no longer wrestle with the angel. The Lord's sword is worn on His thigh (Numbers 5:21; Psalm 45:3; Revelation 19:16). In Nebuchadnezzar's vision the thighs stood for the Grecian empire (Daniel 2:32).

Thorns: Symbol of the curse. Instruments of judgment. Something of no value (Genesis 3:18; Numbers 33:55; Jeremiah 12:13).

Throne: Sovereignty. The seat of authority and rule (Daniel 7:9; Psalm 45:6).

Tongue: Speech. Religious profession. Remorse, torment (Genesis 10:5; Psalm 45:1; 1 Corinthians 13:1).

Tower: Strength. Security (Proverbs 18:10; Zephaniah 3:6).

Travail: Anxiety. Spiritual anguish (Jeremiah 4:31; Galatians 4:19).

Trees: Kings or rulers. People of prominence (Judges 9:8; Daniel 4:10; Revelation 7:1; 9:4).

Trumpet: Clarion call. Judgment. War. Alarm. Summons (Jeremiah 51:27; 1 Corinthians 15:52; 1 Thessalonians 4:16; Revelation 8:6).

Unicorn: Mythical animal. The word so translated in the King James text is probably better translated "wild ox." It symbolizes power, strength, and also the agonies of death (Numbers 23:22; Psalm 22:21).

Veil: Curtain hung between the holy place and the holy of holies in both the tabernacle and the Temple symbolically barring access to God. The veil of the Temple was rent by God when Christ died on the cross; Christ's atoning death removed all that barred the believer from God's immediate presence. It symbolized the fact also that Judaism is obsolete, since, without the veil, all the sacrificial and ceremonial rituals were meaningless (Hebrews 10:20).

Vine: The nation of Israel. Three trees symbolized Israel. The olive anticipates Israel's coming glories in the Millennium; the fig symbolizes Israel between Christ's two advents; the vine symbolizes Israel up to the time of Christ's first advent and His consequent rejection by the nation. Thereafter He proclaimed Himself to be the true Vine (Isaiah 5:1; Jeremiah 12:10; Hosea 10:1; Mark 12:1; John 15:1).

Vipers: Deadly doctrines and their teachers (Matthew 3:7; 12:34).

Virgin: Religious purity. Separation from the world. Spiritual chastity (2 Corinthians 11:22; Revelation 14:4). The ten virgins in the Lord's parable represent the nation of Israel (Matthew 25:1-13).

Vultures: Judgment. Keen vision (Job 28:7; Isaiah 34:15).

Walls: Security (Exodus 14:22; Revelation 21:18).

Water: Water for drinking symbolizes the Holy Spirit. Water for cleansing symbolizes the Word of God. Water also symbolizes human weakness and cleanliness (Psalm 22:14; John 7:38; Ephesians 5:26; Hebrews 10:22). In Revelation 17, water symbolizes the nations.

Waves: Judgment (Psalm 42:7).

Well: Source of satisfaction or blessing (Isaiah 12:3; Psalm 84:6; John 4:14).

Wheat: The Church. True believers (Matthew 3:12; 13:29; John 12:24).

Wheels: Divine government (Proverbs 20:26; Ezekiel 1:15).

Whirlwind: Judgment. God's manifest power (Job 38:1; Proverbs 1:27; Isaiah 66:15; Hosea 8:7).

White: Purity, cleanliness (2 Chronicles 5:2; Psalm 51:7; Revelation 3:4).

Whoredom: Religious apostasy. Spiritual vileness. Idolatry. This symbol derives its strength from the fact that the Canaanite religions, always a snare to Israel, employed temple prostitutes as priestesses in their worship. (Leviticus 19:29; Ezekiel 43:7; Hosea 5:3; Revelation 17:1).

Widow: Desolation (Lamentations 1:1; Revelation 18:7).

Wilderness: Symbol of the world and of a defeated Christian life. A wilderness is also a symbol of affliction and desolation. The wilderness journeys of Israel picture the experiences of the believer in this world while on the way home to heaven. The wilderness *way* was part of the divine plan but the wilderness *wanderings* were a judgment for refusal to enter Canaan. (Song of Solomon 3:6; Revelation 12:6,14).

Wind: The Holy Spirit. God's unseen but felt presence either in grace or judgment. Instability. Intangible and vain expectations (John 3:8; Acts 2:2; Ephesians 4:14; James 1:6; Revelation 6:13; 7:1).

Wine: Joy. Judgment. Natural excitement (Isaiah 55:1; Ephesians 5:18; Revelation 18:13).

Wings: Swiftness of movement. Protection (Daniel 7:4; Isaiah 6:2; Ezekiel 1:6).

Wolves: Cruel enemies of God's people (Acts 20:29).

Woman: Israel. The church, both true and false. Weakness (Jeremiah 6:2; Revelation 12:1; 17:3).

Word, the: Christ (John 1:1-3,14; 1 John 1:1).

Worm: Something contemptible. Death. Eternal remorse (Psalm 22:6; Mark 9:44-48).

Yoke: Restraint. The unequal yoke draws its symbolic value from the unfair practice of yoking together two animals of unequal strength and size. It symbolizes any partnership—business, marital, religious—in which the parties joined together are different in important ways (Matthew 11:29-30; 2 Corinthians 6:14).

5

A Summary of Bible Names

This list contains the more prominent or commonly used names in the Bible. The majority are Old Testament names, which appear to have greater significance than New Testament names— probably because Old Testament names are interwoven with the history of the Hebrew people and hence with the continuing process of divine revelation. Gentile names, unless derived from a Hebrew source, seem to be less significant.

In some cases several alternatives are given. This reflects the uncertainty surrounding the meaning of some of the names, which can be rendered in various ways.

After each name will be found a code number either in Arabic or italicized numerals. This keys the names into the Hebrew and Greek lexicons in the Strong's Concordance and also into Gesenius and Thayer. It will facilitate further study of the names where desired.

Aaron: Enlightened, illuminated (175); High priest of Israel, of the family of Kohath, second son of Levi. Miriam was his older sister, Moses his younger brother. His parents were Amram and Jochebed. His wife was Elisheba. He had four sons: Nadab, Abihu, Eleazar, and Ithamar. He was Israel's first high priest. He died on Mount Hor in Edom at the age of 123.

Abaddon: Destroyer (3); King of the abyss, i.e., the bottomless pit. His name in Greek is Apollyon.

Abana: Permanent, perennial (71); River of Damascus. Its source is 1,150 feet on the Anti-Libanus Mountain. Naaman boasted of this river.

Abdon: Servitude (5658); One of the judges.

Abednego: Servant of Nego (5664); Babylonian name given to Daniel's friend Azariah. He was cast into the burning, fiery furnace.

Abel: Fresh, grassy (59); Place where the Philistines left the ark. Also the name of another place where Joab besieged Sheba.

Abel: Transitory (1893); Second son of Adam and Eve, murdered by his brother Cain.

Abia: God (Jah) is my father (29); Unworthy second son of Samuel. Abia's misbehavior led Israel to desire a king.

Abiathar: Father of the superfluous (54); Eleventh high priest of Israel. He escaped to David when Doeg the Edomite massacred the priests of Nob. He stood by David during the Absalom rebellion but sided with Adonijah and was expelled from the high-priestly office by Solomon.

Abigail: Source of delight (26); Wife of Nabal and, afterward, wife of David. Mother of Amasa, Absalom's captain.

Abihu: He is my father (30); Son of Aaron who, along with his brother Nadab, was destroyed for offering strange fire to God.

Abijah: My father is God (Jah) (29); Son of Rehoboam, whose mother was Maacah, a daughter of Absalom. He succeeded to the throne of Judah. He is also called Abijam. Also the name of several others, including three priests.

Abijam: Father of light (38); Son of Rehoboam who succeeded to the throne of Judah. Also called Abijar.

Abimelech: Father of the king (40); King of Gerar in the time of Abraham and Isaac. A son of Gideon by a concubine. He aspired to be king and was killed by a woman who threw a stone at him. Also the name of several others.

Abinadab: Source of liberality (41); Israelite of the tribe of Judah in whose house near Kirjath-jearim the ark was placed after being returned by the Philistines. Also David's brother, the second son of Jesse. Also a son of King Saul who died at Gilboa along with Jonathan.

Abiram: Father of elevations (48); Reubenite who conspired with Dathan and Korah against Moses and Aaron. He perished. Also the firstborn of Hiel the Bethelite. He died when his father laid the foundations of Jericho.

Abishag: Father of error (i.e., cause of wandering) (49); Woman of Shunem who nursed David in his old age. Adonijah's infatuation with her led to his execution by Solomon.

Abishai: Source of wealth (52); One of David's mighty men. He was David's nephew, son of David's sister Zeruiah, and Joab's brother.

Abner: Father of light (74); Saul's general. He brought the ten tribes to David after being disillusioned in Ishbosheth, Saul's son. He was murdered by Joab.

Abraham: Father of a multitude (85); Youngest son of Terah. Born in Ur of the Chaldees, he was a descendant of Shem. He became the father of the Hebrews and several other peoples, including the Arabs. His name was changed from Abram to Abraham by God in token of his faith.

Abram: High father (87); Abraham's original name.

Absalom: Father of peace (53); David's third son. His mother was Maacah, daughter of Talmai, king of Geshur. He led a strong rebellion against David but died at the hand of Joab when caught by his hair in a wood.

Achan: Trouble (5912); Soldier of the tribe of Judah who stole part of the spoil of Jericho and hid it, a sin that resulted in Israel's defeat at Ai. He was executed by Joshua.

Achish: Serpent-charmer (397); King of Gath to whom David fled to escape Saul's persecutions. Also the name of a king of Gath in Solomon's time.

Achsah: Serpent-charmer (5915); Caleb's daughter and wife of Othniel, Israel's first judge.

Adah: Pleasure (5711); One of Lamech's wives before the Flood. Also the name of one of Esau's wives.

Adam: Of the ground; red earth (120); The first man, placed by God in the garden of Eden and federal head of the human race, the one by whom sin entered the world. Also the name of a city 36 miles north of Jericho on the Jordan.

Adoni-Bezek: Lord of lightning (137); Cruel Canaanite king captured by the men of Judah and Simeon and taken to Jerusalem where he was tortured and killed.

Adonijah: God (Jah) is my Lord (128); David's fourth son, who tried to seize the throne when David was in his extreme age. He was executed by Solomon who suspected him of still harboring regal ambitions.

Adoni-zedek: Lord of justice (139); a Canaanite king slain by Joshua.

Adoram: High honor (151); Officer of David's in charge of the tribute. Also an officer of Solomon's and afterward of Rehoboam's.

Adullam: Resting place (5725); Royal city southwest of Jerusalem. Also the name of a famous cave near the city where David found refuge from Saul.

Agabus: Locust *(13)*; Prophet from Jerusalem who met Paul at Antioch and who foretold a great famine. He also foretold Paul's imprisonment.

Agag: High; warlike (90); Poetic name for Amalek derived from the nation's most prominent dynasty. Haman was an Agagite.

Agrippa: Tamer of wild horses *(67)*; Great grandson of Herod the Great. He became tetrarch of Abilene, Galilee, Iturea, and Trachonitis. Paul gave his testimony to him.

Ague: Gatherer (94); Son of Jakeh (the listener). Author of some of the Proverbs. Some think this is a pseudonym for Solomon.

Ahab: Father's brother (256); Son of Omri and seventh king of Israel. As husband of the Sidonian princess Jezebel he endorsed widespread idolatry in his kingdom and persecuted God's believing remnant. He brought down upon himself the wrath of Elijah. He stole Naboth's vineyard and was told that God's judgment would pursue him in consequence.

Ahaz: He holds (271); King of Judah, son of Jotham, and father of Hezekiah. Ahaz was a weak and wicked king much intimidated by the Assyrians.

Ahaziah: God (Jah) holds or possesses (274); Name of two kings: the son of Ahab and eighth king of Israel; the son of Jehoram (Joram) and fifth king of Judah, a king who is also called Jehoahaz and Azariah.

Ahijah: God (Jah) is a brother (281); Name of half a dozen people, notably the name of a prophet who foretold to Jeroboam the revolt of the ten tribes. Also the name of the father of Baasha who conspired against Nadab, son of Jeroboam and seized the throne for himself.

Ahimelech: Brother of the king (288); Priest murdered by Saul for helping David.

Ahithophel: Foolish brother (302); David's chief counselor and friend. He joined the Absalom conspiracy and hanged himself when his advice was not taken. He was Bathsheba's grandfather.

Ahitub: Good brother (285); Name of several people, notably of the high priest in the days of David.

Aholiab: Father's tent (171); Skilled craftsman of the tribe of Dan entrusted with intricate work on the tabernacle.

Aholibamah: Tent of the high place (173); Pagan wife of Esau.

Ai: Heap of ruins (5857); City near Bethel and about ten miles north of Jerusalem. It was able to repulse Joshua's first attack because of the sin of Achan.

Ajalon: (357); Name of several places, notably of the place where Joshua made the sun stand still. Also a Levitical town.

Alexander: Helper of men *(223)*; The name of some five individuals, notably the son of Simon the Cyrenian who was forced to carry the cross for Christ. Also of an apostate and of a man who opposed Paul.

Alphaeus: Leader; chief *(256)*; Father of James, one of the twelve apostles.

Amalek: Warlike; dweller in the valley (6002); Grandson of Esau whose people, the Amalekites, attacked the rear of Israel when the people were on the way to Canaan. God declared perpetual war against Amalek and they became bitter hereditary foes of Israel.

Amasa: Burden-bearer (6021); David's nephew, whom Absalom made captain over his army of rebels.

Amaziah: God (Jah) has strength (558); King of Judah, the son of Joash.

Ammi: My people; Symbolic name for God's people.

Ammiel: My people is strong (5988); Name of several people, notably the father of Machir who harbored Jonathan's crippled son Mephibosheth.

Amminadab: My people are willing (5992); Name of four people, notably that of a prince of Judah.

Ammon: Fellow countryman (5983); A people descended from Lot through his incestuous union with his younger daughter. The Ammonites had a long history of hostility toward Israel.

Amnon: Faithful (550); The lustful son of David who seduced his half sister Tamar and who was subsequently murdered by Absalom.

Amorite: Mountaineer (567); A race descended from Canaan, fourth son of Ham, whose wickedness was not yet full at the time Abraham entered the land of Canaan. The Israelites were afraid of them but eventually dispossessed them.

Amos: Burden bearer (5986); Herdsman from Tekoa, about six miles south of Bethlehem in Judah, sent as a prophet to the sophisticated city of Samaria.

Amram: Exalted people (6019); Son of Kohath and grandson of Levi. Amran was the father of Aaron, Moses, and Miriam.

Amraphel: Powerful people (569); King of Shinar who invaded Canaan and took Lot captive.

Anak: Giant; longnecked (6061); Son of Arba and ancestor of the Anakim, a race of giants.

Ananias: God (Jah) is gracious *(367)*; Three people bore this name: a man who with his wife Sapphira tried to deceive the apostles about the value of their property and who died instantly as a result; a disciple at Damascus who ministered to Saul of Tarsus after his conversion; and a high priest in Jerusalem hostile to the gospel.

Andrew: Manly (406); Simon Peter's brother and an apostle of Jesus.

Andronicus: Conqueror (408); Kinsman of Paul at Rome.

Aner: Waterfall (6063); Brother of Mamre, an Amorite, and a confederate of Abraham in his rescue of Lot.

Anna: Grace *(451)*; Aged woman in Jerusalem, of the tribe of Asher, at the time of Christ's birth.

Annas: Grace of God (Jah) *(452)*; High priest of Jerusalem in the time of Christ who took a leading role in crucifying Christ and opposing the Church. He was appointed high priest by Quirinius, Roman governor of Syria, after the battle of Actium. He was forced to resign at the beginning of the reign of Tiberius but continued to exert considerable influence.

Anothoth: Answers (6068); City in Benjamin, three miles north of Jerusalem, celebrated as the birthplace of Jeremiah.

Antioch: (490); City in Syria founded by Seleucus Nicator. Christianity took swift root there, fostered by Paul and Barnabas. The disciples were first called Christians there. A second Antioch, in Pisidia, was likewise the scene of missionary activity during the first missionary journey of Paul and Barnabas.

Apollos: A destroyer *(625)*; Eloquent Alexandrian Jew who came to Ephesus preaching an imperfect gospel. Aquila and Priscilla taught him the truth more perfectly. His name was much applauded by one of the factions in the Corinthian church.

Apollyon: Destroyer *(623)*; King of the bottomless pit. In Hebrew his name is Abaddon.

Aquila: Eagle *(207)*; Jew in Corinth who became a friend, convert, and fellow worker of Paul's.

Arabia: Wilderness (6152); Portion of the Arabian peninsula. The original inhabitants were the Horites, so called because of their living in holes and caves. They were supplanted by the Edomites, the Ishmaelites, and the Amalekites. After his conversion, Paul sought out the solitudes of Arabia.

Aram: High, exalted (758); A name used in various ways. Notably it applied to the whole country of Syria but especially the hill country. Aram was founded by one of the sons of Shem.

Ararat: Creation; holy land (780); District of Armenia where the ark of Noah came to rest.

Araunah: Strong (728); Jebusite whose threshing floor David purchased to be the site of an altar and which afterward became the site of the Temple.

Arba: Strength of Baal (704); Father of the Anakim and the Nephilim, a race of giants.

Archippus: Chief groom *(751)*; Probably the son of Philemon. Paul urges him to be faithful.

Areopagus: Mars Hill *(698)*; Famous Athenian court before which Paul was brought to explain his teachings.

Aretas: Pleasing *(702)*; Ethnarch in northern Arabia whose deputy tried to arrest Paul in Damascus.

Argob: Strong (709); A strong division of the kingdom of Og, king of Bashan, containing some sixty cities.

Ariel: Lion of God (740); Symbolic name for Jerusalem used by Isaiah.

Arimathea: Height *(707)*; Another name for Ramah, five miles north of Jerusalem and the home of Samuel. It was also the home of Joseph, the member of the Sanhedrin who donated his tomb in Jerusalem to be the burial place of Jesus.

Arioch: Lionlike (746); King of Ellasar in Assyria who invaded Canaan and took Lot captive. Also the name of Nebuchadnezzar's captain of the guard.

Aristarchus: Best ruler *(708)*; Friend of Paul, who accompanied him on his third missionary journey and on his voyage to Rome.

Aristobulus: Best counselor *(711)*; Person in Rome greeted by Paul. Tradition says he preached in Britain.

Armageddon: Hill of Megiddo *(717)*; Scene of the last battle at the second coming of Christ.

Armenia: Same as Ararat (780); Tradition says it was settled by Haik, son of Togarmah and grandson of Japhat.

Arnon: Rushing river (769); River and its valley which formed the boundary between Canaan and Moab. It rises in the mountains of Arabia and flows into the Dead Sea.

Aroer: Enclosed (6177); Name of three cities.

Artaxerxes: Great king (783); Name of several Persian kings linked with the return of the Jews to Palestine.

Asa: Physician (609); Great grandson of Solomon and one of the kings of Judah.

Asahel: God is a doer (6214); Name of several people, notably one of the sons of Zeruiah, David's sister. He was slain by Abner in self-defense. His brother Joab subsequently murdered Abner under pretense of avenging Asahel.

Asaph: Collector (623); Name of a number of people, notably that of a Levite appointed by David to supervise the service of song in Israel and put in charge of the Temple service by Solomon.

Asenath: Dedicated to Neit (she shall be hated) (621); Wife of Joseph, daughter of Potipherah (priest of On), and mother of Ephraim and Manasseh.

Ashdod: Fortress (795); One of the five cities of the Philistines.

Asher: Happy (836); Eighth son of Jacob, and Zilpah's second son.

Ashkelon: Oak (831); One of the cities of the Philistines.

Ashtoreth: Wife (6252); Idol of the Philistines, Phoenicians, and Sidonians, who was worshiped with immoral rites and became a snare to Israel.

Asia: (778); Asia Minor (now western Turkey), the scene of stirring historical events. It was the scene of the legendary Argonautic expedition and Trojan War. The Persians fought to control it. Alexander the Great marched across it. It was colonized by his successors and eventually came under Roman sway. Some of Paul's key churches were planted here.

Asshur: Level plain (804); One of the seats of Hamitic power after the Flood, founded in the days of Nimrod. When the word is left untranslated, it stands for Assyria.

Athaliah: God (Jah) is strong (6271); Wife of Jehoram, king of Judah, and daughter of Jezebel. She imposed idolatry on Judah and, after the death of her son, Ahaziah, she seized the throne and ruled with despotic power.

Athens: Named after the goddess of wisdom *(116)*; The most famous city of ancient Greece and the center of world culture.

Azariah: God (Jah) is my keeper (5838); Common name denoting over two dozen individuals, notably among them the son of Amaziah and a king of Judah, and a friend of Daniel's in Babylon known as Abed-nego.

Baal: Lord (1168); Chief god of the Canaanites, who long rivaled Jehovah in the affections of the Hebrew people.

Baal-peor: Lord of the opening (1187); Moabite idol. Balaam, unable to curse the people of Israel, taught Balak how to corrupt them into the idolatrous and immoral worship of Baal-peor.

Baalzebub: Lord of the flies (1176); One of the false gods of the Philistines at Ekron.

Baasha: Boldness (1201); Conspirator against Nadab, son of

Jeroboam I of Israel, who then himself seized the throne.

Babel: Gate of God (894); City in the plain of Shinar where Nimrod consolidated his power and where God confounded human language.

Babylon: Confusion (894); Great city on the Euphrates river, which was the seat of Babylonian power and to which the Jews were carried in captivity by Nebuchadnezzar. The world empires of prophecy become such as they take and rule Babylon.

Baca: Weeping (1056); Valley near Jerusalem identified with Ge-Hinnom.

Bahurim: Low ground (980); Village between Jerusalem and the Jordan.

Balaam: Pilgrim; lord of the people (1109); Midianite prophet from the Euphrates, hired by Balak, king of Moab, to curse the Israelites. He is held up as an apostate in the New Testament. He was killed by Joshua.

Balak: Void, waster (1111); King of Moab who hired Balaam to curse Israel.

Barabbas: Son of the father *(912)*; Robber and murderer chosen by the Jews in preference to the Lord Jesus.

Barak: Lightning (1301); Helper of Deborah in the defeat of Sisera and the Canaanites, who became one of the judges.

Barnabas: Son of consolation *(921)*; Levite who donated the money he obtained from the sale of property to the general coffers of the Jerusalem church. He became a friend and fellow missionary of Paul. He is called an apostle.

Barsabas: Son of Saba *(923)*; One of two nominees put forth in the Upper Room as a possible successor of Judas Iscariot.

Bartholomew: Son of Tolmai *(918)*; One of Christ's apostles—same as Nathanael.

Bartimaeus: Son of Timaeus *(924)*; Blind man of Jericho whose sight was restored by Jesus.

Baruch: Blessed (1263); Name of several people, notably Jeremiah's scribe when he was in prison.

Barzillai: Strong, iron (1271); Wealthy Gileadite who befriended David when he fled from Absalom.

Bashan: Fruitful (1316); District on the east side of Jordan renowned for its fertility. It was formerly the kingdom of Og but became part of Manasseh's tribal territory.

Bathsheba: Daughter of an oath (1339); Wife of Uriah seduced by David.

Beersheba: Well of the oath (884); Place in the extreme south of Canaan famous for the well dug there by Isaac. The expression "from Dan to Beersheba" became a synonym for the Promised Land.

Bel: Lord (1078); Babylonian god, thought to be the Babylonian name for Baal.

Belial: Worthless (1100); Epithet denoting any worthless person—"a son of Belial," for instance.

Belshazzar: Lord of lords (1113); Name of a Babylonian king, the last regent of Babylon in the days of Daniel.

Belteshazzar: Lord of lords (1096); Babylonian name given to Daniel.

Benaiah: God (Jah) is intelligent (1141); One of David's outstanding captains.

Benhadad: Son of Hadad (the mighty) (1131); Syrian king who entered into an alliance with Asa, king of Judah, and invaded Israel. Also the name of another Syrian king in the days of Ahab and his son.

Benjamin: Son of my right hand (1144); Name of Jacob's youngest son and of the tribe that sprang from him.

Benoni: Son of my sorrow (1126); The name dying Rachel wanted to give to Benjamin.

Beor: Shepherd (1160); Name of several people, notably the father of Balaam.

Bera: Gift (1298); King of Sodom when Lot dwelt there.

Berea: Region beyond *(960)*; City of Macedonia where Paul preached.

Bernice: *(959)*; Daughter of Herod Agrippa who, along with Agrippa II, heard Paul's defense of the gospel.

Bethabara: Place of the passage *(962)*; Place on the east side of Jordan.

Bethany: House of dates *(963)*; Village on the Mount of Olives famous as the home of Martha, Mary, and Lazarus, devoted friends of Jesus.

Bethel: House of God (1008); Famous place in central Canaan, twelve miles north of Jerusalem, connected with incidents in the life of Abraham and Jacob. Jeroboam made it a center of idolatry as the place where he enshrined one of his golden calves.

Bethesda: House of mercy *(964)*; Renowned pool in Jerusalem near the sheep gate and the scene of one of Jesus' miracles.

Bethlehem: House of bread (1035); Town about six miles south of Jerusalem famous as the city of David and the birthplace of Jesus.

Beth-peor: House of the opening (1047); City of Moab near Mount Peor, east of the Jordan opposite Jericho. It was "over against Beth peor" that God buried Moses.

Bethphage: House of figs *(967)*; Village on the Mount of Olives.

Bethsaida: Place of nets *(966)*; Bethsaida of Galilee—the home of Andrew, Peter, and Philip. The Bethsaida where Jesus fed the 5,000 is thought to be another location on the east side of the lake.

Beth-shan: House of security (1052); City of Manasseh on the west side of Jordan where the Philistines contemptuously nailed up the body of Saul.

Bethshemesh: House of the sun (1053); Town on the northern border of Judah, on the northwest slope of the mountains. When the

Philistines returned the ark to Israel some of the men of Bethshemesh irreverently opened it, peered inside, and were instantly slain by God.

Bethuel: Dweller in God (1328); Abraham's brother.

Beulah: Married (1166); Symbolic name for the Promised Land.

Bezaleel: God protects (1212); One of the Spirit-filled men appointed to help make the tabernacle. He was a craftsman in wood, metal, and stone.

Bichri: Youthful (1075); Father of Sheba, who revolted against David.

Bildad: Son of contention (1085); One of Job's comforters, a descendant of Abraham through his wife Keturah.

Bilhah: Tender (1090); Rachel's maid given by her to be Jacob's wife and afterward seduced by Reuben.

Bithynia: (978); Roman province bequeathed to Rome by Nicomedes III upon his death in 74 B.C. Paul was restrained by the Holy Spirit from evangelizing the area. Peter's first epistle was addressed to Bithynia and elsewhere.

Blastus: Bud (986); Important household servant of Herod.

Boanerges: Sons of thunder (993); Name given to James and John, the sons of Zebedee, because of their hot-tempered zeal.

Boachim: Weepers (1066); Place west of the Jordan and north of Gilgal.

Boaz: Strength (1162); Prince of the house of Judah living in Bethlehem who became the husband of Ruth and an ancester of David.

Bozez: Height; shining (949); Rock near the Michmash ravine not far from Gibea.

Bozrah: Fortification, sheepfold (1224); City of one of the early kings of Edom. Also the name of a place in Moab.

Cabul: Dry, sandy (3521); Name given in disgust by Hiram, king of Tyre, to the twenty cities in Galilee given to him by Solomon.

Caesarea: (2542); Seaport on the coast of Palestine built by Herod the Great seventy miles northwest of Jerusalem and named for Caesar Augustus. Paul was imprisoned there.

Caiaphas: Depression (2503); High priest of the Jews, who handed Jesus over to the Romans after giving Him an illegal trial.

Cain: Acquired (7014); Oldest son of Adam and Eve. He murdered his brother Abel and founded Cainite civilization.

Caleb: Bold; dog (3612); Prince of Judah who, having spied out the land with Joshua, brought back a good report of Canaan. At the age of 85 Caleb asked Joshua to give him the hill country of Hebron from whence he drove out three sons of Anak.

Calvary: Skull (2898); Latin form of *Golgotha,* a little hill outside the walls of Jerusalem where Jesus was crucified.

Cana: Grace, kindness (2580); Village about five miles from

Nazareth where Jesus turned water into wine. It was also the home of Nathanael.

Canaan: Low, flat (3667); Son of Ham and grandson of Noah. It was the name given to the Promised Land, which the descendants of Canaan had occupied.

Capernaum: Village of Nahum *(2584)*; Place on the western shore of Galilee where Jesus did much of His teaching and performed various miracles. He denounced it for its unbelief.

Carmel: Fruitful (3760); Mountain in Palestine projecting into the Mediterranean. It stands between the maritime plain of Sharon and the plain of Esdraelon. It is famous as the site of Elijah's confrontation with Ahab and the prophets of Baal.

Cephas: Stone *(2786)*; The name Jesus gave to Simon Peter.

Chaldea: Astrologer (3778); Region on the Euphrates river from which Abraham migrated and which had Babylon as its capital. Its inhabitants were of Cushite origin.

Chebar: Joining (3529); Tributary of the Euphrates, along the banks of which some of the Jewish exiles lived, and the scene of some of Ezekiel's visions.

Chedorlaomer: Sheaf band (3540); King of Elam who invaded Canaan and took Lot captive.

Cherethites: Executioners (3774); Philistine tribe in the southern part of Canaan.

Cherith: Trench (3747); Brook east of the Jordan in Gilead near Jericho where Elijah hid himself after denouncing Ahab.

Chilion: Pining (3630); Son of Elimelech and Naomi.

Chinnereth: Circuit (3672); District around the sea of Galilee.

Chittim: Terrible; giants (3794); Name for the island of Cyprus.

Chloe: (5514); Woman disciple who brought Paul news about the divisions in the Corinthian church.

Chorazin: (5523); Town two miles from Capernaum on the sea of Galilee where Jesus performed some of His mighty works. It was denounced by Him for its unbelief.

Christ: Anointed (5547); Greek form of the Hebrew "Messiah." A title of the Lord Jesus.

Chushan-rishathaim: Blackness (3572); King of Mesopotamia who oppressed Israel and who was defeated by Othniel.

Cleophas: (2810); Husband of one of the Marys who was a half-sister of Jesus' mother.

Coniah: God (Jah) is creating (3659); Name given to Jehoiachin, the king of Jerusalem who was carried captive to Babylon.

Cornelius: (2883); Roman centurion.

Crete: (2914); Mediterranean island.

Crispus: Crisp *(2921)*; A Corinthian.

Cush: Black (3568); Name of a number of people, notably the eldest son of Ham and a grandson of Noah.

Cushi: Black (3569); Messenger sent to David by Joab to announce news of the victory over Absalom.

Cyprus: (2954); Island in the Mediterranean evangelized by Paul and Barnabas.

Cyrene: (2957); City of Libya in Cyrenaica on the North African coast.

Cyrus: Sun, throne (3566); Founder of the Persian empire, whose coming was foretold by Isaiah. It was he who ended the Babylonian captivity of the Jews.

Dagon: Fish (1712); National god of the Philistines.

Damascus: (1834); Oldest city in the world and capital of Syria.

Dan: Judge (1835); Son of Jacob and Bilhah. The name of one of the tribes and also the name of the most northerly city of Israel. Hence the popular description of the Promised Land, "From Dan to Beersheba."

Daniel: God is the judge (1849); Name of several people, notably the prophet who rose to great power in Babylon and author of the book of Daniel.

Darius: (1867); Name of several rulers of Babylon and Persia.

Dathan: Fount (1885); Reubenite who with Korah and some others led a rebellion against Moses and Aaron and who perished as a result.

David: Beloved (1732); Youngest son of Jesse of Bethlehem in Judah, and Israel's most famous king.

Debir: Speaker (1688); Amorite king. Also a city in the south of Judah near Hebron.

Deborah: Bee, wasp (1683); Prophetess who judged Israel and spurred Barak on to overthrow Sisera. Also the name of Rebekah's nurse.

Dedan: Low (1719); Grandson of Cush and also of a son of Abraham by Keturah. The name is also used of a district near Edom.

Delilah: Languishing (1807); Philistine woman to whom the infatuated Samson told the secret of his strength.

Demas: (1214); Disciple of the apostle Paul who forsook him.

Devil: Accuser (1228); Several words are translated "devil." One Hebrew word literally means "hairy one" or "goat" (Leviticus 17:7; 2 Chronicles 11:15), an interesting fact in the light that goats play in the worship of the Devil. Another Hebrew word means "spoiler" or "destroyer" (Deuteronomy 32:17; Psalm 106:37).

Diana: Artemis *(735)*; One of the chief goddesses of the pagan Greek and Roman world.

Dibon: River course (1269); Name of several towns.

Didymus: Twin *(1324)*; Surname of Thomas.

Dinah: Judged; avenged (1783); Daughter of Jacob and Leah seduced by Shechem.

Dionysius: Reveler *(1354)*; One of Paul's few converts at Athens.

Diotrephes: Nourished by Jove *(1361)*; Disciple who loved to have preeminence.

Doeg: Fearful (1673); Saul's chief herdsman, an Edomite who informed Saul that Ahimelech had helped David and who massacred the priests.

Dorcas: Doe: gazelle *(1393)*; Woman of Joppa renowned for her charity and raised from the dead by Peter.

Dothan: Double feast (1886); City near Mount Gilboa.

Dumah: Silence (1746); Son of Ishmael. Also the name of several places.

Eden: Delight (5731); Garden of God where Adam and Eve lived before the Fall.

Edom: Red (123); Jacob's twin brother who sold his birthright and founded a nation bitterly hostile to Israel.

Eglon: Circle (5700); Name of an Amorite city. Also an oppressor of Israel who was slain by Ehud.

Egypt: Limit, hemmed in (4714); Country on the north coast of Africa which figures prominently in Hebrew history. The Israelites were slaves there until they were delivered by Moses.

Ehud: Strong (261); The second judge.

Ekron: Naturalized (6138); Most northerly of the five cities of the Philistines.

Elah: Oak (425); Valley where David killed Goliath. Also the name of the son of Baasha, a short-lived king of Israel. Also the name of various other people.

Elam: Youth (5867); Son of Shem whose descendants settled an area south of Assyria and east of Persia. Also the name of various other people.

Eldad: God is a friend (419); Prophet in Israel during the days of Moses.

Eleazar: God is my helper (499); Third son of Aaron and the name of various others.

Eli: God (Jah) is high (5941); High priest and judge of Israel who brought up Samuel. His claim to the office of high priest was through Ithamar, the youngest of Aaron's sons.

Eliab: God is my father (446); Name of various people, notably of the eldest son of Jesse and David's elder brother.

Elakim: God sets up (471); Name of various people, notably of King Jehoiakim who was placed on the throne of Judah by Pharaoh-necho.

Elias: God is Jehovah *(2243)*; Greek form of the name Elijah.

Eliel: God is God (447); Name of ten different people.

Eliezer: God is my help (461); Name of Abraham's steward. Also the name of the second son of Moses and the prophet who rebuked Jehoshaphat, and various others.

Elihu: God himself (453); Name of one of Job's friends and of various others.

Elijah: God is Jehovah (452); Famous prophet who withstood Ahab and Jezebel and the Baal cult.

Elim: Palm trees (362); Second encampment of Israel after leaving Egypt.

Elimelech: My God is King (458); Bethlehemite in the days of the judges who took his family to Moab and whose son married Ruth.

Eliphaz: God dispenses (464); One of Job's comforters. Also the name of one of Esau's sons.

Elisabeth: God swears *(1665)*; Wife of Zacharias the priest and mother of John the Baptist.

Elisha: God saves (477); Elijah's successor as prophet.

Elishama: God hears (476); Joshua's grandfather. Also the name of one of David's sons and of various others.

Elkanah: God possesses (511); Samuel's father. Also the name of various others.

Elon: Oak, strong (356); One of Esau's fathers-in-law. Also the name of two others (including one of the judges) and of a town in Dan.

Emims: Terrible ones (368); Name of a race of giants.

Emmanuel: God with us *(1694)*; Name of the Lord Jesus.

Emmaus: *(1695)*; Village about seven or eight miles from Jerusalem.

Endor: Fountain of Dor (5874); City of Manasseh south of Tabor where Saul consulted the witch.

Engedi: Fountain of God; kid (5872); Town on the west shore of the Dead Sea.

Enoch: Initiated; teacher (2585); Cain's eldest son to whom Cain dedicated a city. Also a godly descendant of Seth translated to heaven before the Flood.

Enos: Mortal man (583); Son of Seth and grandson of Adam.

Ephraim: Doubly fruitful (669); Joseph's second son and patriarch of the tribe which at times gave its name to all ten of the northern tribes. Also the name of two towns.

Ephratah: Fertility (672); Ancient name of Bethlehem.

Ephron: Strong (6085); Hittite from whom Abraham purchased a burying place for Sarah.

Er: Watcher (6147); Judah's oldest son, slain by God for his behavior.

Esau: Hairy (6215); Jacob's twin brother and founder of the Edomite kingdom so hostile to Israel.

Eschol: Cluster of grapes (812); Brother of Mamre, a confederate of Abraham. Also the name of a place near Hebron visited by the ten spies.

Esther: Planet Venus (635); Benjamite orphan, adopted by Mordecai, who became queen of Persian king Ahasuerus (Xerxes).

Ethan: Ancient (387); Name of various people, notably a sage famous in the days of Solomon.

Ethbaal: Baal's man (856); King of Sidon and father of Jezebel.

Ethiopia: (3568); Country in Africa, south of Egypt, populated by the descendants of Cush, son of Ham.

Eunice: Victorious *(2131)*; Timothy's mother.

Euodias: Fine traveling *(2136)*; Quarrelsome woman at Philippi.

Euphrates: Bursting, sweet (6578); Famous river flowing out of Eden, eastern boundary of the Promised Land. The Euphrates also flows through Babylon and figures largely in Bible prophecy.

Eutychus: Fortunate *(2161)*; Young man of Troas whom Paul raised from the dead.

Eve: Life-giving (2332); The first woman.

Evil-merodach: Soldier of Merodach (192); Son and successsor of Nebuchadnezzar. He released Jehoiachin who had been kept in prison by Nebuchadnezzar for 37 years.

Ezekiel: God is strong (3168); Priest who prophesied to the exiles in Babylon.

Ezion-geber: Backbone of a mighty one (6100); One of Israel's stopping places in the wilderness. Later a naval base of Solomon and where Jehoshaphat lost his fleet.

Ezra: Help (5830); Scribe who led a contingent of Jews to the Promised Land from Babylon and who then led religious reforms among the remnant in the land.

Felix: Happy *(5344)*; Unscrupulous Roman procurator of Judea who heard Paul's case.

Festus: Festal *(5347)*; Successor of Felix as Roman procurator of Judea. When Festus heard Paul's testimony he told him he was mad.

Gabbatha: Elevated place *(1042)*; Place where Pilate tried Jesus.

Gabriel: God is mighty (1403); Herald Angel.

Gad: Seer (1408); Seventh son of Jacob and firstborn of Leah's maid Zilpah. He became founder of the tribe of Gad. Also the name of a prophet who joined David in the hold and who advised him to abandon it as a place of refuge.

Galatia: (1053); Roman province and scene of Paul's early and most fruitful missionary journeys.

Galilee: Circle *(1056)*; District of Naphtali. After the captivity, Galilee comprised all the Promised Land north of Samaria, and was the scene of much of Christ's ministry.

Gallio: (1058); Roman proconsul of Achaia who was indifferent to the charges of Jews in his district against Paul. He was a younger brother of the famous Roman scholar Seneca.

Gamaliel: God recompenses *(1583)*; Assistant of Moses in the wilderness. More notably, the name of a famous teacher among the Jews who was a tutor of Saul of Tarsus.

Gath: Wine press: Fortune (1661); One of the five cities of the Philistines, celebrated as the home of Goliath.

Gath-hepher: Winepress of the well (1662); Jonah's birthplace in the tribe of Zebulun.

Gaza: Strong place (5804); One of the five cities of the Philistines.

Gedaliah: God (Jah) is great (1436); Governor of Judah appointed by Nebuchadnezzar after the destruction of Jerusalem. Also the name of several others.

Gehazi: Diminisher (1522); Servant of Elisha who deceived Naaman and who was consequently smitten with Naaman's leprosy.

Gennesaret: Heart-shaped *(1082)*; Another name for the sea of Galilee.

Gera: Enmity (1617); Father of Shimei, the man who cursed David.

Gerizim: Waste places (1630); Mountain upon which God's blessings were pronounced on Israel.

Gershom: Stranger (1648); Firstborn of Moses and Zipporah. Also the name of the eldest son of Levi and several others.

Gethsemane: Wine press *(1068)*; Garden in Jerusalem where Jesus prayed the night before his crucifixion.

Gezer: Precipice (1507); Town conquered by Joshua and given to the Kohathites.

Gibeah: Height (1390); City in the highlands of Judah.

Gibeon: Height (1391); One of four cities that conspired to deceive Joshua into making a treaty with them. It was given to Benjamin and became a Levitical city.

Gideon: Feller, hewer (great warrior) (1439); Judge who delivered Israel from the Midianites.

Gihon: Stream (1521); River of Eden. A place near Jerusalem where Solomon was proclaimed king.

Gilboa: Bubbling fountain (1533); Hilly area of Manasseh on the west side of Jordan where Saul was slain. Mount Gilboa was six miles from Bethshan.

Gilead: Strong; rocky (1568); Mountainous area on the east side of Jordan occupied by parts of Reuben, Gad, and Manasseh. In New Testament times it was called Peraea. Also the name of several individuals, including the father of the judge Jephthah.

Gilgal: Circle, wheel (1537); Place on the western side of the Jordan near Jericho where Israel first camped when they entered the Promised Land.

Gittites: Wine press (1663); Inhabitants of Gath.

Gog: High, mountain (1463); Prophetic name for Russia.

Golan: Circle (1474); City of refuge in Manasseh on the east side of Jordan in Bashan.

Golgotha: Skull *(1115)*; Small hill where Christ was crucified.

Goliath: Exile; soothsayer (1555); Philistian giant slain by David.

Gomer: Completion; heat (1586); Eldest son of Japheth and father of Ashkenaz and Togarmah. Gomer founded the Cimerian tribes and other Celtic families. He is mentioned as a confederate of Russia in the last days. Also the name of Hosea's unfaithful wife.

Gomorrah: Fissure; submersion (6017); Sister city of Sodom and likewise overthrown by God.

Goshen: (1657); Area of Egypt in which Joseph settled his brothers. It seems to have been in the eastern part of the country toward the Promised Land.

Habakkuk: Courier (2265); Prophet who was troubled by God's warnings that Judah would be overthrown by the Babylonians.

Hadad: Mighty (1908); Name of several people related to Esau and Ishmael.

Hagar: Wandering (1904); Sarah's Egyptian maid who became the mother of Abraham's first son, Ishmael.

Haggai: Festive (2292); Minor prophet who prophesied after the end of the Babylonian captivity.

Haggith: Festive (2294); One of David's wives and mother of Adonijah.

Ham: Swarthy (2526); Youngest son of Noah.

Haman: Celebrated (2001); Grand vizier of Ahasuerus (Xerxes) whose hatred of Mordecai led him to plot the extermination of the Jews.

Hamath: Defensed, walled (2574); City of Syria populated by people of Hamitic origin.

Hamor: Large donkey (2544); Prince of Shechem whose son seduced Dinah the daughter of Jacob.

Hanani: Gracious (2607); Name of half a dozen individuals, including the brother of Nehemiah who became governor of Jerusalem.

Hananiah: God (Jah) is gracious (2608); Name of about fourteen people, including the friend of Daniel who was given the name *Shadrach* by the Babylonians.

Hannah: Grace (2584); Mother of Samuel.

Haran: Strong; enlightened (2039); Abraham's youngest brother whose children were Lot, Milcah, and Iscah (whom Joseph says was Sarah). Also the name of several other people, as well as of a city in Padan-aram where Abraham halted on his way to Canaan.

Hashabiah: God (Jah) is associated (2811); Name of several individuals, mostly Levites.

Havilah: Circle, district (2341); Name of a place connected with the garden of Eden. Also the name of several people.

Hazael: God sees (2371); Official in the court of Ben-hadad of Damascus who consulted Elisha about the king's illness. Thereafter he murdered his royal master and seized the throne for himself. Some time before, Elijah had secretly anointed him king of Syria.

Hazor: Enclosed (2674); Fortified city ruled by Jabin. It had been burned by Joshua and its site given to Naphtali.

Heber: Companion (2268); Name of several people, including the husband of Jael who killed Sisera.

Hebron: Ford; company, fellowship (2275); City of Judah about twenty-two miles south of Jerusalem. Also the name of a couple of individuals.

Heman: Faithful (1968); One of David's musicians.

Hephzibah: My delight is in her (2657); Hezekiah's wife, thought by some to be the daughter of Isaiah. She was the mother of King Manasseh. The name is also used poetically of the future Jerusalem.

Hermon: Prominent; rugged (2768); High mountain in Lebanon, thought by many to be the site of Christ's transfiguration.

Herod: Hero (2264); Herod the Great was procurator of Judea under Julius Caesar and king under Augustus. His son, Herod Antipas, was tetrarch of Galilee and Peraea. He murdered John and mocked at Jesus. Herod Agrippa I murdered James, imprisoned Peter, and died under God's judgment. Herod Agrippa II heard Paul's testimony and said he was "almost persuaded" to be a Christian.

Herodias: Heroic (2265); Granddaughter of Herod the Great, who married her uncle Philip but left him for his brother Herod Antipas. She instigated the murder of John the Baptist.

Hezekiah: God (Jah) is strong (2396); Great and good king of Judah during the days of Isaiah and the Assyrian invasion.

Hezron: Blooming (2696); Name of several people, including a grandson of Judah, an ancestor of Jesus.

Hiddekel: Rapid (2313); Ancient name of the Tigris, one of the rivers of the garden of Eden, which flowed toward Assyria.

Hinnom: Free (2011); Person after whom a notorious valley in Jerusalem was named, in which human sacrifices were offered to pagan gods. The name became a synonym for hell.

Hiram: Whiteness; noble (2438); King of Tyre friendly to David and Solomon, who supplied materials and labor for the Temple.

Hittites: Terror (2850); Descendants of Canaan occupying the hill country of Judah.

Hivites: Villagers (2340); Descendants of Canaan occupying part of the Promised Land and tending to be peaceable and trade-minded.

Hobab: Beloved (2246); Also called Raguel (Raiel) and identified with Jethro the father-in-law of Moses, although some identify him as Moses' son-in-law.

Hophni: Strong (2652); One of the wicked sons of Eli the priest.

Hor: Mountain (2023); Place where Aaron died on the boundary of Edom.

Horeb: Waste (2722); Range of mountains dominated by Sinai.

Horim: Cave dwellers: (2752); Original inhabitants of Mount Seir who lived in the cave dwellings in the cliffs especially at Petra and were driven out by Esau's descendants.

Hosea: God (Jah) is my help (1954); One of the minor prophets.

Hoshea: God (Jah) is my help (1954); Original name of Joshua. Also the name of the last king of Israel.

Huldah: Weasel (2468); Prophetess consulted by King Josiah about a recently discovered book of the Law.

Hur: Free, noble (2354); Name of several people, notably of one of the men who held up the arms of Moses as he interceded for Joshua and Israel as they fought with Amalek. According to Jewish tradition he was the husband of Miriam.

Huram: Noble, free (2361); Name of several people, notably a craftsman from Tyre employed by Solomon for work on the Temple.

Hushai: Quick (2365); One of David's friends, sent by him to Absalom to defeat the counsel of Ahithophel.

Ibzan: Splendid (78); One of the judges.

Ichabod: The glory is gone (350); Son of Phinehas, the wicked son of Eli the priest. Ichabod was born at the time the Philistines captured the ark.

Iddo: Favorite, festal, opportune, honorable (5714); Name of several people.

Idumea: Territory of Edom (123); Greek form of the name Edom.

Illyricum: (2437); Part of the Roman empire on the east coast of the Adriatic Sea.

Isaac: Laughter (3327); Abraham's son and heir, and father of Jacob and Esau.

Isaiah: God (Jah) is our helper (3470); Greatest of all the writing prophets, who ministered for about sixty years and warned Israel of the impending Assyrian invasion. He was a close friend and supporter of Hezekiah of Judah.

Iscariot: Son of Kerioth *(2469)*; Name for Judas who betrayed Jesus.

Ishbi-benob: Dweller on the mount (3430); One of the sons of the giant Goliath.

Ish-bosheth: Man of shame (378); Son of Saul set up as a puppet and rival king of David by Abner, Saul's general.

Ishmael: God hears (3458); Son of Abraham by Hagar and father of the Arab peoples. Also the name of several other individuals.

Israel: Prince with God (3478); Jacob's new name after he wrestled with the Jehovah-angel at the Jabbok. Also the name given to the nation which descended from him.

Issachar: Bearing hire; reward (3485); Ninth son of Jacob, and Leah's fifth son, father of the tribe that bears his name.

Ithamar: Coast of the palm tree (385); Youngest son of Aaron the priest.

Ittai: Being, living (863); Gittite captain in David's army when David fled from Absalom.

Jabal: Moving (2989); Antedeluvian who taught people to herd cattle.

Jabbok: Running, flowing (2999); Small river dividing Israel from Ammon. It rises in the hills of Bashan and runs into the Jordan halfway between the sea of Galilee and the Dead Sea. Here Jacob wrestled with the angel.

Jabesh: Dry place (3003); Abbreviation for Jabesh Gilead.
Jabesh-gilead: (3003;1568); City in Gad near Bethshan.
Jabez: Height (3258); Outstanding man of Judah. Also a city.
Jabin: Intelligent (2985); Name of two kings of Hazor, notably the one who oppressed Israel for twenty years and who was overthrown by Barak.
Jacob: Supplanter (3290); Son of Isaac and Rebekah, and Esau's twin. He became the father of the twelve patriarchs who gave their names to the twelve tribes of Israel.
Jael: Chamois (3278); Wife of Heber the Kenite who assassinated Sisera.
Jair: God (Jah) enlightens (2971); Name of several people, notably one of the judges.
Jairus: One who enlightens *(2383)*; Ruler of the Capernaum synagogue, whose young daughter Jesus restored to life.
Jambres: *(2387)*; Egyptian magician at Pharaoh's court in the days of the Exodus.
James: Greek form of the name Jacob *(2385)*; Name of a number of people, including two of the Lord's disciples, and the Lord's brother.
Jannes: *(2389)*; Egyptian magician at Pharaoh's court who opposed Moses.
Japheth: High *(3315)*; Second son of Noah.
Jared: To go downward (3382); Enoch's father.
Jason: Healing *(2394)*; Believer at Thessalonica who entertained Paul and Silas.
Javan: Effervescent (3120); Son of Japheth whose descendants populated Greece.
Jebus: Trodden down (2982); Old name for Jerusalem.
Jebusites: Belonging to Jebus (2983); Branch of the Canaanite family who dwelt near and in Jerusalem until David wrested it from them.
Jeconiah: God (Jah) will establish (3204); Godless king of Judah.
Jedaiah: God (Jah) knows (3042); Name of several priests.
Jedidah: Beloved (3040); Wife of Amon, king of Judah, and mother of Josiah.
Jedidiah: God (Jah) is a friend (3041); Name given to Solomon by the prophet Nathan.
Jeduthun: Choir of praise (3038); Levite whose name is connected with the song service in the temple.
Jehiel: God is alive (3171); Name of about a dozen people.
Jehoahaz: God (Jah) upholds (3059); King of Israel, a son of Jehu, and father of Joash. Also the name of a king of Judah also called Shallum, the son of Josiah. He was deposed by Pharaoh-necho.
Jehoash: God (Jah) supports (3060); King of Judah, son of Ahaziah, and father of Amaziah. Also the name of a king of Israel, son and successor of Jehoahaz, and father of Jeroboam II.

Jehoiachin: God (Jah) established (3078); Son of Jehoiakim, king of Judah, who was set on the throne by Nebuchadnezzar. He was eventually deported to Babylon.

Jehoiada: God (Jah) knows (3111); Name of half a dozen people, notably the high priest who hid Joash from Athaliah and made him king.

Jehoiakim: God (Jah) sets up (3079); Son of Josiah who was made king of Judah by Pharaoh-necho in place of Jehoahaz. His original name was Eliakim.

Jehonadab: God (Jah) is liberal (3082); Son of Rechab, also called Jonadab.

Jehoram: God (Jah) is high (3088); Name of a king of Judah, son of Jehoshaphat. He is often called Joram. Also the name of a king of Israel, a son of Ahab, slain by Jehu. Also the name of a priest.

Jehoshaphat: God (Jah) is judge (3092); Name of several people, including the father of Jehu. Notably the name of one of Judah's good kings. The name is also given to a valley in Jerusalem where the Lord will eventually judge the nations.

Jehovah: The Existing One (3068); Form of the name of God by which He was known in the Old Testament.

Jehu: God (Jah) is he (3058); Name of several people, notably a vigorous king of Israel anointed by Elijah to make an end of the dynasty of Ahab.

Jemima: Pure (3224); One of Job's daughters.

Jephthah: Opposer (3316); One of the judges.

Jephunneh: Appearing (3312); Caleb's father.

Jeremiah: God (Jah) is high (3414); Name of half a dozen people, notably one of the major prophets.

Jericho: Fragrant (3405); Canaanite city near Jordan taken by Joshua and laid under a curse.

Jeroboam: Enlarger (3408); Name of two kings of Israel.

Jerubbaal: Contender with Baal (3378); Name given to Gideon by his father.

Jerusalem: Place of peace (3389); Capital city of the Jews since the days of David.

Jesse: God (Jah) exists (3448); Father of David.

Jesus: Savior *(2424);* Name of the promised Messiah of the Jews and the Savior of mankind.

Jethro: Preeminence (3503); Priest of Midian and Moses' father-in-law.

Jezebel: Without cohabitation; Dunghill (348); Wicked daughter of Ethbaal, king of the Zidonians. She became the wife of Ahab and was also the mother of the notorious Athaliah.

Jezreel: God sows (3157); Name of several people and places. Hosea gave the name symbolically to his son to represent the nation of Israel.

Joab: God (Jah) is my father (3097); David's nephew and unscrupulous commander-in-chief.

Joash: God supports (3101); Name of various people, including several kings.

Job: Hated, i.e., persecuted (347); A Semite dwelling in Uz, whose sufferings gave rise to the book that bears his name.

Jochebed: God (Jah) is honor; God my glory (3115); Mother of Moses, Aaron, and Miriam.

Joel: Jehovah (Jah) is God (3100); Name of more than a dozen people, notably the prophet of that name.

Johanan: God (Jah) is gracious (3110); Name of at least a dozen people.

John: Favored of Jehovah *(2491)*; Forerunner of Jesus. Also the name of one of the Lord's most intimate disciples.

Jonadab: God (Jah) is liberal (3122); Also called Jehonadab, a Rechabite.

Jonah: Dove (3124); Hebrew prophet sent to preach to Nineveh.

Jonathan: God (Jah) is given (3129); Name of various people, notably the son of Saul who befriended David.

Joppa: Height, beauty (3305); Seaport in the tribal territory of Dan.

Joram: God (Jah) is high (3141); Name of both a king of Israel and a king of Judah, both called Jehoram and both of whose names were thus abbreviated.

Jordan: Descender (3383); Chief river of Canaan, rising from two springs in the valley between Lebanon and Hermon. It descends on a twisted course to lose itself in the Dead Sea. In Bible typology it symbolizes death.

Joseph: One who increased (3130); Son of Jacob and Rachel, brother of Benjamin, and father of Ephraim and Manasseh. Also the name of various other people, including Joseph, husband of the virgin Mary and foster father of Jesus, and of Joseph of Arimathea who gave Jesus his tomb.

Joses: Same meaning as Joseph *(2500)*;

Joshua: God (Jah) saves (3091); Name of various people, notably the captain of Israel's armies who conquered Canaan.

Josiah: God (Jah) supports (2977); One of Judah's godly kings.

Jotham: God (Jah) is perfect (3147); Youngest son of Gideon who escaped Abimelech's massacre of his brothers. Also the name of a king of Judah.

Jubal: Stream; to bring forth (3106); Antedeluvian who invented musical instruments.

Judah: Praise (3063); Fourth son of Jacob and Leah, and father of the royal tribe from which Jesus came.

Judas: Praise *(2455)*; Disciple who betrayed Jesus, also called Iscariot. Name of various other people, notably a disciple of Jesus also called Lebbaeus and Thaddaeus.

Kadesh: Holy (6946); Place in the wilderness sometimes called Kadesh-Barnea on the west of Edom, where Moses sent out the spies to reconnoiter Canaan. It was here the children of Israel turned back in unbelief from the conquest of the Promised Land and were consequently condemned to wander forty years in the wilderness.

Kedesh: Holy (6943); Levitical city of refuge in Naphtali, west of Lake Merom.

Keilah: Enclosed (7084); City of Judah in the hill country toward Philistia whose people, having been saved from the Philistines by David, subsequently betrayed him to Saul.

Keturah: Fragrance (6989); Woman whom Abraham married after the death of Sarah.

Kidron: Turbid (6939); Stream flowing through the valley between Jerusalem and the Mount of Olives and running on to the Dead Sea. Jesus crossed this brook on His way to Gethsemane.

Kirjath-arba: City of Arba (7153); Father of Anak, one of the giants of Canaan. The city which bore his name was afterward called Hebron.

Kirjath-jearim: City of forests (7157); Benjamite city eight miles west of Jerusalem.

Kirjath-sepher: City of books (7159); Judean city not far from Hebron. Also called Kirjath-Sannah (city of instruction), and Debir (speaker).

Kish: Bow, power (7027); Name of various people, notably the father of King Saul.

Kishon: Winding (7028); Stream arising in Mount Tabor which flowed westward along the foot of Carmel to the Mediterranean. The place where Elijah killed the prophets of Baal.

Kohath: Assembly (6955); Levi's second son, and ancestor of Moses and Aaron. The Kohathite family were entrusted with the transportation of the holiest objects in the tabernacle.

Korah: Baldness (7141); Name of several people, notably of a great grandson of Levi who joined Dathan and Abiram in a conspiracy against Moses and Aaron and who consequently perished. Also the name of another grandson of Levi whose descendants became prominent musicians and to whom a number of psalms are ascribed.

Laban: White, glorious (3837); Jacob's father-in-law, whose two daughters were Rachel and Leah.

Lachish: Height (3923); Ancient Amorite city captured by Israel and later besieged by the Assyrians in the days of Hezekiah.

Lahai-roi: The Living One sees me (883); A well associated with Isaac.

Lazarus: Without help *(2976)*; Friend of Jesus, brother of Martha and Mary of Bethany. Jesus raised him from the dead. Also the name of a beggar in one of Christ's stories.

Leah: Weary (3812); One of Jacob's wives.

Lebanon: White, snowy (3844); Mountain range from Tyre to Syria almost parallel with the sea coast and climbing in places to a height of 9,000 feet.

Lebbaeus: Man of heart *(3002);* One of Jesus' disciples. He was surnamed Thaddeus and is sometimes identified with Jude, the brother of James.

Levi: Joined (3878); Third son of Jacob and Leah, and father of the Levitical tribe entrusted with the service of the tabernacle. Israel's priests were all from this tribe. Also the name of Matthew, one of the Lord's disciples, formerly a tax collector.

Lo-ammi: Not my people (3818); Symbolic name given by Hosea to the son born to Gomer.

Lo-debar: No pasture (3810); Place beyond Jordan in Gilead where Mephibosheth hid after the fall of Saul's house.

Lo-ruhamah: Unpitied, unloved (3819); Symbolic name given by Hosea to a daughter born to Gomer.

Lot: Concealed, dark (3876); Abraham's nephew and incestuous father of Moab and Ammon.

Lucifer: The shining one (1966); Name for Satan.

Luke: Light *(3065);* Physician and companion of Paul who wrote the Gospel and Acts.

Maachah: Depression (4601); Absalom's mother. Also the name of several people and of a place in Syria.

Macedonia: (3109); Region north of Greece evangelized by Paul.

Machir: Salesman (4353); Son of Manasseh. Also the name of a man living near Mahanaim who befriended Mephibosheth.

Machpelah: Winding, spiral (4375); Field in Mamre near Hebron purchased by Abraham as a burying place for Sarah.

Magdala: Tower, greatness *(3093);* Home of Mary Magdalene, three miles north of the Sea of Galilee.

Magog: (4031); Son of Japheth. Also the name given by Ezekiel to the Russian homeland.

Mahanaim: Two camps (4266); Town on the east side of the Jordan, south of the Jabbok river.

Mahlon: Mild (4248); Eldest son of Elimelech and Naomi, and husband of Ruth.

Malachi: Messenger of God (Jah) (4401); Old Testament prophet.

Malchus: A king *(3124);* Servant whose ear Peter cut off.

Mamre: Firmness, vigor (4471); Place two miles north of Hebron connected with Abraham. Also the name of an Amorite friendly to Abraham.

Manaen: Comforter *(3127);* Boyhood friend of Herod, who became a prophet of the church at Antioch.

Manasseh: Causing forgetfulness (4519); Son of Joseph, and father of one of the tribes. Also the son of Hezekiah and one of Judah's wickedest kings.

Manoah: Rest (4495); Samson's father.

Marah: Bitter (4785); Israel's first encampment on the east of the Red Sea where the water was undrinkable.

Mark: (3138); Author of the Gospel of Mark, and cousin of Barnabas.

Martha: Lady (3136); Sister of Mary of Bethany and of Lazarus.

Mary: Bitter *(3137);* Name of seven women in the New Testament.

Mattaniah: Gift of God (Jah) (4983); Jehoiakim's brother, made king of Judah when his nephew Jehoiakim was deposed by Nebuchadnezzar. He is also called Zedekiah and was the last king of Judah.

Matthew: Gift of God *(3156);* Disciple of Jesus also called Levi.

Matthias: Gift of God (3159); Man the apostles chose to replace Judas Iscariot.

Medad: Love (4312); Prophet in the camp of Israel in the days of Moses.

Medes: Middle (4074); The people of Media in league with, but also subject to, Persia.

Megiddo: Place of God (4023); City west of the Jordan and site of the last battle at Christ's coming.

Melchizedek: King of righteousness (3198); Priest-king of Jerusalem to whom Abraham paid tithes.

Menahem: Comforter (4505); Murderous king of Judah.

Mephibosheth: Utterance of Baal (4648); Jonathan's lame son befriended by David.

Merab: Increase (4764); Saul's elder daughter promised to David but given to Adriel.

Merari: Bitter; excited (4847); Youngest son of Levi.

Meribah: Strife (4809); Place in Rephidim where Moses struck the rock.

Meshach: (4336); Babylonian name of Michael, Daniel's friend.

Meshech: Sowing; possession (4902); Name of several people. Also the name of a part of Russsia mentioned by Ezekiel.

Mesopotamia: Between two rivers (763); The country between the Euphrates and Tigris rivers.

Methuselah: When he dies it shall come (4968); Enoch's son.

Micah: Who is like God (Jah)? (4319); Name of various people, notably an apostate in the days of the judges. Also the name of one of the minor prophets.

Micaiah: Who is like God (Jah)? (4321); Prophet who foretold Ahab's doom.

Michael: Who is like God? (4317); Name of various people. Also the name of the archangel who upholds Israel's cause.

Michal: Who is like God? (4324); Saul's younger daughter and David's wife.

Michmash: (4363); Benjamite city seven miles north of Jerusalem.

Midian: Contention (4080); Son of Abraham and Keturah. Also their country on the east side of Jordan.

Milcah: Counsel (4435); Near relative of Abraham's. Also the name of a daughter of Zelophehad.

Miphkad: Appointment (4663); One of the gates of Jerusalem.

Miriam: Fat, strong (4813); Elder sister of Moses and Aaron.

Mishael: Who is what God is? (4332); Name of several people, notably a friend of Daniel's whose Babylonian name was Meshach.

Mizpah: Watchtower (4709); Name of a number of cities.

Mizraim: Hemmed in (4714); Second son of Ham from whom the Egyptians descended.

Moab: A father's water (4124); Son by incest of Lot and his eldest daughter, and father of the Moabite people on the east side of the Dead Sea.

Moloch: Counselor, king (4432); Fierce god, to whom little children were offered in the fire.

Mordecai: Dedicated to Mars (4782); Esther's cousin and guardian.

Moriah: God (Jah) provide (4179); Place where Abraham offered Isaac, later the site of the Temple.

Moses: Drawn out (4872); Great emancipator and lawgiver of Israel.

Naamah: Pleasant; Wife of Lamech. Also the name of Rehoboam's Ammonitess mother.

Naaman: Pleasant (5279); Syrian leper healed by Elisha.

Nabal: Fool (5037); Rich man who insulted David, and husband of Abigail.

Naboth: Prominence (5022); Godly Israelite murdered by Jezebel because he refused to sell his vineyard to Ahab.

Nadab: Liberal (5070); Aaron's eldest son slain by God for offering strange fire on the altar. Also the name of several others, including one of Israel's kings.

Nahash: Oracle (5176); Name of two Ammonite kings. Also the name of Zeruiah's sister.

Nahor: Piercer, slayer (5152); Name of Abraham's grandfather. Also the name of Abraham's brother.

Nahum: Comforter (5151); Minor prophet who predicted Nineveh's fall.

Naioth: To rest at home (5121); City where David vainly sought refuge from Saul.

Naomi: Pleasant (5281); Ruth's mother-in-law.

Naphtali: Wrestling (5321); Sixth son of Jacob and second son of Bilhah, Rachael's maid.

Nathan: Giver (5416); Name of various people, notably the prophet who denounced David for his sin with Bathsheba.

Nathanael: Given of God *(3482)*; Disciple of Jesus, otherwise called Bartholomew.

Nazareth: (3478); Boyhood home of Jesus.

Nebat: Look, cultivation (5028); Father of Jeroboam I of Israel.

Nebo: Height (5015); Name of various places, notably a mountain east of Jordan in view of Jericho, part of the Abarim range with Pisgah as its summit, where Moses died.

Nebuchadnezzar: (5019); Babylonian king who took the Jews into captivity.

Nehemiah: God (Jah) comforts (5166); Name of several men, notably the cup bearer of Artaxerxes who rebuilt the walls of Jerusalem.

Ner: Light (5369); Saul's grandfather. Also the name of Abner's father.

Nethaneel: God gives (5417); Name of ten people in the Old Testament.

Nicodemus: Innocent blood *(3580)*; Member of the Sanhedrin who converted to Christ.

Nicolas: Conqueror of the people *(3532)*; One of the first seven deacons.

Nimrod: Rebel; strong (5248); Builder of Babel and founder of Nineveh.

Noah: Rest (5146); Man who built the ark.

Nob: Height (5011); City in Benjamin whose priests were murdered by Saul and Doeg.

Nod: Wandering (5113); Land east of Eden settled by Cain.

Nun: Continuation (5126); Father of Joshua.

Obadiah: Serving God (Jah) (5662); Servant of Ahab. Also minor prophet.

Obed: Serving (5744); Name of several people, notably the son of Boaz and Ruth, the father of Jesse.

Obed-edom: Servant of Edom (5654); Name of several people.

Og: Long-necked; giant (5747); King of Bashan whose land was given to Manasseh.

Olivet: Olives (2132); Short ridge of hills east of Jerusalem.

Omri: God (Jah) apportions (6018); King of Israel and father of Ahab.

On: Sun (204); Place a little north of Memphis in Egypt, capital of lower Egypt, whose priest's daughter Joseph married.

Onesimus: Profitable *(3682)*; Runaway slave who was converted by Paul in Rome and sent back to his master Philemon at Colossae.

Ophel: High place (6077); Part of Jerusalem on the east of Zion.

Ophir: Far; rich (211); Celebrated place in south Arabia famous for its gold and wealth.

Ornan: Strong (771); A Jebusite.

Orpah: Back, neck, stiffneck (6204); A Moabitess.

Othniel: God is forceful (6274); Caleb's younger brother who judged Israel after the death of Joshua.

Padan-aram: Plain of Aram (6307); Plains of Mesopotamia where Laban lived.

Palestine: Emigration (6429); The Promised Land.

Paran: Full of caverns (6290); Part of the wilderness east of Edom.

Pathros: (6624); Upper Egypt.

Patmos: (3963); Barren island in the Aegean Sea where John was imprisoned.

Paul: Little *(3972);* Great apostle to the Gentiles who wrote much of the New Testament.

Pediah: God (Jah) delivers (6305); Name of several people.

Pekah: Watchfulness (6492); King of Israel.

Pekahiah: God (Jah) watches (6494); King of Israel.

Peleg: Division (6389); Descendant of Shem in whose days the earth was divided.

Peniel: The face of God (6439); Where Jacob wrestled with the angel.

Penuel: The face of God (6439); Another name for Peniel.

Peor: Opening (6465); Place in Moab where Balak brought Balaam so that he might curse the Israelites.

Peter: Stone (4074); One of the disciples.

Pharaoh: The sun (6547); Egypt's king.

Pharez: Breach; breaking forth (6557); Judah's son by Tamar, and ancestor of Jesus.

Pharpar: Rapid (6554); River of Damascus.

Phichol: Great, strong *(6369);* Abimelech's captain.

Philip: Lover of horses *(5376);* An apostle. Also the name of one of the first deacons.

Philistia: Migration (6429); Land of the Philistines.

Phinehas: Oracle (6372); Name of several priests, notably one of Aaron's sons who fought for Moses in the matter of Baal-peor in the wilderness. Also the name of one of Eli's evil sons.

Pilate: Firm, close-pressed *(4091);* Roman procurator who sentenced Jesus to death.

Pisgah: Peak (6449); Ridge of mountains of which Nebo is the peak.

Pison: Freely flowing (6276); One of the four rivers of Eden.

Pithom: (6619); Treasure city in Egypt built by the slave labor of the Hebrews.

Potiphar: (6318); Captain of Pharaoh's guard to whom Joseph was sold.

Potiphera: (6319); Priest of On whose daughter married Joseph.

Priscilla: Little Prisca; ancient *(4252);* Wife of Aquila who with her husband instructed Apollos more perfectly in the things of God, and a devoted co-worker with Paul.

Publius: Common, popular *(4196);* Chief of the island of Crete where Paul was shipwrecked.

Pudens: Shamefaced *(4196);* Friend of Paul's.

Pul: Strong (6322); Assyrian king who invaded Israel.

Raamses: Son of the son (7484); Treasure city in Egypt built with the slave labor of the Israelites.

Rabbah: Great (7237); Capital of Ammon twenty-two miles east of the Jordan.

Rab-shakeh: Head of the cupbearers (7262); Sennacherib's officer who tried to persuade Hezekiah to surrender Jerusalem.

Rachel: Lamb (7354); Jacob's favorite wife.

Raguel: God (Jah) is a friend (7467); Moses' father-in-law.

Rahab: Breadth (7343); Harlot of Jericho who sheltered the two Hebrew spies, married into the royal family, and became an ancestress of Jesus.

Ramah: Height (7414); Name of several cities, in one of which Samuel lived.

Rameses: Son of the sun (7486); Egyptian city.

Ramoth: Heights (7216); Levitical city in Gad. Same as Ramoth-Gilead.

Rebekah: Flattering (7259); Isaac's wife, and mother of Esau and Jacob.

Rechab: Companionship (7394); Name of several people, notably the father of the Rechabites, a tribe that adopted certain customs of the Hebrews.

Rehoboam: Emancipator of the people (7346); Solomon's foolish son and successor on the throne, who lost ten of the twelve tribes to Jeroboam.

Rehoboth: Enlargement (7344); One of Isaac's wells.

Rephaim: Strong (7497); Valley in Jerusalem. Also the name of a race lodged south of Jerusalem.

Rephidim: Plains (7508); Place where Israel murmured for water and Moses smote the rock.

Reuben: Behold a son (7205); Firstborn of Jacob and Leah, and founder of a tribe.

Reuel: God is a friend (7467); Son of Esau. Also the name of Moses' father-in-law.

Rezin: Dominion (7526); Syrian king slain by the Assyrians.

Rhoda: Rose (4498); Woman in the house of Mary the mother of Mark.

Rimmon: Pomegranate (7417); Name of various places. Also the name of a Syrian god similar to Adonis.

Rizpah: Variegated (7532); One of Saul's concubines later married to Abner.

Rogelim: Place of the fuller (7274); City in Gilead and home of Barzillai.

Rufus: Red (4504); Son of Simon the Cyrenian.

Ruth: Friendship (7327); Moabite woman who faithfully returned to Judah with her mother-in-law Naomi and then was "redeemed" and married by Boaz.

Samaria: Watch (8111); Capital of the kingdom of Israel forty-two miles north of Jerusalem.

Samson: Distinguished (Shining like the sun) (8123); One of the judges, famous for his strength.

Samuel: Levite (8050); Last of the judges and first of the prophets of Israel.

Sapphira: Sapphire *(4551)*; Wife of Ananias who died for lying to the Holy Spirit.

Sarah: Princess *(8283)*; Wife of Abraham, and mother of Isaac.

Sarai: God (Jah) is prince *(8297)*; Abraham's wife, whose name was changed by God to Sarah. She was Abraham's half-sister.

Satan: Accuser, hater (7854); Name for the Devil.

Saul: Asked (7586); Name of Israel's first king. Also the given name of the apostle Paul.

Sennacherib: (5576); Assyrian king who invaded Judah in the days of Hezekiah and Isaiah.

Serahiah: God (Jah) is a prince (8303); Name of a number of people.

Seth: Compensation (8352); Son of Adam and Eve born after the murder of Abel.

Shadrach: (7715); Babylonian name of Hananiah, one of Daniel's friends.

Shallum: One who recompenses (7967); Murderous king of Israel who was himself murdered.

Shalmaneser: (8022); Assyrian king.

Shamgar: Cupbearer; one who flees (8044); One of the judges.

Shammah: Fame (8048); Name of several people, notably one of David's brothers.

Shapan: Sly (8227); Name of several people, notably a scribe close to godly King Josiah.

Sharon: Plain (8289); Rich pasture land between Joppa and Caesarea.

Shealtiel: Asked for from God (7597); Son of Jeconiah, and father of Zerubbabel.

Sheba: (7652); Name of several people. Also the country from which the Queen of Sheba came to Solomon. A different word meaning "oath" or "covenant" is used in connection with the name Beer-sheba. Also the name of a Benjamite who rebelled against David.

Shechem: Shoulder (7927); One of the cities of refuge. Also the name of several people, including the man who seduced Jacob's daughter.

Shem: Name, renown (8035); Son of Noah, and founder of the Semitic families.

Shemaiah: God (Jah) is famed (8098); Name of two dozen people, including a prophet sent to Rehoboam to warn him to accept the rebellion of the ten tribes and the establishment of the northern kingdom.

Shiloh: To be happy (7887); City in Ephraim where the tabernacle was lodged until the days of Samuel. Also a mystical name for the Messiah.

Shimei: God is famed (8096); Name of about twenty people, including the Benjamite who cursed David and was executed by Solomon.

Shinar: (8152); Babylonia. The place where the tower of Babel was built.

Shunem: Uneven (7766); City in Issachar on the steep face of Gilboa. The name *Shulem* probably refers to the same place; if so, the Shulamite who won Solomon's attention came from there.

Shushan: Lily (7800); Capital of Persia on the river Ulai.

Siddim: Extension (7708); Region where the cities of Sodom and Gomorrah were located.

Sidon: Fortified (6721); Famous Phoenician seaport twenty miles north of Tyre.

Sihon: Great, bold (5511); Amorite king.

Sihor: Turbid; slimy (7883); Stream sometimes called "the river of Egypt." The word is also applied to the Nile. It marks the boundary of the Promised Land.

Silas: (4609); Fellow missionary of Paul, also called Silvanus.

Simeon: Hearing (8095); Second son of Jacob and Leah. Also the name of various other people, including Simon Peter.

Simon: Hearing (4613); Name of two of the apostles. One was the brother of Andrew and the other was known as Simon the Canaanite or Simon Zelotes.

Sin: Cliff (5512); Desert between Elim and Sinai.

Sinai: Cliff (5514); Mountain with three peaks between the gulfs of Suez and Aquaba, where God gave the Law to Moses.

Sisera: Meditation; array (5516); Captain of the army of Jabin, king of Canaan, killed by Jael.

Smyrna: Myrrh (4667); One of the cities of Asia Minor.

Sodom: Place of lime (5467); Vile city where Lot lived, overthrown by a singular fiery judgment of God along with Gomorrah and several other cities.

Solomon: Peace (8010); David's son, a king of Israel famous for his wealth and wisdom.

Sorek: Vineyard (7796); Valley between Ashkelon and Gaza.

Stephen: Crown (4736); First martyr of the Church.

Succoth: Booths (5523); Name of several places.

Syntyche: Accident (4941); Quarrelsome woman in the church at Philippi.

Syria: High land (758); Israel's northern neighbor, usually hostile to Israel.

Tabitha: Gazelle *(5000)*; Woman whom Peter raised from the dead.

Tabor: Mountain (8396); Name of several places, notably a solitary mountain in Galilee.

Tamar: Palm (8559); Widow of Er, married by Judah against his will, and an ancestress of Jesus. Also the name of several others, including Absalom's sister who was seduced and shamed by Amnon.

Tarshish: Hard (8659); Believed to be Tartessus in Spain, one of the outposts of the Phoenician commercial empire.

Tarsus: *(5019)*; Capital of Cilicia in Asia Minor, renowned as the birthplace of the apostle Paul.

Teman: South (8487); Area from which one of Job's comforters came.

Terah: Turning, wandering (8646); Abraham's father.

Thaddaeus: *(2280)*; Another name for Lebbaeus, one of the Lord's disciples.

Theophilus: Loved of God *(2321)*; Nobleman to whom Luke addressed his Gospel and the book of Acts.

Thomas: Twin *(2381)*; An apostle called Didymus (twin).

Tiberias: Pertaining to the river *(5085)*; City on the west side of the sea of Galilee built by Herod Antipas (murderer of John the Baptist) and named for the Emperor Tiberius. It became the seat of rabbinical learning and was considered almost as holy as Jerusalem, Hebron, and Safed by the Jews after the time of Christ.

Tiberius: Pertaining to the river *(5086)*; The reigning Caesar when Jesus was born.

Timnath: A portion assigned (8553); Place where Samson went to get a wife.

Timothy: Honored of God (5095); A half-Jew circumcised by Paul after his conversion, and a fellow laborer with Paul.

Tirzah: Delight (8656); City, famed as the capital of the ten tribes before the building of Samaria, and to which Solomon likened the Shulamite.

Titus: *(5103)*; Greek disciple of Paul's.

Tobiah: God (Jah) is good (2900); Name of several people, notably of the Ammonite who opposed Nehemiah.

Tola: Warm. Crimson (8439); One of the judges. Also a son of Issachar.

Tophet: Altar (8612); Place in the valley of Hinnom in Jerusalem where sacrifices were offered. The name became a synonym for hell.

Tubal: *(8422)*; Son of Japheth always associated with Meshech in enmity to God's people.

Tyre: Rock (6865); Imperial city of the Phoenicians assigned to the tribe of Asher but never taken by them.

Uriah: God (Jah) is light (223); Name of several people, notably Bathsheba's husband, whom David had murdered.

Uzzah: Strength (5798); Man who died for touching the sacred ark. Also the name of several others.

Uzziah: God (Jah) is strong (5818); Powerful king of Judah who became a leper for intruding into the priests' office.

Vashti: (2060); Queen deposed by Ahasuerus.

Zacchaeus: Pure *(2195)*; Tax collector of Jericho.

Zachariah: God (Jah) had remembered (2148); Common Hebrew name, notably that of one of the later kings.

Zacharias: God (Jah) is renowned *(2197)*; Greek form of Zechariah, notably the father of John the Baptist.

Zadok: Righteous (6659); Name of a number of people, notably a priest in the days of David.

Zaphnath-paaneah: Savior of the world (revealer of secrets) (6847); Name Pharaoh gave to Joseph.

Zebedee: God (Jah) gives *(2199)*; Father of James and John, and husband of Salome.

Zebulun: Dwelling (2074); Son of Jacob and Leah, and founder of one of the tribes.

Zechariah: God (Jah) is renowned (2148); Name of over a score of people in the Bible, notably one of the minor prophets.

Zedekiah: God (Jah) is might (6667); Name of several people, notably the name given by Nebuchadnezzar to Mattaniah when he made him king in place of the deposed Jehoiachin.

Zelotes: Zealot or partisan *(2208)*; One of the Lord's disciples also called the Canaanite.

Zephaniah: God (Jah) is darkness (6846); One of the minor prophets. Also the name of several others.

Zerubbabel: Shoot of Babylon; sown in Babylon (2216); Man who led a group of captives back from Babylon. He was the grandson of Jehoiakim.

Zeruiah: Balm (6870); David's sister, and mother of Joab, Abishai, and Asahel.

Ziba: Plantation (6717); Servant of Saul appointed by David to serve Mephibosheth and who slandered Mephibosheth to David.

Ziklag: Winding (6860); City associated with David's fugitive years.

Zillah: Protection, screen (6741); One of the wives of Lamech.

Zilpah: Dropping myrrh (2153); Leah's maid who conceived children by Jacob.

Zimri: Celebrated (2174); Murderous king of Israel who was himself murdered.

Zion: Fortress (6726); Southwest hill of Jerusalem, sometimes called the city of David. A poetic name for Jerusalem.

Ziph: Refining place (2128); Name of a place in Judah. Also the name of a person.

Zippor: Sparrow (6834); Father of Balak, the king of Moab who hired Balaam to curse Israel.

Zipporah: Little bird (6855); Wife of Moses.
Zoan: (6814); Important Egyptian city.
Zoar: Little (6820); City to which Lot fled when God destroyed Sodom. Afterward a Moabite city.
Zophar: Hairy, rough (6691); One of Job's friends.

6
Helpful Books for Study

Charles H. Spurgeon, known as the "prince of preachers," once said:

> Even an apostle must read. Some of our very ultra-Calvinistic brethren think that a minister who reads books and studies his sermon must be a deplorable specimen of a preacher. A man who comes into the pulpit, professes to take his text on the spot, and talks any quantity of nonsense, is the idol of many . . . . How rebuked are they by the apostle! He is inspired, and yet he wants books! He has been preaching at least for thirty years, and yet he wants books! He has seen the Lord, and yet he wants books! He had had a wider experience than most men, and yet he wants books! He had been caught up into the third heaven, and had heard things which he said it was unlawful to utter, yet he wants books! He had written the major part of the New Testament, and yet he wants books! The apostle says to Timothy and so he says to every preacher: "Give attendance to reading." The man who never reads will never be read; he who never quotes will never be quoted . . . Paul cried, "Bring the books"—join in the cry.

Wilbur M. Smith, in an address on "The Pastor and His Reading" delivered at a special pastors' session of the Moody Bible Institute *Founders' Week* Conference in 1960, said:

> A Christian minister . . . has more areas of vital interest than a man of any other calling. These areas include the vast subjects of systematic, Biblical, and historical theology, in which of course, the person and work of Christ takes first place; the history of the Christian Church; hermeneutics; the manifold aspects of homiletics; the growth and principles of missions; the biographies of those men and women who have made vital contributions to the extension of the Kingdom of God and the knowledge of His Word through the centuries; worship; church architecture; pastoral psychology; the history and geography of the Near East; apologetics; the philosophy of religion, and so on.
> No one can in a lifetime examine even superficially the major works, old and new, in all these areas, and only a few have the ability for mastering the entire literature or even one of these subjects, as Latourette has done with the history of missions, or R. H. Rowley with the literature pertaining to the Old Testament.

Nobody knows, for instance, how many books have been written directly relating to the Lord Jesus Christ. One authority estimates that over 10,000 books have been written about Him in English alone in the last 200 years (W. M. Smith, *The Minister in His Study* Chicago: Moody Press, 1973, p. 53).

Preachers, as well as Bible class and Sunday school teachers, have their work cut out for them. Their first problem, assuming they are serious about their calling to preach and teach the Word, is to decide what books will help them in their study. Some books have received great acclaim but are really worthless. Other books contain a mixture of material, some of it useful, some of it not. Even "sound" writers cannot always be uniformly recommended. Sound authors are not always helpful—and a particular writer, regardless of how sound, may not appeal to everyone.

Which books are best? What I can do here is provide a list of titles that many persons have found helpful. Readers will have to decide for themselves, by trial and error, which authors help them most.

The present list is suggestive, not exhaustive. Not all the good books on a given subject are cited among these titles. Some of the books are out of print but can at times be found in secondhand bookstores. Not all books by any given author are listed, but, generally, if readers find a book by a particular writer helpful, they will probably find other books by the same person helpful. One further word of caution is necessary, however. Some authors excel in certain areas but have questionable views in other areas; Bullinger and Pink, for instance, must be read with discrimination. (Discernment is always desirable, of course, in whatever aspect of life.)

The following list will get readers started in a given area, and everyone can add to this bibliography as he or she becomes more at home in it.

So then, "Give attendance to reading" (1 Timothy 4:13).

INTERPRETATION

Rightly Dividing the Word, Clarence Larkin (2802 N. Park Ave., Philadelphia, PA: Larkin Estate) 1958 reprint.
An excellent study of things that differ in the Bible. The book contains 29 chapters and 55 charts, aptly illustrating the truths taught. The book is an excellent introduction to the fundamental doctrines of the Christian faith.

Protestant Biblical Interpretation, Bernard Ramm (Boston: Wilde Co.), 1958 revision.
A modern approach to hermeneutics. Very helpful. A standard Bible School textbook.

Biblical Hermeneutics, J. E. Hartill (Grand Rapids: Zondervan), 1947.
A basic overview of Biblical principles of interpretation. Very helpful.

Knowing the Scriptures, A. T. Pierson (Springfield, MO: Gospel Publishing House), 1910, (now reprinted by Zondervan).
Packed with helpful sidelights on the Scripture. An old classic by an able Bible teacher. The book contains 50 chapters on Bible interpretation and has much useable material.

Biblical Hermeneutics, Milton S. Terry (Grand Rapids: Zondervan), 1976 reprint.

A classic. A standard seminary text. Very thorough for those who want to go into the subject at depth.

How to Enjoy the Bible, E. W. Bullinger (London: Eyre & Spottiswoode), 1907.

Filled with interesting sidelights on the Bible illustrating various principles of Bible interpretation. Many helpful comments on the original languages.

Dispensational Truth, Clarence Larkin (Philadelphia: Larkin Estate), 1918.

The best available charts on prophecy, God's dealings with the race, perspectives of Bible truth. Also helpful commentary. One of the best places to begin a study of prophecy.

Dispensationalism Today, Charles C. Ryrie (Chicago: Moody Press), 1965.

Puts the subject into perspective. Defends this basic hermeneutical approach against its critics. Shows the weakness of Covenant theology.

Principles of Expository Preaching, Merill F. Unger (Grand Rapids: Zondervan), 1955.

This Dallas Seminary professor brings his classroom expertise to bear on the subject. The book contains some basic hermeneutical principles and an interesting chapter on logic.

BIBLE HISTORY, GEOGRAPHY, AND CULTURE

Manners and Customs of Bible Lands, Fred H. Wight (Chicago: Moody Press), 1953.

Lives up to its title. Gives useable facts about the way people lived in Bible times. The 31 chapters cover all kinds of everyday customs in Bible lands: houses, meal-time customs, education, religion, marriage customs, sickness, death, slavery, and many other topics. A valuable information source.

Manners & Customs of the Bible, James M. Freeman (Plainfield, N.J.: Logos International), 1972 reprint.

A helpful handbook about the way people lived and thought in Bible times. It begins with Genesis and, in a series of 893 notes on related matters, takes the reader book by book through the Bible to Revelation. A helpful Analytical Index enables one to locate comments on religious, civil, political, military, social, and domestic customs.

A Book about the Bible, George Stimson (New York: Harper), 1945.

An unusual book, filled with odds and ends of information (for instance, what is the middle verse of the Bible?) as well as pages of facts, answers to all kinds of questions about the Bible, and much pertinent information. Do you want to know who divided the

Bible into chapters and verses? How many hairs are on the average person's head? How long is a Bible generation? How many times does the word *and* occur in the Bible? This book contains the answers.

The International Standard Bible Encyclopedia (4 vols.), James Orr, ed. (Grand Rapids: Eerdmans).
An outstanding, complete reference dictionary, explaining every significant word in the Bible as well as in the Apocrypha. Gives detailed information on archaeological discoveries, the language and literature of Bible lands, customs, family life, occupations. Gives the historical and religious environments of the Hebrew people.

The Westminster Dictionary of the Bible, John D. Davis (revised by Henry S. Gehman), (London: Collins), 1944.
A compact, comprehensive Bible dictionary. An invaluable mine of information. Interesting maps. Conservative in scholarship and doctrinal emphasis.

Unger's Bible Dictionary, Merrill F. Unger (Chicago: Moody Press), 1957.
A book that should be within reach at all times. Packed with vital, useable information. Four emphases mark this dictionary: the archaeological, historical-geographical, biographical, and doctrinal.

Illustrations from Biblical Archaeology, Donald J. Wiseman (Grand Rapids: Eerdmans), 1958.
An internationally famous archaeologist who is also a conservative is rare. Wiseman is such a scholar.

Bible History: Old Testament (4 vols.), Alfred Edersheim (Grand Rapids: Eerdmans), 1956 reprint.
A Christian Jew's view of God's dealings with His people in historic Old Testament times. Factual and accurate—reads like a story.

The Life and Times of Jesus the Messiah (2 vols.), Alfred Edersheim, (Grand Rapids: Eerdmans), 1959 reprint.
Written by a Christian Jew, this is the classic on the subject. Invaluable for understanding the background, culture, and customs in the Holy Land in Jesus' day. (Be sure to get the two-volume set rather than the condensed version of this monument of learning.)

In the Steps of the Master, H. V. Morton (London: Rich & Cowan), 1934.
Morton traveled widely in Bible lands prior to the rebirth of the State of Israel. He observed life as it had been for centuries. This travelog is full of interesting information about Palestine and its peoples.

Through Lands of the Bible, H. V. Morton (London: Methuan & Co.), 1938.
This inquisitive and informed traveler kept his eyes open and his Bible and notebook handy as he went from place to place. The

book contains all sorts of sidelights on lands of vital interest to all who study the Scriptures.

In the Steps of St. Paul, H. V. Morton (London: Rich and Cowan), 1936.

A keen observer, Morton has filled his book with much interesting and helpful information about places and events in the life of Paul.

The Land and the Book, W. M. Thomson (Grand Rapids: Baker), 1954.

A classic that will never get out of date. It is difficult for the traveler in modern Israel to picture what the land was like in Bible times, when old Bible names are now associated with modern cities. Thomson toured the country at a time when it was still relatively undisturbed by modern civilization. His book is full of helpful information about Palestine as it was in Bible times.

Archaeology and the New Testament, Merrill F. Unger (Grand Rapids: Zondervan), 1962.

The book covers Palestine in the days of Jesus, the Roman world so well known to Paul, as well as a brief commentary on Palestine between the Testaments. Full of interesting information and numerous illustrations.

Archaeology of the Old Testament, Merrill F. Unger (Grand Rapids: Zondervan), 1954.

A standard work, thoroughly conservative, which faces the deeper problems. A good introduction to the subject. Good bibliographies. The student will probably want the companion volume on the archaeology of the New Testament.

The Geography of the Bible, Dennis Baley (New York: Harper), 1941.

A helpful introduction to the geographical features of the Holy Land and its Middle East neighbors by one who spent years in Bible lands. It enters into the deeper implications of geographic factors. The book contains 97 photographs, 47 maps and diagrams, a considerable bibliography, and a readable text.

The MacMillan Bible Atlas, Yohanan Aharoni and Michael Aui-Yonah (New York: MacMillan), 1968.

This book contains 262 maps covering Palestine from the time of the Canaanites to the Jewish revolt against Rome. The epitome of secular scholarship, some of its orientation would not be ours. The atlas, however, is packed with helpful maps which shed much light on Bible events.

Eerdmans' Atlas of the Bible (Grand Rapids: Eerdmans), 1983, First American Edition.

This small volume contains graphic maps in color and a section on all the places in the Bible giving brief information on those places. An interesting little book.

An Atlas of the Acts of the Apostles, John Sterling (Westwood, N.J.: Revell), 1966, Third Edition.

An excellent companion when studying the journeys of Paul. Contains 22 maps and a sketch of Jerusalem locating the events occurring there in the days of the apostles.

An Atlas of the Life of Christ, John Sterling (Westwood, N.J.: Revell), 1966, Fourth Edition.
Edited by a member of the British and Foreign Bible Society. It contains 20 maps and a two-page chart of the events of passion week. Very useable.

Rand McNally Bible Atlas, Emil Kraeling (Chicago: Rand McNally), 1956
The outstanding feature is the text, about 235,000 words. Though liberal in places, the book is valuable for describing the actual locations of the various episodes in the life of David, the conquests of Solomon, etc. There is an excellent discussion of the crossing of the Red Sea, the geographical features of the life of Gideon, the archaeology of the life of Saul, recent discoveries at Nazareth, the question of whether or not Paul visited Spain, and a chapter on a rarely treated subject—the geography of the Revelation.

The Atlas of the Bible, L. H. Grollenberg (Nashville: Nelson), 1956.
A Catholic work singularly free of bias. The index itself is almost a dictionary of geographical terms. The atlas contains the name of every town, village, mountain, valley, region, river, country, and people occurring in the Bible.

Hammond's Atlas of the Bible Lands (New York: Hammond), 1960.
Chiefly maps and illustrations accompanied by a few lines of text. Very moderately priced.

Baker's Bible Atlas, C. F. Pfeiffer (Grand Rapids: Baker), 1984.
Very helpful view of Bible geography. Includes colored maps and an informative commentary. Also an updated chapter on Biblical archeology. The atlas reflects recent happenings in the Middle East. A geographic gazetteer (69 pages) gives the location and pertinent information about Bible places.

WORD STUDIES AND BIBLES

The Exhaustive Concordance of the Bible, James Strong (New York: Abingdon), 1890, reprint.
The single most useful and functional Bible concordance. Other authorities on the Greek and Hebrew words of the Bible are now being coded into the lexicons which appear at the back of this concordance.

Analytic Concordance to the Bible, Robert Young (Grand Rapids: Eerdmans), 1975 reprint.
Young's Concordance differs from Strong's in the way material is organized. Young's is particularly useful for the student who wants to study every occurrence of a given Old or New Testament

word, since this concordance groups all Bible references under the given Hebrew or Greek word.

Gesenius' Hebrew-Chaldee Lexicon to the Old Testament Scriptures, S. P. Tregelles, trans. (Grand Rapids: Baker), 1979.

A comprehensive treatment of Old Testament words (more than 12,000 entries). Be sure to get the edition keyed to Strong's Concordance. A valuable tool.

Greek-English Lexicon of the New Testament, J. H. Thayer (Grand Rapids: Baker).

An exhaustive dictionary of New Testament words. Be sure to get the edition keyed to Strong's Concordance. A valuable tool.

A Critical Lexicon and Concordance to the English and Greek New Testament, E. W. Bullinger (London: Bagster), 1957, (now reprinted by Zondervan).

An excellent guide to the vocabulary of the Greek New Testament. Its plan of organization makes it very easy to use.

The English and Hebrew Bible Student's Concordance, Aaron Pick.

Does for the Old Testament what Bullinger's Critical Lexicon does for the New. Organized on the same plan, but is not always as helpful as Bullinger's work.

The New Scofield Reference Bible, C. I. Scofield, updated by E. Schuyler English and Committee (New York: Oxford University Press), 1967.

Some of the notes in this Bible are the best in any Bible. The note on the seventy weeks of Daniel, for instance, is the most helpful one to be found on this difficult passage. It is almost impossible to exaggerate the usefulness of this Bible for all who wish to rightly divide the word of truth.

The Emphasized Bible, J. B. Rotherham (Grand Rapids: Kregel), 1968.

Rotherham's unique system enables the reader to know just what and how much emphasis should be placed on any given word when reading the Bible. Very helpful at times.

The Companion Bible, E. W. Bullinger (London: Bagster).

Packed with helpful marginal comments on the Hebrew and Greek text. Rarely fails to give help with difficult passages. The structural outlines alone are worth the price of the book. The 198 appendixes are packed with valuable information. Students must beware of Bullinger's ultra-dispensationalism. Some of his dating is no longer valid.

Word Studies in the New Testament (4 vols.), M. R. Vincent (Grand Rapids: Eerdmans).

A cross between an exegetical commentary and a dictionary, this set opens up the force of New Testament words in their lexical sense, their etymology, history, inflection, and usage.

Wuest's Word Studies from the Greek New Testament (4 vols.), Kenneth S. Wuest (Grand Rapids: Eerdmans), 1966.

Excellent. Kenneth Wuest taught N.T. Greek at Moody Bible Institute. Anything he wrote deserves a place in the Bible student's library. You will find yourself consulting him often.

Word Pictures in the New Testament (6 vols.), A. T. Robertson (Nashville: Broadman).
Covers the New Testament book by book, commenting verse by verse, phrase by phrase, and, at times, word by word on the Greek text.

The New Testament for English Readers (4 vols.), Henry Alford (Grand Rapids: Baker).
Alford's work has been the classic in the field of commenting on the New Testament with special reference to the Greek text.

An Expository Dictionary of Biblical Words, W. E. Vine, Merrill F. Unger, and William White (Nashville: Nelson), 1984.
This combines W. E. Vine's famous *Expository Dictionary of New Testament Words* with a comparable treatment of Old Testament words. This valuable tool deserves a place in every Bible student's library.

BIBLE NAMES

Names of God, Nathan Stone (Chicago: Moody Press), 1944.
Brief but informative. Nathan Stone, a Hebrew Christian, taught Hebrew at Moody Bible Institute. This book is a reverential treatment of God's primary way of revealing His character in Old Testament times.

The Names of God in Holy Scripture, Andrew Jukes (Grand Rapids: Kregel), 1967.
A classic introduction to a vital subject.

A Dictionary of the Proper Names of the Old and New Testament Scriptures, (Neptune, N.J.: Loizeaux), 1946 reprint.
A list of all Bible names and their meanings.

The Proper Names of the Bible, John Farrar (London: Kelly), n.d.
Hard to find, but a classic. Gives not only the meaning of Bible names but information on the places and people.

BIBLE SURVEY

From Eternity to Eternity, Erich Sauer (Grand Rapids: Eerdmans), 1954.
A survey of God's dealings with mankind. The book is in three parts. Part 1 deals with God's overall plan of redemption in Christ. Part 2 deals with the Bible as the record of God's dealings with man. Part 3 deals with the coming kingdom, with special emphasis on various objections to the pre-millennial view of the return of Christ.

Triumph of the Crucified, Erich Sauer (London: Paternoster Press), 1951.

A survey of God's dealings with mankind during the New Testament period. Factual and interesting, the book is exact and thorough in setting forth New Testament doctrine. It contains some 3,700 Scripture references and many useful comments.

Dawn of World Redemption, Erich Sauer (London: Paternoster Press), 1951.
A survey of God's dealings with the human race during the Old Testament period. Many interesting sidelights on Bible truth add luster to this book, which reviews the whole process of divine redemption that culminates in Christ. Contains about 2,200 Scripture references and is a useful compendium of Old Testament theology.

Explore the Book, J. Sidlow Baxter (Grand Rapids: Zondervan), 1977 reprint.
An excellent survey of the whole Bible. Contains many helpful insights. The broad picture of Scripture unfolds in chapter after chapter. This book is thorough and very helpful.

Exploring the Scriptures, John Phillips (Chicago: Moody Press), 1978 revision.
A brief but useful overview of the whole Bible. Helpful maps and charts. Alliterated outlines give verbal road maps to each book of the Bible.

The Unfolding Drama of Redemption (3 vols.), W. Graham Scroggie (London: Pickering and Inglis), 1953.
Anything Scroggie wrote deserves a place in the Bible teacher's library. This series combines charts, tabulations, and commentary, to give a comprehensive, fast-paced overview of the whole Bible.

Know Your Bible: Old Testament and New Testament, W. Graham Scroggie (London: Pickering and Inglis), 1956.
Brief introductions to each book of the Bible. Pithy comments and good outlines. The New Testament section is more thorough than the Old Testament section.

The New Bible Handbook, G. T. Manley, G. C. Robinson and A. M. Stibbs (Downers Grove, Ill.: InterVarsity Press), 1956 reprint.
Helpful introductions to each book of the Bible. Critical problems are addressed and the claims of liberal theology explained and exposed.

Living Messages of the Books of the Bible, G. Campbell Morgan (Westwood, N.J.: Revell), 1912.
This great expositor captures the heart and essential message of each book of the Bible.

PARABLES AND TYPES

The Study of the Types, Ada R. Habershon (Grand Rapids: Kregel), 1973 reprint.
A classic treatment of the subject by a painstaking author.

Camping with God, Stephen Olford (Neptune, N.J.: Loizeaux), 1971.
A study on the tabernacle by a gifted expositor. Very devotional and practical. Stephen Olford learned his typology among
the Plymouth Brethren who excelled in this approach to the
Old Testament.

The Parables of the Lord Jesus Christ, Thomas Newberry (Glasgow:
Pickering & Inglis), n.d.
The author of the famous and once popular *Newberry Bible* brings
his scholarship and expertise to bear on this specialized area of
Bible truth.

Notes on the Parables of the Lord, Richard C. Trench (London: Kegan,
Paul, Trench, Trubner), 1906.
This is the classic on the subject. Not everyone will agree with
some of Archbishop Trench's conclusions. (Be sure to get the edition in which the Latin footnotes are translated.)

Lectures on the Tabernacle, Samuel Ridout (Neptune, N.J.:
Loizeaux), 1945.
A very useful introduction to an important area of Bible typology.

The Tabernacle, Walter Scott (London: Alfred Holmess), n.d.
Well-known for his classic work on *Revelation,* Walter Scott brings
his Biblical insights to bear on this area of typology.

The Parables and Metaphors of the Lord, G. Campbell Morgan (London: Marshall, Morgan, Scott), 1944.
Excellent treatment. At times, however, the author's weakness in
the area of prophecy shows. Overall, very helpful.

All the Parables of the Bible, Herbert Lockyer (London: Paternoster),
1963.
The more important books on the parables have been digested,
and their views explained, along with the author's own sane interpretation. Most helpful.

Pictures and Parables, G. H. Lang (London: Paternoster), 1955.
Always interesting, sometimes controversial, often very helpful
treatment of all the parables and illustrations of the Bible.

Preaching from the Types and Metaphors of the Bible, Benjamin Keach
(Grand Rapids: Kregel).
This old classic has been reprinted. It presents the entire range of
Bible symbolism. It is heartily recommended by Herbert Lockyer,
who acknowledges his indebtedness to this volume in producing
some of his own works.

The Study of the Parables, Ada R. Habershon (London: Pickering &
Inglis) n.d.
A comprehensive overview of the parabolic method in both the
Old and New Testaments. Some details might be questioned but
no one will deny the way this book stimulates one's own thoughts.

The Tabernacle, The Priesthood and The Offerings, Henry W. Soltau
(London: Morgan & Scott), 1850.
Probably the most helpful single book on the subject. Be sure to

get the author's companion volume on the furniture of the tabernacle, *The Holy Vessels and Furniture of the Tabernacle*, reprinted
by Kregel.

PROPHECY

Millennialism: The Two Major Views, Charles L. Feinberg (Chicago:
Moody Press), 1980 revision.
  Dr. Feinberg was raised on Biblical Hebrew in a strictly orthodox Jewish home, with a view to becoming a rabbi. This book is
an authoritative treatment on the millennialist and
a-millennialist views of Bible prophecy and of the schemes of interpretation lying behind the two views. Scholarly—and
devastating for a-millennialism.

The Rapture Question, John F. Walvoord (Grand Rapids:
Zondervan), 1979 revised and enlarged.
  A thorough-going examination of the four views of the
church's role in the tribulation: partial rapturism, pre-
tribulationism, mid-tribulationism, and post-tribulationism.
Dr. Walvoord is noted for his staunch defense of the pre-
tribulation position and as the scholarly and erudite president
of Dallas Theological Seminary.

Things To Come, J. Dwight Pentecost (Findlay, Ohio: Durham), 1958.
  A monumental work which lays the foundation for all sound understanding of the prophetic Scriptures. Dr. Pentecost shows the
important part played by exegesis, synthesis, hermeneutics, and a
consistent theological system in grasping eschatology.

The Lamp of Prophecy, H. A. Ironside (Grand Rapids: Zondervan),
1940.
  An introduction to Bible prophecy by the beloved former pastor
of Moody Memorial Church. Dr. Ironside specializes in making
truth simple. An excellent place to begin a study of prophecy.

The Coming Prince, Sir Robert Anderson (Grand Rapids: Kregel
Publications reprint), 1954.
  A scholarly investigation of the person and work of the Antichrist.
Contains an epochal chapter on the chronology of Daniel's seven-
ty weeks.

Rays of Messianic Glory, or Christ in the Old Testament, David Baron
(London), 1888.
  This has been called one of the most precious volumes on Messianic prophecy ever written by a great Christian Hebrew scholar
who was not only an able expositor, but also a man filled with love
and adoration for Christ. Long out of print, but find it if you can.

Great Prophecies of the Centuries concerning Israel and the Gentiles, G.
H. Pember (London: Hodder & Stoughton), 1895.
  One of the greatest books on the prophecies of the Old Testament
relating to the Gentiles and the Jewish nation. Not all Pember's

conclusions can be accepted, but his book remains a masterpiece.

The Great Prophecies of the Centuries concerning the Church, G. H. Pember (London: Hodder & Stoughton), 1909.
Pember was a profound student of prophecy. The prophetic passages of Matthew receive special attention in this book.

Exploring the World of the Jew, John Phillips (Chicago: Moody Press), 1981.
A look at the Jew in history and prophecy. Traces the development of the Talmud and its influence on the Jew down the ages. A chapter on pseudo-Messiahs gives information overlooked by many Christians. The author was in Palestine for the last two years of the British mandate and saw firsthand many of the events that led up to the rebirth of the State of Israel. A book for all who wish to know more about the fascinating Jewish people.

The Roman Empire in the Light of Prophecy, W. E. Vine (London), 1916.
Many books have been written about the final alignment of the nations of Europe at the time of the appearance of Antichrist. Many are fanciful. This book is based on a sound, sane investigation of Scripture. It contains five excellent maps of the Roman empire in different periods of history.

The Divine Program of the World's History, H. Gratton Guinness (London), 1888.
A magnificent, authoritative treatment of prophecy as unfolded by "The Adamic Program," "The Noahic Program," "The Abramic Program," "The Mosaic Program," "The Davidic Program," "The Daniel Program," "The Christian Program."

Exploring the Future, John Phillips (Nashville: Nelson), 1983.
An up-to-date look at the prophecies of the Bible: a synopsis of Daniel, Revelation, and Zechariah; chapters on the dying prophecy of Jacob, the astonishing prophecies of Balaam, and the Lord's great Olivet prophecies. The book also contains chapters on Israel, Russia, and her satellites, the Bible and the Bomb, the rapture, the coming occult invasion, and much more. Useful maps and charts.

CHRISTOLOGY

The Crisis of the Christ, G. Campbell Morgan (New York: Fleming H. Revell) 1903.
This series of studies on the birth, baptism, temptation, transfiguration, crucifixion, resurrection, and ascension of the Lord Jesus comprise this author's greatest work (published when he was forty years of age). Rereading it when much older, he said, "I wouldn't change a word of it."

The Great Physician, G. Campbell Morgan (New York: Fleming H. Revell) 1937.
A look at the Lord Jesus as the healer of bodies and souls as revealed in the Gospels and the book of Acts. An incisive study of the Lord at work. A book to come back to again and again.

The Life of Christ, James Stalker (New York: Revell) 1891.
Traces the life of the Lord from His birth, through His infancy and youth, to His death. A tender and inspiring commentary on the life and times of our loved Lord. A classic.

The Trial and Death of Jesus Christ, James Stalker (London: Hodder & Stoughton), 1894.
A devotional history of the last days of the Lord. The book begins with Christ's arrest, reviews His various trials, traces His sufferings before and on the way to Calvary. It contains vivid sketches of Herod, Pilate, Judas. It enables us to draw near to the groups around the cross, listen to the Lord's last words, and reverently contemplate His sufferings. An unforgettable book.

Who Moved the Stone? Frank Morrison (London: Faber & Faber), 1930.
Most will not agree with the final conclusion, but the road along the way is so interesting that this book is hard to put down. It brings to life the story of the trial of Jesus and the events leading up to His death and burial.

Your God Is Too Small, J. B. Phillips (New York: MacMillan), 1967.
A fascinating study in two parts. The first part deals with most people's wholly inadequate concept of God. The second part tells what we might expect to happen if God became a man. Not surprising—it is just what happened. Very readable.

The Lord from Heaven, Sir Robert Anderson (Grand Rapids: Kregel), 1978 reprint.
A Bible study on the Sonship of the Lord Jesus. All who read this book will come away with a deeper appreciation of the Lord. This book has stood the test of time—it is one hundred years old.

The Life of Christ (2 vols.), Frederick W. Farrar (London: Casses, Pelter & Galpin), 1874.
Farrar's liberal views are overruled in this book by his masterly treatment of the story of Jesus. Contains much helpful material as, for instance, comments on the apocryphal stories of Christ's childhood.

The Search for the Twelve Apostles, William S. McBirnie (Wheaton: Tyndale), 1973.
The author has unearthed an astonishing amount of information about the Lord's disciples and other apostles not numbered among the twelve. The author's travels and diligence in studying and researching every scrap of evidence and information, digging it out, sifting it, and placing the results of his study before us are commendatory. Interesting and illuminating.

The Master and His Men, J. Stuart Holden (London: Marshall Morgan & Scott), 1953.
What do we know about James, son of Alphaeus, or Lebbaeus (Thaddaeus)? By what other name do we know Bartholemew? Here is a penetrating study of the Lord's disciples. The author introduces us to these men as though he had known them all his life.

Jesus Christ Our Lord, Alexander Whyte (Grand Rapids: Zondervan), 1953 reprint.
Thirty-five vivid chapters by a master of the art, devoted to the most wonderful Person who ever lived. Reading this book for the first time is an unforgettable experience.

MISCELLANEOUS

Figures of Speech Used in the Bible, E. W. Bullinger (London: Eyes & Spottiswoode), 1898.
Unsurpassed. The author identifies and explains 200 Bible figures of speech and gives examples of their use. A classic.

Numbers in Scripture, E. W. Bullinger (London: Lamp Press), 1952 reprint.
Undoubtedly the classic treatment of the subject. Absolutely unsurpassed.

Thy Word Is Truth, Edward J. Young (Grand Rapids: Eerdmans), 1957.
This book deals with the Biblical doctrine of inspiration and is one of the finest books on the subject from a conservative viewpoint. Faces major problems.

Systematic Theology (8 vols.), Lewis Sperry Chafer (Dallas: Dallas Seminary), 1947–1948.
An indispensable set for every serious student of Scripture. It needs to be read and well marked. There are many works on theology on the market but this one is the best for the initial foundation.

Dictionary of Theology, Everett Harrison (Grand Rapids: Baker), 1960.
Helpful on the whole. It contains articles on all kinds of theological issues, including an interesting article on "The Fate of the Heathen."

Major Bible Themes, Lewis Sperry Chafer and John Walvoord (Grand Rapids: Zondervan), 1980 reprint.
A useful handbook of 52 Bible doctrines. One could profitably read one a week.

The Principles of Theology, W. H. Griffith Thomas (London: Church Book Room Press Ltd.), 1951 reprint.
This former vicar of St. Pauls, London, looks at the 39 Articles of the Church of England and expounds them. We might not agree with all his positions but we can certainly profit from many of them.

Bible Characters (6 vols.), Alexander Whyte (Grand Rapids: Zondervan), 1968 reprint (one vol.).
Unsurpassable. You'll soon get hooked on Alexander Whyte and want to read everything he wrote. Not all his "characters" are equally well treated, but when he excels he does so surpassingly.

Saul Called Paul, Alexander Whyte (Grand Rapids: Zondervan), 1955.
Whenever Alexander Whyte touches a Bible character he brings that individual to life. This masterly series of studies in the life and ministry of Paul is unsurpassed.

COMMENTARIES

The Pulpit Commentary, (23 vols.), H. D. M. Spence and J. S. Exell, eds. (Grand Rapids: Eerdmans), 1950 reprint.
This old timer still has much to say. Introductory essays deal with critical issues for each book. The commentary, by various authors, is in the form of verse-by-verse exposition of the text. Then follows homiletical material (of varying value) on the passage just exegeted. Generally very helpful.

Commentary on the Old Testament, (10 vols.), C. F. Keil and F. Delitzsch, eds. (Grand Rapids: Eerdmans), 1971.
A classic of conservative Biblical scholarship. Good exegetical insight and a rich source of information. Wilbur M. Smith claimed there was nothing to compare with this set.

The New International Commentary on the New Testament, (17 vols.), (Grand Rapids: Eerdmans).
Wilbur M. Smith considered this series to be the most important commentary on the New Testament. It is by various authors, so their doctrinal bias needs to be taken into consideration.

Tyndale New Testament Commentaries (20 vols.), R. V. G. Tasker, ed.
A popular series of paperback commentaries. Not too technical nor unhelpfully brief. Written by a number of evangelical scholars. Critical questions are fully considered in introductory sections and in additional notes.

Expositions of Holy Scriptures (32 vols.), Alexander MacLaren (Grand Rapids: Baker), 1910, reprinted 1975 (17 vols.).
Often called the "prince of expositors," MacLaren's works are always helpful. The drawback with this set is that the author does not expound all the passages in a given Bible book. If you find one you need, however, on which MacLaren has a sermon, you will usually have found a gold mine.

The Expositor's Bible (6 vols.), W. Robertson Nicoll, ed. (Grand Rapids: Baker), 1956.
This work is patchy—much depends on which author is writing. Not all the authors are sound, so the commentary needs to be used with discretion. Parts of it are valuable, however, Sir George

Adam Smith, for instance, on the Minor Prophets, provides excellent flashes of insight into the backgrounds against which the twelve ministered—although his liberal bias shows. Not a set for everyone.

The New Testament and Wycliffe Bible Commentary, Charles F. Pfeiffer and Everett Harrison, eds. (Chicago: Moody Press), 1962.
A phrase-by-phrase treatment of the Bible by a variety of Old and New Testament scholars. The book is printed in two columns, the Bible text in one and the commentary alongside in the other. Since the 48 contributors come from more than 15 denominational backgrounds and include professors from 25 schools of Christian higher education, differences of interpretation among the authors surface. Still, the work is worth consulting as a one-volume commentary.

Commentary on the Whole Bible, Jamieson, Fausset & Brown (Grand Rapids: Zondervan), n.d. (Reprint. One vol.)
Originally published in a series of volumes, this condensation is handy and usually helpful. Each Bible book has an introductory essay followed by verse by verse exposition of the text. A lot of information is packed into a relatively small space.

The Student's Commentary on the Holy Scriptures, George Williams (London: Thynne & Co.), 1932 reprint.
This one-volume commentary is devotional and helpful. Special attention is paid to typology. You will find yourself underlining almost all of it. In some places the comments are too brief. The spiritual lessons of the Old and New Testaments are ably presented.

Genesis to Deuteronomy: Notes on the Pentateuch, C. H. Mackintosh (Neptune, N.J.: Loizeaux), 1972 reprint (one vol.).
Devotional and inspirational. Lacks clear outlines. Emphasizes types and shadows that speak of Christ in the Pentateuch.

The Genesis Record, Henry M. Morris (Grand Rapids: Baker), 1976.
The author describes this as "a scientific and devotional commentary." A very helpful book, one you will refer to constantly when studying Genesis.

The Pocket Commentary of the Bible: Genesis, Basil F. C. Atkinson (Chicago: Moody Press), 1957.
A verse-by-verse commentary. Always helpful. Brief but meaty.

Gleanings in Genesis, Arthur W. Pink (Chicago: Moody Press), 1922.
One has to beware of Pink's hyper-Calvinism. Apart from that, this is an excellent commentary, especially for those interested in typology.

Exploring Genesis, John Phillips (Chicago: Moody Press), 1980.
Alliterated outlines. Readable commentary. Helps bring to life the people who throng the pages of this important Old Testament book. Useable and preachable.

The Pocket Commentary of the Bible: Exodus, Basil F. C. Atkinson (London: Henry Walker Ltd.), n.d.
Atkinson was under-librarian of Cambridge University in England. His plan is to trace Christ in all the Scripture. He brings an acute and believing mind to the study of the Bible and his reverent meditations are worth considering. This book has hundreds of references to other passages of the Bible. Worth consulting even if all his conclusions cannot be accepted.

Gleanings in Exodus, Arthur W. Pink (Chicago: Moody Press), 1962.
Arthur W. Pink was a gifted expositor, able at times to soar to flights of considerable eloquence. No one can read him without getting some help, even though one cannot always accept his extreme teachings on divine sovereignty.

Lectures on the Tabernacle, S. Ridout (Neptune, N.J.: Loizeaux), 1945.
A helpful book on this often neglected portion of Exodus. Ridout excels at drawing out the spiritually significant lessons of the tabernacle.

The Pocket Commentary of the Bible: Leviticus, Basil F. C. Atkinson (London: Henry Walker Ltd.), n.d.
When approaching the first seven chapters of Leviticus one needs to see Christ or else conclude these chapters have little to say to us today. This commentary will show you Christ and also yourself. Helpful though brief.

An Outline of Leviticus, C. A. Coates (Kingston-on-Thames: Stowhill Bible and Tract Co.), n.d.
C. A. Coates is hard to read because he follows no discernible outline. His thoughts are devotional and Christ exalting. He represents a school of thought that specializes in typology. If you find him useful, you will probably want his other commentaries on the books of Moses.

The Law of the Offerings, Andrew Jukes (Grand Rapids: Kregel), n.d. Reprint.
If you are studying the difficult chapters of Leviticus dealing with the offerings you will find this book indispensable. You will end up underlining nearly all of it.

The Pocket Commentary of the Bible: Numbers, Basil F. C. Atkinson (London: Henry Walter Ltd.), 1956.
Homiletical, expository, and devotional; a mine of wealth. The book brings out the spiritual lessons, the clear types, and the Christology of the book of Numbers.

Conquest and Victory: Studies in Joshua, Carl Armerding (Chicago: Moody Press), 1967.
Dr. Armerding underlines the great spiritual truths underlying the book of Joshua. He shows how every advance is challenged by the enemy. He presents the lessons of the various battles, the cities

of refuge, the altar of witness. He brings out the believer's possession, provision, and protection in today's spiritual battle.

Victorious Christian Living: Studies in the Book of Joshua, Alan Redpath (Westwood, N.J.: Revell), 1955.
Alan Redpath transforms the truth of Joshua from history into dynamic Christian living. He seeks to enable us to bridge the gap between what we believe and how we behave.

The Land and Life of Rest, W. Graham Scroggie (London: Pickering & Inglis), 1950.
Five thought-provoking Bible studies delivered at the famous Keswick meetings in England. Devotional and challenging. Small but powerful.

Lectures on the Book of Judges, Samuel Ridout (Neptune, N.J.: Loizeaux), n.d.
A devotional commentary that grasps the essence of the disastrous days of the Judges. The author brings out the parallel between Israel's military, social, and religious struggles in Canaan and our spiritual struggles in the heavenlies. He reveals our failures as well as our victories.

A Critical and Expository Commentary on the Book of Judges, A. R. Fausset (London: Nisbet), 1885.
An old classic. A verse-by-verse commentary with special attention to background detail.

Israel's Iron Age: Sketches from the Period of the Judges, Marcus Dods (London: Hodder & Stoughton), 1874.
This out-of-print survey of the leading characters in the book of Judges is priceless. Half-a-dozen key Bible characters are studied and made to live.

Boaz and Ruth, August VanRyn (Fort Dodge, Ia.: Walterick), n.d.
A delightful study of a charming book by a warm-hearted, original, and interesting author.

All the Kings and Queens of the Bible, Herbert Lockyer (Grand Rapids: Zondervan), 1961.
This informative book covers not only the kings and queens of Israel and Judah but also other Gentile monarchs whose histories impinged on that of God's people. Filled with useful information.

A History of Israel, John J. Davis and John C. Whitcomb (Winona Lake: BMH Books), 1969–1971.
The book is a historical commentary on the history of Israel from the conquest to the exile. It belongs on the shelf along with Edersheim's great work on *Bible History.* Since this book reflects more recent scholarship than Edersheim's work it is particularly helpful in settling matters of dates and chronology in the light of our increased knowledge of ancient times.

Psalms, W. Graham Scroggie (Old Tappan, N.J.: Revell), 1948.
A classic. Each Psalm is briefly introduced. Of special value is the

appendix, a mine of information on the Psalms and on Hebrew poetry in general.

The Book of Psalms, A. F. Kirkpatrick (London: Cambridge University Press), 1902.
A gold mine on the Psalms. Sometimes the author expresses critical views with which we would disagree; otherwise an invaluable help.

The Treasury of David (3 vols.), C. H. Spurgeon (McLean, Va.: MacDonald).
The classic on the Psalms. Probably the most-quoted author on this important segment of Bible poetry. Each psalm is presented in three parts: a general verse-by-verse exposition, explanatory notes and quaint sayings, hints to preachers.

Studies in the Psalms, J. B. Rotherham (London: Allenson Ltd.), 1911.
Another old-timer packed with helpful information. The author is particularly helpful in discussing the occasion that gave each psalm its birth. He emphasizes the dispensational character of the Psalms. His translation and special treatment of what words should be emphasized are very helpful.

Exploring the Psalms (5 vols.), John Phillips (Neptune, N.J.: Loizeaux), 1985–1987.
Clear, useable alliterated outlines open up each psalm in visual form. The exposition is sound and filled with practical illustrations. Attention is paid to the circumstances lying behind each psalm. The prophetic element in the Psalms is recognized and given due prominence.

An Exposition of Proverbs, Charles Bridges (Jenkintown, Pa.: Sovereign Grace Publishers), 1959 reprint distributed by Zondervan.
Books on the Proverbs are rare. This verse-by-verse commentary is a good one. The author's definition of a proverb: "The great object in each of the Proverbs . . . is to enforce a moral principle in words so few that they may be easily learned . . . "

A Homiletic Commentary on the Book of Ecclesiastes, Thomas Leale (London: Dickinson), 1877.
Out-of-print, but worth having if you can find it. This is a verse-by-verse commentary with critical notes introducing each section.

Exploring the Song of Solomon, John Phillips (Neptune, N.J.: Loizeaux), 1984.
There are more differing views on the Song of Solomon than on any other book of the Bible except Revelation. The author takes the view that the Shulamite, having given her heart to her Shepherd, is tempted by Solomon, using all this world's glory as a bait, to switch her affections to him. A Christ-exalting book and a study in temptation. Alliterated outlines help the reader keep on course.

Isaiah, W. E. Vine (London: Oliphants), 1946.
A verse by verse commentary by the gifted author of the famous *Expository Dictionary of New Testament Words.* Brief, but
very helpful.

Studies in Isaiah, F. C. Jennings (Neptune, N.J.: Loizeaux), n.d.
The classic commentary on Isaiah. The author comments on the
book paragraph by paragraph. The approach is scholarly,
premillennial, and spiritual.

The Book of Isaiah, George L. Robinson (Grand Rapids: Baker),
1958.
It would be hard to find another book packing so much helpful information on Isaiah in such a short space. The book is a series of
15 studies that put the man, the times, and the message together
in a vivid way.

Studies in the Prophecy of Jeremiah, G. Campbell Morgan (Westwood,
N.J.: Revell), 1958 reprint.
The author brings his considerable skills to provide the broad
movements of the book of Jeremiah against the background of
the tragic events behind it. Many an incisive comment causes one
to stop and think and apply the truth personally.

The Book of Daniel, Clarence Larkin (Philadelphia: Larkin Estate),
1929.
A helpful verse-by-verse commentary enlivened by the author's unique charts. The author has drawn on the ablest
scholars and the best books available to him to give a very understandable commentary.

The Climax of the Ages: Studies in the Prophecy of Daniel, F. A. Tatford
(London: Marshall Morgan & Scott), 1953.
The author has read and digested everything available to him on
the subject. A valuable verse-by-verse commentary. The book
contains a useful appendix by F. F. Bruce on "The Chronology of
Daniel 1:1" as well as a summary of relevant dates.

In and Around the Book of Daniel, Charles Boutflower (London: Society for Promoting Christian Knowledge), 1923.
Brings the cream of archaeological research to bear on the book
of Daniel. An informative book combining commentary with illustrations from archaeology.

The Minor Prophets (2 vols.), E. B. Pusey (Grand Rapids: Baker) 1953
reprint.
This old classic is hard to read because of the very small type in
which it is set. Nor would we agree with all the author's comments. But for a book on the lives and times of the prophets, this
one is hard to beat.

The Twelve Minor Prophets, George L. Robinson (Grand Rapids:
Baker), 1952 reprint.
A handbook of great value and readability. If you are studying

this section of Scripture you will want to read this book first to give you orientation.

The Major Messages of the Minor Prophets, Charles Lee Feinberg (New York: The American Board of Missions to the Jews).

Hosea (1947)

Joel, Amos, and Obadiah (1948)

Jonah, Micah, and Nahum (1951)

Habakkuk, Zephaniah, Haggai, and Malachi (1951)

Zechariah (1952)

These books are indispensable, written by a Hebrew Christian scholar. They are readable and shed much light on these neglected books of the Bible.

A Guide to the Gospels, W. Graham Scroggie (London: Pickering and Inglis), 1948.

Everything Scroggie wrote deserves a place on your book shelf. The author works through the Gospels three times—first synthetically, then analytically, and finally Christologically. Packed with useful information and enhanced with visual aids.

The Four Gospels, Samuel Ridout (Neptune, N.J.: Loizeaux), 1947.

The Gospels are looked at nine different ways in this notable book. The chapter on the typical and symbolic representations of the four Gospels is especially interesting.

The Four Gospels (4 vols.), G. Campbell Morgan (London: Oliphants) 1956 reprint.

You will find yourself consulting these books again and again. Although the outline is sometimes obscure, the author specializes in bringing the broad sweep and scope of the Gospels before us. He mixes in a liberal measure of background material and a reverent love for the Lord.

The Fourfold Gospel, J. W. McGarvey and P. Y. Pendleton (Cincinnati: Standard), n.d.

A chronological commentary on the four Gospels, combining a harmony of the Gospels with a rich, lively text.

Studies in the Sermon on the Mount (2 vols.), D. Martyn Lloyd-Jones (Grand Rapids: Eerdmans), 1959–1960.

The classic on the subject. The book consists of a series of sermons preached by the author at Westminster Chapel in London. The approach is expository. Although the author takes issue with dispensationalism, the books are devotional, heartwarming, and challenging.

Studies in Mark's Gospel, A. T. Robertson (Nashville: Broadman Press), 1958 revision.

This is not a verse-by-verse exposition but a series of studies on the themes in Mark's Gospel (Christ's parables, miracles, teaching). The author traces Peter's influence on Mark.

The Gospel of Mark, W. Graham Scroggie (Grand Rapids: Zondervan), 1979 reprint.

A verse-by-verse commentary by one of the great Bible teachers of our times.

A Commentary on the Gospel of Luke, F. Godet. E. W. Shalders, trans. (Edinburgh: T & T Clark), 1890.
An old classic. This verse-by-verse commentary reveals the author's scholarship as well as mastery of the subject. Always helpful and thorough.

John: His Record of Christ: W. E. Vine (London: Oliphants), 1948.
A verse-by-verse commentary with special attention paid to the glories of Jesus as the Son of God. Rich and reverent.

The Acts of the Apostles, G. Campbell Morgan (New York: Fleming H. Revell), 1924.
"Each new page flames with some surprise, and one is held in suspense to the end—and then left to dream dreams of all that has not been recorded—and of all that follows after" (from the author's introduction). G. Campbell Morgan, too, never fails to surprise us with his skill as an expositor.

Commentary on the Book of the Acts, F. F. Bruce (London: Marshall Morgan & Scott), 1954.
Fast becoming a classic. A lively commentary is accompanied by extensive footnotes equally as interesting and informative. F. F. Bruce relegates to footnotes enough meat to make an entire book for lesser authors.

Exploring Acts, John Phillips (Chicago: Moody Press), 1986.
Clear outlines, graphic commentary. The Holy Spirit as seen in Acts is dealt with. Exposes the errors of the charismatic movement.

Life of St. Paul, James Stalker (Grand Rapids: Zondervan), n.d.
One of the best brief studies of Paul's life and ministry. A valuable background to a study of Acts and the Pauline epistles.

The Life and Epistles of Paul, W. J. Conybeare and J. S. Howson (Grand Rapids: Eerdmans), 1959 reprint.
The classic on the subject. Packed with information on the times in which Paul lived, the places he visited, the story of his life, and the circumstances that gave birth to his epistles. The book contains a translation of Paul's letters with comments.

The Epistle to the Romans, W. E. Vine (Grand Rapids: Zondervan), 1957.
A verse-by-verse commentary with special attention paid to the meaning of the words in the Greek text.

Romans, Verse by Verse, William R. Newell (Chicago: Moody Press), 1938.
A comprehensive commentary by one of the masters of Bible exposition.

Exploring Romans, John Phillips (Chicago: Moody Press), 1969.
Alan Redpath says of this book, "I was immediately captivated, not only by its sound and thoroughly evangelical exposition, but also by the practical application . . . This is a book every minister

will find of immense value . . . I would find this volume hard to beat . . . " This book is enhanced by alliterated outlines that reflect the teaching of the Biblical text.

The Corinthian Letters of Paul, G. Campbell Morgan (Westwood, N.J.: Revell), 1946.
The "charismatic problem" was not nearly so great a problem when Morgan wrote as today. For help on this one must look elsewhere. Still, this is a good book in which the author displays to the full his great talent for getting to the heart of a passage of Scripture.

The New Century Bible Commentary: I and II Corinthians, F. F. Bruce (Grand Rapids: Eerdmans), 1971.
Brief comments on each verse with some reference to problems brought on by the charismatics. Bruce makes us aware of his scholarship and mastery of the Greek text.

First Corinthians, W. E. Vine (Grand Rapids: Zondervan), 1951.
An indispensable book to have handy when studying this epistle. W. E. Vine's grasp of the Greek text comes through clearly.

The Royal Route to Heaven: Studies in I Corinthians, Alan Redpath (Westwood, N.J.: Revell), 1960.
Messages preached at Chicago's Moody Church by a pastor deeply burdened by the urgency and relevancy of the truths of this important epistle. It is typical of Alan Redpath that he should tread lightly down the controversial 12th and 14th chapters and major on the challenging 13th chapter.

The Corinthian Catastrophe, George E. Gardiner (Grand Rapids: Kregel), 1974.
This little book is the answer to the charismatics. George Gardiner was reared in the Pentecostal tradition and at one time was zealous for that doctrinal position. He came to understand the Scriptures better and became a vocal and able apologist for the traditional, conservative view on the Holy Spirit and His gift.

The Second Epistle to the Corinthians, Handley C. G. Moule (London: Pickering and Inglis), 1962.
All this man's books (on Romans, Ephesians, Philippians and Colossians) should be on one's shelf and deserve to be studied. A scholar, the Bishop of Durham (England), a gifted teacher, and a choice servant of God, Handley Moule's books are always illuminating—especially his insights into the original text.

Blessings out of Buffetings: Studies in II Corinthians, Alan Redpath (Westwood, N.J.: Revell), 1965.
The former pastor of Moody Church in Chicago brings all his skill as an expositor to bear on this practical treatment of the most autobiographical of all Paul's letters.

The Epistle to the Galatians, C. F. Hogg and W. E. Vine (Grand Rapids: Kregel), 1921.

Here is a sound and reliable commentary. Questions of a historical or textual nature are faced. Here is a verse-by-verse,
clause-by-clause, sense-for-sense exposition for all who thought-
fully study the Scriptures.

Govett on Galatians, A. Govett (London: Thynne & Co.), 1930.
Another title for this book is "Moses or Christ?" Govett is known
for his logic, independence, orderly handling of material, simplic-
ity, and faithful adherence to Scripture. This is a helpful
verse-by-verse commentary.

The Epistle to the Ephesians, F. F. Bruce (Westwood, N.J.: Revell),
1961.
Concise and coherent evaluation of critical questions surrounding
the circumstances of the epistle. A verse-by-verse commentary
with special help in hard places.

The Wealth, Walk and Warfare of the Christians, Ruth Paxson (London: Oliphants) 1939.
A devotional commentary with special emphasis on living the
higher life.

Philippian Studies, H. C. G. Moule (London: Hodder & Stoughton),
1897.
"The whole aim is towards edification" says the author of this
commentary. Each segment is treated exegetically and then
homiletically. We are aware that we are walking with a scholar and
a saint as we study Ephesians in the company of this great teacher.

The Epistles to the Philippians and Colossians, W. E. Vine (London:
Oliphants)
In early days, W. E. Vine was a schoolmaster. His habits of grammatical, textual, and historical accuracy are evident in his
commentaries. This is a verse-by-verse commentary with attention paid to the original Greek text.

Joy Way (Philippians), Guy King (London: Marshall, Morgan &
Scott), 1952.
This commentary on Philippians reveals the author's gift for clear
outlines and concise comments.

Crossing the Border (Colossians), Guy King (Fort Washington, Pa.:
Christian Literature Crusade), 1957.
Guy King's commentaries are always a favorite with busy preachers because of his clear outlines and helpful comments. This book
on Colossians follows the usual pattern.

Colossians and Philemon Studies, Handley C. G. Moule (Westwood,
N.J.: Revell), n.d.
Another in the series of great commentaries by this gifted Bible
teacher and scholar. Very helpful and devotional.

Studies in Philemon, W. Graham Scroggie (Grand Rapids: Kregel),
1977.
Eight short but pregnant chapters from a gifted author on a neglected New Testament memo. Excellent.

A Leader Led (I Timothy), Guy King (Ft. Washington, Pa.: Christian
Literature Crusade), 1951.
   The author's desire was to bring out of this epistle all that applies
to us and to our conditions of life today. The author's Anglican
background can occasionally be detected. A worthwhile book on
I Timothy.
The Second Epistle to Timothy, H. C. G. Moule (Grand Rapids: Baker),
1952.
   The chapters are short, but there are 48 of them. Each one yields
something of profit.
To My Son (II Timothy), Guy King (London: Marshall, Morgan &
Scott), 1944.
   Chapter titles tell us much about the author's way with words:
"The Gospel Gold-Mine," "At the End of the Road," "Snapshot of
Six Soldiers." A good commentary.
The Epistle to the Hebrews, W. E. Vine (Grand Rapids: Zondervan),
1952.
   Another in the author's usual verse-by-verse exposition accompa-
nied by helpful comments and references to the Greek text.
The Hebrews Epistle, Sir Robert Anderson (London: Nisbet), 1911.
   A lesser-known of Sir Robert Anderson's works, one of his best.
In this book the author brings his keen mind to bear on the Penta-
teuchal types in Hebrews. It shows clearly how dependent
Christian revelation is on the divine religion of Judaism as en-
shrined in the Old Testament.
Exploring Hebrews, John Phillips (Chicago: Moody Press), 1977.
   A verse-by-verse exposition of Hebrews with alliterated outlines
that graphically open up the text and enable the reader to keep on
course while studying the epistle. Special attention is paid to the
five warning passages and to the "Westminster Abbey of the
Faith," the great picture gallery of Hebrews (chapter eleven).
Helpful illustrations enliven the text. A Christ-exalting book.
A Belief That Behaves (James), Guy King (London: Marshall, Morgan
& Scott), 1941.
   Some chapter titles: "All in the Same Boat," "The Short-
Sighted Usher," "A Subject That Is in Everyone's Mouth,"
"Camel-Knees." The book lives up to expectations. A brief but
pertinent commentary.
Practical and Social Aspects of Christianity, A. T. Robertson (New
York: Hodder & Stoughton), 1915.
   This is a valuable commentary on the epistle of James. Expository
in character, scholarly in style, helpful in essence.
James Your Brother, Lehman Strauss (Neptune, N.J.: Loizeaux),
1956.
   All of Lehman Strauss's commentaries are worth including in
one's library. The author has been a successful pastor of a large
church, a well-known radio teacher, and a popular conference

speaker for many years. He has a gift for making difficult passages plain and challenges the reader with practical applications of truth.

Epochs in the Life of Simon Peter, A. T. Robertson (New York: Scribners), 1933.
The two epistles of Peter are included in this survey. Through it we get to know this giant of faith for ourselves. A readable book.

The Epistles of John, F. F. Bruce (Grand Rapids: Eerdmans), 1970.
A look at some of the more difficult books of the New Testament by a noted scholar. Verse-by-verse exposition. Practical and helpful.

The Epistles of John, W. E. Vine (London: Oliphants), 1965.
A verse-by-verse devotional commentary of three epistles written at a time when heresy was making tremendous inroads into the church. Helpful and practical.

The Fellowship (I John), Guy King (London: Marshall, Morgan & Scott), 1954.
The author takes the word *fellowship* as the key to this complex little epistle. He opens it up with his usual clear outlines and helpful comments.

Jude: The Acts of the Apostates, S. Maxwell Coder (Chicago: Moody Press), 1958.
Dr. Coder was Dean of Education at Moody Bible Institute for many years, and a gifted teacher. Here are nineteen chapters on one chapter of the Bible. The author does a fine job of opening up this dynamic epistle on apostasy.

The Apocalypse, G. A. Seiss (Grand Rapids: Zondervan), 1964 reprint.
This work has gone through numerous editions. It was originally published in three volumes although it is now published in the one-volume edition listed here. Probably one of the most interesting and practical works of an expository nature, brilliant in places. Some chapters, however, are based on wrong conceptions—as, for instance, the author's interpretation of the woman in Revelation 12.

Exposition of the Revelation of Jesus Christ, Walter Scott (London: Pickering and Inglis), n.d.
Very satisfactory as a verse-by-verse commentary on this book. Never fails to shed light on difficult passages. Because the book lacks an outline, the reader sometimes gets lost in details. Also, the author wrote before many of the events of our age cast their light on the prophetic Scriptures.

The Apocalypse or the Day of the Lord, E. W. Bullinger (London: Eyre & Spottiswoode), 1935.
Bullinger's hyper-dispensational position can be seen in his handling of the seven churches. Apart from that, this book is a gem, a

verse-by-verse commentary by a very able scholar and writer. Bullinger must be read cautiously—but he deserves to be read.

Revelation, A. C. Gaebelein (New York: Our Hope Publishers), 1915.

A much neglected book, which still has much to say about the book of Revelation. The author knew his subject and treats it well.

The Book of Revelation, Clarence Larkin (Philadelphia: Larkin Estate), 1919.

A helpful commentary by one who in his day was almost without peer in his ability to open up the prophetic Scriptures.

Exploring Revelation, John Phillips (Chicago: Moody Press), 1974.

A verse-by-verse commentary with useful alliterated outlines. Makes a serious attempt to interpret Revelation in the light of current events. The author shows how the crucial 38th and 39th chapters of Ezekiel (dealing with the coming Russian invasion of Israel) fit in relation to other events in the Apocalypse. Reverential and Christ-exalting.